GIRL GONE WILD

THE HOLLYWOOD MISADVENTURES
OF A SMALL-TOWN GIRL

"*Girl Gone Wild* is fiery, sparkly, spicy. It's brash. It's just—
wild. It's a fire sign on the page."
–Chloé Caldwell, author of *Women* and *Trying*

GIRL GONE WILD

by Courtney Kocak

TRIO HOUSE PRESS

Kocak, Courtney
1st edition

ISBN: 978-1-949487-54-1
Library of Congress Control Number: 2025948172

Interior design by Natasha Kane
Cover design by Joel W. Coggins
Editing by Kris Bigalk and Lili Gourley

Trio House Press, Inc.
Minneapolis
www.triohousepress.org

for the dreamers

"Every woman is a rebel, and usually in wild revolt against herself."
–Oscar Wilde

"Almost everything has been stolen from us by the patriarchy.
Our creativity has been stolen, our creative energies, our religion.
I want it back."
–Mary Daly

AUTHOR'S NOTE

This book contains explicit language and candid depictions of drugs, sex, and other adult subject matter. Some content may be offensive to certain readers—including my own mom—and inappropriate for unsupervised minors. Reader discretion is advised.

I changed the names of most people in this book and changed identifying details to protect the privacy of people in my life who aren't exhibitionists. I occasionally omitted people, places, events, and other details for clarity and cohesion. Dialogue in this memoir has been recreated from memory, intended to reflect the spirit and meaning of what was said. The language is accurate to its day, though I fully embrace evolving norms.

Memory is fallible and perspective is unique to each of us, yet I did my best to tell the truth as I experienced it and fact-check myself wherever possible. But beyond anything, this book is a product of my emotional truth.

Aside from commentary on my personal experience briefly working for the brand in 2005, this work has no commercial relationship of any kind with the adult entertainment company Girls Gone Wild, which has been under new ownership since 2014.

I do not speak on behalf of any groups or identities or other people, I only speak for myself.

TABLE OF CONTENTS

Prologue: Opening Curtain 3
Born to Be Wild 7
Waiting for Guffman 8
6th Period Math 15
History Lesson 16
Theatre of Religion 19
Desperately Seeking Sparkle 24
Sweet Sixteen & Never Been Kissed 29
Raked 36
Let's Rail 41
Grand March 47
Border Crossing 51
Smothered, Covered & Chunked 63
Peep Show, Interrupted 69
The Blue House 77
The Boji Mile 88
Miss Adderall USA 98
Model Mayhem 103
1311 Nasty Frat 108

Intermission 1 115

The Poisoned Court 117
How Not to Make It in Hollywood, Part 1 125
Seeking: Model 4 Massage 133
The Dregs of Summer 140
Girl Gone Wild 147
Hollywood Cleaners 160
Dear Derek 163
Woozy Blues 168
Mr. Skin 177
How to Set Your Own Trap 182

Intermission 2   211

A Noise Within   212
Tragedy + Time   215
Day of the Dead   227
I Cum All Over My Closet Floor   237
The Self-Esteem Police   241
Things Don't Always Stay Where You Leave Them   249
Dr. Donna   261
How I Talk About My Abortion (Now)   267
Exposure Therapy   278
What Happens in Vegas   286
Epilogue: Curtain Call   293

Acknowledgments   299
About the Author   303

PROLOGUE:

OPENING CURTAIN

Wind ripped through my long, tangled hair, window at half-mast, as I drove out to California in a gray Chevy Corsica. The sky was honey-soaked as the heavy sun sagged toward its swollen end in the scorching, record-breaking heat of summer 2005. I had just acted in my second independent film, lured to Hollywood by the beacon of the West—where dreamers and rugged individualists have prospected for their fortunes since the Gold Rush.

I jammed a cassette wired to my Discman into the player and ran through a rousing medley of my favorite CDs. I belted my heart out to the Dixie Chicks' "Wide Open Spaces," hit the high notes to Maxwell's "This Woman's Work," put my quivering soul into Ben Harper's "Sexual Healing (LIVE)," and sang Lisa Loeb's "Stay (I Missed You)," preserved in the amber of my adolescent muscle memory, perfectly three times in a row. I had to sing to stay awake.

I'd driven through the night before and pulled over on the shoulder of the Interstate that morning. Semi trucks tore by at 75 miles per hour while I took a nap.

I startled awake from my sweaty mid-day slumber to the sound of rapping on the window. The dark silhouette of a police officer peered in the driver's side window.

"If you're tired, I want you to get your rest. But I don't want you to get hit in the process. There's an exit seven miles up." He'd pulled over to nudge me along on the Eastern plains of Colorado.

Back on the road, one hand on the wheel, one hand in my purse, I pulled out a pill bottle to get an Adderall. The faint rattle made me wince. Only five left. *Shit*, I thought, I would have to ration. I bit off a sensible 10 milligram chunk and turned up the radio as I waited for the amphetamine salts to kick in. Soon my heart began to beat faster, and I rode my second wind all the way through the Rockies.

Adderall kept me fast-tapping the steering wheel to the greatest hits of my early aughts CD collection. It gave me an artificial buzz, a double-time cadence. When it started to wear off, I stopped for curly fries in Grand Junction against a pink and orange explosion of sunset. Driving out of town past a Super 8, the hotel barely registered—I was determined to make it to LA before noon the next day. As twilight introduced purple to the horizon, my eyes began to droop.

I whizzed past a sign that read, "No services for 110 miles" amid the red rocks. I looked down at my gas gauge: less than a quarter. At exit 160, I got off to fill my tank in Green River, Utah. I bought myself two Diet Mountain Dews to jazz me up for the next two hours. But the caffeine wasn't enough—it just made me have to pee on the most desolate stretch of interstate in the entire U.S.; no gas, food, hotels, or civilization until Salina.

After nearly an hour of nothingness, I was bleary-eyed, shouting lyrics into the Utah void, trying to force my eyelids open with imaginary forks. Almost like a mirage, a "View Area" sign entered my periphery. Just 10 more miles, and I could rest. I bounced in my seat, anticipating. If I stayed in motion, I could stay awake.

When I finally pulled off in the overlook parking lot, bugs swarmed the solitary lamppost as it flickered. Darkness cloaked my view of the craggy red rocks, but I wasn't there to take in the beauty. Despite the fullness of my bladder and the cramped recline of my seat, desperate to shut my aching eyes, I fell asleep almost immediately.

I awoke to a harsh flash of headlights. As I pushed myself upright, a white pickup pulled in right next to me in the totally vacant parking lot. The pickup's engine idled aggressively. The outline of a man loomed menacingly. It's just us. Me and the man in the pickup and the pitch-black night. I could feel his eyes on me. Not wanting to make eye contact, I stared ahead but felt a pang of bad fate in my stomach. *I'm going to die because I wouldn't spend $80 on a hotel* *room*, I thought, willing my muscles to move as fast as possible. I scrambled for my keys in the center console, grabbed the right one, put it in the ignition, turned it, put the car into drive, drove fast, drove fast, drove fast. The danger alarm in my mind beeped wildly. *Go, go, go.* I gripped the wheel and, when the speedometer hit 80, back on the Interstate, I finally unclenched my jaw.

When you grow up in Minnesota, you know the road can be tempestuous. In high school, several of my classmates lost their lives on the road. Because it's icy and dangerous and people like to drink. So Minnesota girls know how to drive. Spinning out on the ice, learning how to recover without slamming on the brakes. And after your close call, you have to get back out on the road and make it home. There will be more snowstorms. There will be more icy roads. There will be more places to go.

A small-town dreamer with big city ambitions, cars were my freedom. The promise of possibility, access to the highway of life. And I wanted mine to take place in Hollywood. As soon as I got my driver's license, I drove myself to act in plays in nearby towns. In the five years since I'd turned 16, my range and castability gradually evolved from von Trapp children and Dickens' ghosts, to ditzy bimbos and dead hookers.

Freedom begets danger, which I kept encountering during those drives to and from LA. I was broke and dumb and didn't know how to do anything right. I was always driving straight through on Adderall crumbs, never wanting to spend my precious money on a hotel room—which wasn't entirely dumb because I didn't have much of it. I drove old clunkers through the desert mountains in the middle of the night. I once accepted a ride from a strange man alongside an interstate in Colorado, when my new-used Oldsmobile blew its transmission.

The road almost killed me. Not just once, but again and again. And it wasn't my only predator. Being self-made requires risk. Not being able to afford the trip, and taking it anyway. Sleeping on the shoulder and waking up to a bear of a man watching you like his next meal. Having to save your own ass NOW.

I was always going to go. But when I heard most accidents happen within five miles of home, I knew the risk was worth it. I could die not chasing my dreams, so I might as well try my luck down the big wide open road.

BORN TO BE WILD

I was born first and fast, covered in a thick layer of what looked like
    parmesan cheese.
When I was a baby, I shat on my mom's lap so ferociously, she
    couldn't move for two hours until my dad returned home from
    coaching a basketball game.
My first memories are of being bad.
A rageful scream at the end of a tantrum.
Ripping my clothes off as soon as I got home from daycare.
Telling neighbor kids that pellets of rabbit poop were raisins.
Encouraging them to eat it.
I came clean before they actually did it... but I wanted to see if
    they would.
I had good qualities, too.
Rabid curiosity. Always wanting to know: *how, why, what's next?*
A playful eccentricity—dramatically sweeping my long bangs across
    one eye like a pirate, an actor on her tiny world of a stage.
Despite my attraction to struggle, I had an earnest longing for
    rightness, fairness. Rules are okay… as long as they can be
    broken sometimes.
The bad and the good swirled together. Not an angel and a demon,
    just a girl. One ravenous girl. One ambitious tornado.
An erratic driver with a sturdy engine, a heavy foot, and a lust for
    the open road.
My parents chuckle and say that kids' personalities come out fully
    formed.
When I think back to the beginning, I was wild all along.

WAITING FOR GUFFMAN

In Christopher Guest's cult classic *Waiting for Guffman*, the Blaine, Missouri, community theater troupe rehearses their sesquicentennial musical revue in eager anticipation of theater agent Mort Guffman, their supposed ticket to Broadway, who never shows. I grew up waiting for Guffman.

When I finally saw the 1996 mockumentary starring indie icon Parker Posey in college—while pursuing my BFA in Theater Arts with an Acting emphasis (that last part was really important to me)—I understood the sardonic comedy and fell in love with the (slightly?) exaggerated characters. But a large part of me watched earnestly. I knew exactly how these characters felt.

I wanted to be an actress more than anything in the whole wide world for as long as I could remember. I loved TV and movies and beauty and attention and, most of all, drama, regardless of its delivery method. The idea of crying *as a job* blew my mind. The purge, the emotional release, the hysteria. "*That* is what I want to do when I grow up," I thought—and frequently said out loud, much to my parents' chagrin and occasional eye-rolls.

Acting unlocked my fantasy world, though I don't remember finding the key—one of my earliest memories is performing in front of a mirror. It was there from my beginning, like the entire universe is made of stardust from the big bang.

In fact, I remember *only* wanting to be an actress, which is a pretty strange thing to want to be. All eyes on me, performative, playing pretend well into adulthood. Anything else I entertained as an occupation was a blip on the radar—usually my consideration was piqued after watching a movie that made a job look kinda sexy. Investigative journalism after I saw Denzel Washington and Julia Roberts in *The Pelican Brief*, advertising for a half a second after I saw *Picture Perfect* with Jennifer Aniston, even a nun after I saw Whoopi Goldberg in *Sister Act*—I told our priest that with a straight face during an event in the church hall, but as soon as it came out of my mouth and I heard my mom giggle, I knew it wasn't true.

I wanted to *play* a nun, not *be* a nun.

Choosing acting meant choosing it all. And I felt confident that it would work out, that I would "make it," despite my dad's best efforts to get my head out of the stars and bring me back down to Earth, guide me down a more realistic path, as he felt was his duty. One night, in my teens, he cornered me at the dining room table and showed me a graph of all the people who try to make it and the one person out of a thousand who actually does. It was a professional document, printed on high-quality cardstock. I have no idea where he got it—a basketball or teaching conference?—or the intended purpose of this chart, but to him, those 999 light gray dots were a visual representation of risk. *My* risk in becoming an actress.

He jabbed at the graphic with his finger and demanded, "What happens if you're not that person?"

He wanted me to reckon with the delusion of it. Forget the fantasy, and pick something more practical. But I didn't internalize it. I knew I was the one person out of a thousand who would make it. I knew that I was a black dot.

As a child stuck in Jackson, Minnesota, population 3,559, I didn't know anyone in the entertainment industry, aside from members of the community theater—if that counts for anything (it doesn't). But I wasn't going to let that stand between me and a little fantastical thinking. By this point in my life, with eleven years of wisdom under my belt, I was familiar with a dozen or so accounts of young talent being "discovered." Kate Moss at an airport, Natalie Portman at a pizza place, Julia Roberts walking down the freaking street. Agents of the industry could be anywhere. *My Guffman could be around literally any corner*, I thought.

Jackson didn't have a local mall to hang out at, so I had to be proactive. Whenever we went out of town, I was on high alert. I had to scout for any potential scouters to make one hundred percent sure that they scouted me during their mission, however covert. The safest bet was just to be "on" all the time—they wouldn't be able to miss me. If I was to have a career as a child actor, I couldn't afford to be overlooked. I was almost twelve, I was running out of time!

Luckily, I had a lead: my mom's cousin Jill would be attending my Aunt Robyn's wedding. Jill grew up outside of LA and was now living in New York City. Technically she was my second cousin once removed. I thought even that had a chic ring to it. Jill worked at Random House and brought treasure troves of books whenever she came to visit and sent them as gifts in her absence. I saw her as a sort of cosmopolitan Santa Claus, one who could deliver my acting dreams like a Christmas present. She would notice my "It" factor, rescue me from my drab rural tedium, and launch me into a glamorous life in show business.

Jill had all the necessary qualifications: She lived on the actual island of Manhattan. She was the co-lessee of a romantically tiny apartment (which surely had a couch big enough for a child). She smoked cigarettes unabashedly, not caring what her parents thought. She had cool fashion and her clothes were always inventively styled—a denim jacket with fringes, big gold, ornate buttons on her chiffon blouse, crinkle paper as a belt! She dated a revolving door of D-list or friend-of-celebrity boyfriends, and she had an epic story about the time she beat a guy with her purse in Times Square after he tried to steal it from her. She'd done a brief stint at the American Academy of Dramatic Arts in Pasadena, so she was pretty much a full-fledged actress. She was my hero. She would save me.

I'd met Jill on two prior occasions. Once when my great-grandfather died, then again for my grandparents' fiftieth anniversary. She was thirty years old and one of the most beautiful people I'd ever met—blonde, piercing blue eyes, perfect bone structure. She must *really* be choosy with her roles, I thought, or she'd be working all the time.

Knowing Jill would be a guest at Robyn's wedding, I planned for weeks to impress her. It was a loose plan—I had to leave some room for improv—but it contained ample opportunity to knock her socks off. I was regimented in my preparation: I spent a lot of time contemplating which scrunchie would best accessorize each outfit for the wedding as if I were competing in a beauty pageant (drivingwear, wedding, reception), practicing exaggerated accents like Eliza Doolittle at the beginning of *My Fair Lady*, and trying to casually insert the term "feature film" into conversations.

If my scheme worked, I would be moving into Jill's studio apartment (which sounded very luxurious by the way) just a week or two after the wedding. After she worked out all the details with my parents. Of course, they would raise a stink about me leaving home and they'd want to know when I would be back, but it would have to be between movies. I didn't want to miss out on any more opportunities. My career was the most important thing in my life.

On the day of the wedding, I'd finagled a primo travel arrangement for the two-hour drive to the festivities: bouncing in between Jill (!) and my grandpa in his white Chevy S10 pickup, freshly cleaned for the occasion, though it still smelled like a work truck. Outside endless acres of flat farmland blurred together in a green and brown smear as we sped west on I-90. It was a clear, crisp day, and I felt like a sunbeam. I wore acid-washed denim on acid-washed denim with a cool headband for the car ride. I wanted Jill to get a peek at my street fashion before donning a dress for the main event.

They picked me up around noon. By 1:30 we'd driven by hundreds of fields of corn, beans, and wheat, and I'd already said "feature film" at least as many times. I no longer bothered to veil it in conversation; sometimes I would just shout it in the general direction of Jill or Grandpa Joe. "Feature film!" I was on a roll.

My grandpa was probably itching to turn on his favorite AM talk radio, but I would not shut up. I had Jill's undivided attention for hours—I had to take full advantage. She had no choice but to acknowledge again and again how seriously I took my acting. What a fine actress I clearly already was! Plucky, precocious, perfect for the industry. And I obviously knew the lingo already, so we wouldn't have to waste any time on that.

The drive to the wedding was sublime—even better than expected. I knew I was "breaking a leg" (standard showbiz speak) because of the rush I got delivering my monologue. Sermon, really. I could *feel* how well it was going. I said things like "You know how it feels when you're not where you're supposed to be in life, like physically and emotionally?" and "I make myself cry for fun every day!" and "Some people are normal and some people are touched with a special gift they have to share," and "This might be redundant, but I think I'm ready for the big time."

I broke all the legs, nothing but slaughtered limbs in my grandpa's truck.

Once we arrived at the church, I changed into my knee-length button-down red ditsy-print dress and took a brief moment to congratulate myself in the bathroom mirror as I adjusted the shoulder pads. *You're crushing it, kid*, I told myself. This would be a great story for the *People* magazine interview I'd inevitably do when promoting my first movie—excuse me, *feature film*—sometime early next year. But don't just coast on a stellar car performance, I warned myself, keep your eye on the prize. Entertain this woman for the rest of the night. *It's the least you can do*, I thought, *you'll be living with her soon.*

So that's what I did. I sat in the third pew and performatively teared up during the vows. I demonstrated different dialects, casually working them into conversation at the reception. As I tore into a piece of wedding cake, I mused on maybe being into dating Richard Gere if he and Cindy Crawford ever broke up. Jill played with her necklace and snickered from across the banquet table.

"What's funny?" I looked at her sideways.

She shook her head. "It's not appropriate."

Now I had to know. "Tell us," I demanded. My uncle nodded in agreement.

She raised her eyebrows, "You don't know about the gerbil?" Everyone at our table leaned in to hear the unsubstantiated slander. *Wow, Jill knows all the best Hollywood gossip*, I thought.

When the dance portion of the evening got underway, I really let it rip. The lights were bright in the banquet hall and the dance floor was just a six-foot square. I'm not even sure if there was music, but I didn't let that stop me. I gyrated every dance move I could think of, many of them original. Jill, looking impossibly chic in her fitted periwinkle skirt suit and matching purse, stood off to the side talking to other adults, but I made sure she could see me, dropping by to say "hi" or throw her a wave or a peace sign every few minutes. I was a very sober eleven-year-old completely drunk

on adrenaline. Wasted. Exhilarated. I even negotiated to stay later
and return via the earlier arrangement with my grandpa and Jill,
instead of riding back with my parents.

When I finally got home that night, I skipped up to my
bedroom and took a bow in front of the mirror. My hair was messy,
shoulder pads askew. I was exhausted from auditioning for Jill, yet
I was still beaming. *You nailed it, sweetie.* I winked at my reflection
and smiled.

Then, still in my wedding attire, I crawled into bed and
passed out. Visions of Broadway danced in my head.

"WHAT IS WRONG WITH YOU?!" my mom snarled in my face
like the Big Bad Wolf, blowing the sleep right out of my eyes.

"I don't know what you're talking about…" I responded
groggily, rubbing my face.

As far as I was concerned, things with me were going great.
The sun was streaming in through the windows, creating a sheen
on the wood paneling, and today would be my grand finale at Jill's
brunch send-off. Yet I knew something was very wrong from the
way my mom had just shaken me awake.

"What did you say to Jill?" she asked through gritted teeth.

"I don't know, I said a lot of things… about acting?" I
replied, adjusting the comforter.

"Well, she thinks your dad is abusing you," my mom said
flatly, the sentence landing with a thud.

Oh, no! The reviews of my performance were in, and they
were not good. I had been grossly misinterpreted. In fact, it had
gone so poorly that the finale was canceled—I had been uninvited
from brunch.

In retrospect, I did say some weird things, but nothing I can trace to
this conclusion. Being openly horny for an older man, maybe? But
Richard Gere was only forty-six at the time and the whole culture
had a predilection for pedophilic age-gaps. Perhaps she thought
auditioning that hard to sleep on her couch was a sign something
must be wrong at home. The only thing "wrong" was how bad I

wanted to be an actress.

A few weeks later the leaves were turning orange. My mom and I ran a bank errand to Alpha in the maroon minivan. I propped my feet up on the dashboard and pressed seek on the radio past ads for ag services and sports updates until I recognized a song I liked.

"You're so vain. I bet you think this song is about you," I crooned.

My mild-mannered Minnesota mom unclenched her death grip on the steering wheel to reach over and turn up the volume.

She never turned up the volume. I stopped singing immediately.

"This song reminds me of YOU," she shouted over Carly Simon.

"Why?!" I looked at her for an explanation.

"It was Robyn's wedding day, and you couldn't help but put on a show," she glowered back.

"You're *still* mad at me about Robyn's wedding? Look, I'm sorry—I didn't mean to!"

"Why don't you apologize to Robyn... and your dad."

"I already did!" I said with a huff.

Still not satisfied, she sneered, "Everything's not about you, you know."

I looked out the window at the freshly harvested fields surrounding us for miles and miles, all the way to the horizon line. There would be no grand escape to New York City this year. I sighed and resigned myself to more waiting.

Next time, I would need to choose my Guffman more wisely... maybe figure out how to be my own Guffman? And most importantly: save the drama for the stage.

6TH PERIOD MATH

The seat of my school desk caught me by surprise. In fifth grade, sixth period. Right after lunch. Looking for more excitement than math.

Algebra was too easy. I was bound to distract myself with something harder.

Sitting in the quad of desks next to the chalkboard, I couldn't even look out the window. I'd already memorized the bulletin boards. Jittery with pent up energy, I rocked forward in my seat, and my tender little vagina bumped against the wooden ridge.

Oh! I was not expecting such a blunt force sensation, such a good sensation. I wanted to bump it again and again and again.

It was a curious vagina—sheltered, as it should have been, but also where I frequently rested my hand while I watched TV. I'd played a few games of softcore doctor, playdate check-ups with vague sexual undertones. Yes, I was sheltered, but I still had a pulse. And my vagina was discovering that she had a pulse too.

Mrs. Driscoll was teaching math equations from the front of the room, but once we felt the ridge, we couldn't unfeel it. And we couldn't resist bumping into it again.

Mrs. Driscoll was my teacher, but I knew her first from church. She sat in the fourth row every Sunday during Mass, where I could see her from the balcony, in my sightline to Father Neudecker as a stand-in for God.

I clenched my jaw, still missing my permanent molars, and rode the desk's ridge, over and over and over against the ridge, and oh my god, that feels goo—

"Courtney." Mrs. Driscoll snapped.

Oh! Oh no! The thrill in my eyes disintegrated into shame as she stared back with stern pupils. Her accusing eyes burned through me. My cheeks turned bright pink. She was on to me.

That's how I learned a math equation I would struggle to unlearn for decades: Pleasure = shame. They would tug-o-war long after I traded that desk for other sources of distraction and delight.

HISTORY LESSON

"I thought sweatshop was another word for gym," a stupid boy confessed from across the room.

Tall and gangly, he spit a little when he talked. He wore a striped crew neck, probably made in a sweatshop.

We were in seventh grade history class and Mr. Albrecht was teaching us about sweatshops—poor people working for peanuts in dangerous conditions. In old-timey New York, there was the Triangle Shirtwaist Factory fire, in third-world countries, our Nikes were made today. I knew of sweatshops from a *60 Minutes* segment, but this type of labor condition was a foreign concept to most of my classmates. An invisible fact of life.

"I'm sure they'd give you a good workout!" I jabbed, jumping on the opportunity to poke fun at the stupid boy in the striped crew neck.

"Yeah, but you'd probably have to quit the basketball team," my best friend Karissa added, punctuated by a snort.

The class erupted in laughter.

"You." Mr. Albrecht—with his bald-gray horseshoe hair, his drab rotation of sweater vests, and his velcro shoes—pointed at me. "And you." He pointed at Karissa. "Get down on the floor."

"What?" I asked, still giggling, confused.

Karissa and I were active participants in class, for better or worse. But I'd never gotten in trouble like this before.

"Get down on all fours and crawl around on the floor like animals," he said, his tone dead serious.

Disoriented by both the request and the energy of the room, I slid off my desk chair awkwardly, briefly catching Karissa's eye as she too sank to the floor.

"Now crawl," Mr. Albrecht instructed with a wry smile on his face.

Karissa and I shared another look of hesitation before submitting. We crawled on our hands and knees, picking up debris from the cold floor.

Amid a chorus of cheers and jeers from the faces overhead,

Mr. Albrecht pointed out a path zigzagging through the rows of desks, directing us around the room. Karissa and I were uncharacteristically quiet and kept our eyes on our classmates' ankles.

"All the way around," he said like a gluttonous king, delighted to be holding court over the mayhem.

I could feel the grit jabbing into my palms.

When Mr. Albrecht finally told us we could stand, I rose with a blank dizziness and dusted off my red knees. I couldn't wait to wash my hands.

"What were you doing on the floor in Mr. Albrecht's class, Courtney?" my dad asked at the dinner table that night. He wasn't accusing, he was inquiring.

"How do you know about that?" I said sheepishly.

"Your Uncle Tom called me."

"How did he find out?"

"The small-town gossip mill moves fast, Cork," he said. "So, tell me, what happened?"

I picked at my vegetable medley. "I know he was making a point—we were being disruptive—but the punishment seemed kinda… strange." I segregated the carrots to the far side of my plate. "I just can't imagine the boys in our class being forced to crawl around on the dirty ground, regardless of what they had done."

For some reason, saying it out loud made it seem even worse than it had felt on my knees.

"Courtney, Karissa, can you stick around for a minute?" Mr. Albrecht asked before dismissing our class the next day.

We covertly rolled our eyes at each other as our classmates filed past.

When the room was empty aside from us, Mr. Albrecht started softly, "I would like to apologize for yesterday… That wasn't an appropriate punishment." His eyes darted down at his hands as he continued.

There would be no more crawling on the floor.

"Did he apologize?" my dad asked, peppering his potato at dinner that night.

"Oh yeah," I said, pouring myself a glass of water.

"I don't think it will happen again, but let me know if it does."

I nodded.

Up to that point in my life, I'd felt like my dad could protect me when it mattered. That day in history class, I got my first official lesson on sweatshops and my first official lesson on sexism. Stabbing my green beans, I began to realize that both problems were sprawling and complicated. If I wasn't careful—reading labels and doing research—I could easily buy something made in a sweatshop. I could easily exploit garment workers trapped in inhumane conditions. And if I didn't protect myself—how exactly, I still wasn't sure—I could find myself crawling on the ground at the pervy whims of an old man in a sweater vest, entrusted with my safety.

I took a big bite and chewed, deep in thought. I wasn't sure what to do with this information. Guys like Mr. Albrecht were everywhere.

THEATRE OF RELIGION

One winter Wednesday night, our teacher, Marianne Callahan, told us demurely, "I have been blessed with the gift of speaking in tongues," as she stroked her cross necklace.

"What?!" "No way!" We couldn't believe it.

We were seventh graders, gathered at the musty Catholic church school for our weekly catechism classes—an event that I wasn't allowed to skip unless I was actively vomiting. We met upstairs, in a classroom at the end of the hall on the second floor. My aunts and uncles had attended the school as kids and it hadn't changed much since the '60s. The same tile, chalkboard, chairs. Fluorescent lights bright enough to keep the devil away.

In a few years, we would be confirmed, becoming adult members of this wildly popular cult with ancient roots in Judea. For now, we were learning about the sacraments, patron saints, and a (highly selective) history of the religion. On this night, we were learning the gifts of the Holy Spirit. Speaking in tongues was one of the most fantastical. We were beside ourselves that we knew someone who could actually do it.

"I prayed for the gift and one day it came to me," Marianne explained, her hands folded in prayer, their natural resting place. Marianne had more faith than anyone I'd ever met, but even she was surprised when her request was finally granted, unknown words babbling out of her mouth, the only witness, her newborn baby.

After a flabbergasted moment of silence, the room spoke in unison. My classmates and I had so many questions.

Marianne held her hand up. "Hold on, one at a time."

"Have you done it more than once?" asked Ethan Anderson.

"Yes, many times."

Ethan looked at the rest of the class with his jaw slack, in disbelief. We looked back at him the same.

"Do you understand what you're saying when you speak in tongues?" I chimed in.

"No, that would require the gift of *receiving* tongues, which

I don't yet have. I am praying for it though."

"Please show us!" we begged.

"Maybe someday, but not tonight," Marianne said with a smile.

No matter how much we begged, she wouldn't show us.

"It's a direct connection to God, not a party trick," she said firmly, "To abuse it would be blasphemy."

We were foaming at the mouth. A dozen Doubting Thomases, we had to see it for ourselves.

I was never a believer, but I was a very good student. The Biblical lessons we were taught in class felt more like trivia than holy scripture from a higher power. As early as I can remember, the whole thing seemed far-fetched. Even as a kindergartner, my tiny world already felt too big, the veins traversing my little body too complicated to have been thought up by some faceless man. I'd seen *The Wizard of Oz*—the man behind the curtain wasn't real.

The details were actually horrific when, if, I let them sink in: God, the most powerful entity in existence, publicly executed his only son for our sins. Wait, why do we worship this guy? How is he all-powerful, yet so much of his process seems like trial and error? Also, the timeline seemed off. I struggled to understand which parts were literal and which were metaphorical. Why would he make this a riddle?

When I saw *Schindler's List* in fifth grade, the ruse was up. I'd already been a skeptic, but after I saw people hiding for their lives in port-a-potties and much, much worse, the cognitive dissonance became too heavy a load. I couldn't believe it. It didn't make sense.

"I just don't understand why God would let horrible things happen," I told my mom in a panic late one night. "Why would he let the Holocaust happen? Or slavery?"

Either God wasn't real or he was a real asshole.

Despite my lack of piety, there I was every Sunday and Wednesday, taking in the word of the Lord as a present to my parents. Really a self-serving gift. Mutually beneficial, let's say. They got to pretend they had a fully faithful family and were doing their job as parents, and in exchange, I was allowed privileges, like hanging out with my friends and doing after-school activities.

I couldn't disobey my parents too much; it was a miserable thing to do. Even though we already had different worldviews, I knew that they wanted well for me, and rebelling against their bedrock principles (you have to go to church, you have to try hard in school, and you have to look the server in the eyes while you're ordering) would make my life a living hell.

A couple weeks later, we had not forgotten what Marianne told us. We would beg to see it every chance we got. On this night, Marianne must have been in the mood. She adjusted her cross necklace and took a deep breath. "Let's stand in a circle." We rushed into formation. "Hold hands with the people next to you," she instructed. We gripped each other's hands enthusiastically and exchanged grins around the circle. "I can't control when it happens," Marianne warned us. We nodded seriously. "Okay, let's say the Lord's Prayer together." She closed her eyes and we recited together.

> *Our Father, Who art in heaven, hallowed be Thy name; Thy kingdom come; Thy will be done on earth as it is in heaven. Give us this day our daily bread; and forgive us our trespasses as we forgive those who trespass against us; and lead us not into temptation, but deliver us from evil—*

Suddenly, Marianne started to sway and her face began to flush as she broke into a chant in a language none of us had ever heard. My chin dropped and my eyes grew wide. I squeezed my cousin Ashley's hand tightly and she squeezed back. *It was really happening!* Marianne's energy when she was speaking in tongues was dramatically different from her usually meek housewife persona. She chanted for a minute—a long minute stretched with our amazement as we tried to latch onto the foreign syllables that rushed out of her in our feeble attempt to comprehend the miracle before us. I almost forgot I didn't believe in God. What an excellent recruiting tool!

Then, as quickly and intensely as it began, it was over and

everything was back to normal. It was almost like she was set on fire and then extinguished without getting burned. For her, this God stuff was real, and she took it more seriously than any job. To me, she wasn't just a believer, she was a witch or an excellent actress. Either way, I was entranced enough to keep up the charade.

A few years later, in preparation for the sacrament of confirmation, our parish's good-natured priest came to visit our class. We were in a different room, right across from the office. The Holy Spirit had not visited us since that night with Marianne and my belief in the Holy Trinity was waning.

Father Quinn sat on a rickety wooden chair at the front of the class and we sat cross-legged around him. I took this visit as an opportunity to interrogate him about the timeline and forensics of Catholicism. "I just want more proof... I saw this episode of *60 Minutes* where they carbon dated the Holy Shroud and the dates were all wrong. They don't even know if it's real. Can't they do DNA testing?"

A knowing smile formed on Father Quinn's lips as he launched into a sermon on faith.

But that didn't answer my question.

There were so many questions, and not a lot of satisfying answers.

Given as much, it felt insincere to get confirmed in a religion I didn't believe in. I told my mom that, which I thought was a pretty mature perspective on the matter and, thus, I should get a pass. But she did not agree.

"Oh, you are getting confirmed, end of story," she said. She didn't find it hypocritical in the least. She found it mandatory.

"Okay," I relented.

Soon it was time to pick a confirmation name. Trading card depictions of the saints were laid out on a table for us to peruse. I wanted to choose my confirmation name as a statement of protest. I wanted to subvert expectations. My first choice was Saint Sebastian, patron saint of archers, pin-makers, athletes, and of a holy death—

who looked very hot getting maimed by arrows in the Renaissance paintings depicting his martyrdom. Going with a male saint was funny, I thought, and if I was going to go through with this, I at least needed to have fun with it. As an alternative, I could go with Saint Ferdinand, patron saint of engineers.

I carried on like this for months, cycling through every masculine saint in Christendom.

My mom and grandma lost their minds at the idea of me naming myself Saint Sebastian. Meanwhile, my instructors kept asking me to confirm my confirmation name.

The education director (who was also one of my Grandma Betty's brunch buddies) cornered me after class a few weeks before the ceremony, "We really need to lock this in, Courtney." They needed to print programs and make name cards. I was holding things up. I had to make a decision. "Pick something that would make your grandma proud," she prodded.

My Grandma Betty was a very devout woman, but not in a stuffy, pretentious way. One evening, after a family dinner, she grabbed my hand and said, "We need to talk about your confirmation name." I wanted to say "Saint Sebastian or bust, I don't even believe this shit," but she had already moved into a sincere speech about how I was hurting my mom's feelings and her feelings and, worse, "making a joke out of your confirmation name is making a joke out of God." I thought my mom was being unreasonable, but I didn't want to hurt my grandma, so begrudgingly, I landed on Saint Clare of Assisi instead, the patron saint of TV. A cool patronage, sure, but not the rebellion I was after. It was an acquiescence after all.

I took solace in the ticking clock. In just a couple short years, I would run away and join the circus. I would choose a different church: the theater. I would worship a different holy trinity: Shakespeare, Sam Shepard, and Eve Ensler. Ironically, acting felt more honest than Catholicism.

But it was too late to make a clean getaway. I'd already soaked up the Catholic guilt, forever branded with its indelible ink—the need to be good, the not wanting to disappoint, the distance it put between me and my family, and the everlasting dissonance of it all.

DESPERATELY SEEKING SPARKLE

I drove my big blue boat of an Oldsmobile Cutlass Ciera—a hand-me-down from Grandma Betty—along the winding country road to Matt Erickson's house in Lakefield, the next town over from Jackson. The school districts in our respective hometowns were so tiny they had consolidated into one a few years prior. And in the time since, Matt had become one of my closest guy friends.

It was the dog days of August, and the sweltering heat made my thighs stick to the faux leather seats. But I was hell-bent on making good use of this last little sliver of freedom before school started up again.

Matt might have had a crush on me, and I might have had a crush on him too, but any romantic feelings were fleeting. We were two positively charged magnets, there was too much sameness, no attraction, no pull. And then there was the issue of our hair. Matt had a Bob Ross 'fro and I had a frizzy Jennifer Aniston 'do, mangled by a local hairdresser thrilled at the opportunity to experiment. Neither of us had suitable tresses for the late summer Minnesota humidity.

He was awkward, and I hated that he was a mirror to show me that I was too. Any time I would start thinking *maaaybe*, I would catch a glimpse of the beige brillo pad atop his head and call the whole thing off in my mind.

Still, we hung out all the time after acting in several school musicals and plays together, including *A Christmas Carol* and *The Pajama Game*, a musical about unionizing garment workers. In the upcoming school year, we would go on to play a middle-aged married couple in the one-act play *Crawling Arnold* and star-crossed lovers in the Holocaust play *I Never Saw Another Butterfly*. We also competed in Speech, Math League, and were attorneys for Mock Trial together. There was nothing else to do in our rural area… except maybe drugs. At sixteen, I'd never so much as smoked a cigarette, but I was more than ready to have some wild experiences offstage, as well. At the top of my list was weed.

My parents were teetotalers. They're both control freaks, and since they hadn't seen any good come from drinking, they didn't feel like they were missing out. I had never seen them so much as sip on a beer or puff a cigarette. Their expectation was that I would be the same. While I could understand their perspective, I didn't entirely agree.

Thanks to DARE and one of my favorite movies at the time, *The Basketball Diaries*—

"Mom, can you give me some money, please? Mom, can you give me some money, please? STOP FUCKING AROUND!"

"Ooo, are you desperate, baby? Who's a whore now?"

(I could probably still recite most of the movie from memory.)

—I was aware that drugs were dangerous and could mess up my life. I even went down to the local senior center along with a few other kids to read essays about how bad drugs were from the perspective of sixth graders who'd never done drugs.

Sure, drugs could be bad. But they also looked kinda sexy. They also looked kinda fun.

I stayed good as long as I could. But I had been trapped in this little bumfuck town for far too long. Eventually, boredom won. Plus, I hated being sheltered. I yearned to know the world more intimately—the good, the bad, and everything Jonas got to feel in *The Giver*—and that wasn't going to happen if I didn't seek out the worldliness I was after.

I was determined to check marijuana off my list by the end of the summer. I was about to be a junior and needed to lose at least one of my V-cards before going back to school in the fall, so I started asking around the marching band at flag corps practice and calling friends on the landline. Karissa and Ashley didn't know anything. Unfortunately, my friends were mostly straightedge, but Matt promised to get us some pot after I'd threatened to inquire with some notorious bad boys. He'd smoked two or three times prior. Thus, he considered himself something of an expert. And I think he liked the idea of being my guide.

Enthusiastically taking him up on the offer, I followed up several times to no avail. Then finally, he called me after getting a dime bag from a slightly older boy. It was go time.

The heavy steel door of my Oldsmobile slammed behind me and I skipped across Matt's lawn. I let myself in the side door and found him right inside, in his computer room, where he was burning CDs of pirated music off of Napster, one of his favorite pastimes. "I can't wait to get hi-iiiigh!" I sang and did a little dance. A wide smile crawled across Matt's face. "I'll show you what I scored," he said, cautiously pulling a baggie out of his pocket.

It was very shitty weed, even I knew that, evidenced by the fact that it was about thirty percent seeds and smelled more like mildew than what I'd smelled wafting off the cute burnouts at school. It couldn't be helped. Who was going to sell their best weed to try-hard nerds in rural Minnesota?

"So this must be considered schwag," I said matter-of-factly. I had learned the stoner lexicon from the movie *Half Baked*. "It will still get you high," Matt reassured me.

"Oh shit, we're gonna need a piece." Suddenly remembering we would need a smoking device, Matt set to work, first fashioning an unsuccessful rig out of an apple. "I think it's too moist," he said after a few unsuccessful hits. "Too moist?" I repeated and we giggled. "Let's try a pop can," he said, pulling an empty Sprite can out of the recycling bin. He took a hit to test the Sprite contraption. It was marginally better.

"We shouldn't smoke in the house," Matt said, trying to hold his breath. He herded me outside, exhaling a tiny cloud once we were firmly in the yard. He thought we should smoke in his car in case his parents came home, so we drove around in his blue boat (ugh, we even had similar cars). We followed Highway 86 to the tar road by the golf course until it turned into gravel. Then it was back to Highway 86. The windows wouldn't roll down, so we stopped every mile or so to inhale from the Sprite can. Sure, it wasn't very discreet, but I wasn't worried about looking suspicious, only about getting high.

"I'm not feeling anything yet," I complained as we drove back to his place, passing rows of modest homes and kids playing in the park. A lawnmower buzzed in the background.

Upon our return, Matt fumbled around the living room,

trying to set a mood. From the couch, I watched the giant wall clock tick off the intervals of monotony. *Tick tock.*

Matt stood by the light switch, attempting to create some kind of strobe effect, as if that might help throw us into an altered state. He flicked the light on. *Tick tock.* Then flicked it back off. *Tick tock.* Nothing.

I followed him up the stairs to his room, doing a body scan as we climbed. "Yeah, I'm just not feeling it," I said, plopping onto his bed. "Maybe this will help," he said, turning on the ceiling fan.

We lay side-by-side on his bed, our hands almost touching. We both stared up at the ceiling, watching the blades whip around and blur as they tried to catch each other. My breathing seemed to sync up with the fan's hypnotic drone as I tried to identify the individual blades within the opaque, never-ending spiral.

My mind began to blur similarly as I pondered. I wondered how many minutes would go by until the weed finally kicked in. I wondered how many days it would take for me to be lying on a bed with a boy who I actually wanted to kiss. I wondered how many years would go by before this unexciting first was a far-off memory. I wondered how different my life would feel after I'd done more drugs and kissed more boys.

I felt a melancholy pang simultaneously coming from a distant galaxy and somewhere inside the house.

All of a sudden I sat up straight and sighed, "Whelp, this was a bust. Not everyone feels it on their first time, I guess."

Disappointment washed over Matt's face. "I'll get some better stuff for next time," he promised.

I watched my feet as they made their way down the stairs, searching for some perceptible difference that would tell me I was high. A clear sign that I was no longer a pot virgin.

I slid onto my Oldsmobile's cream leather seat and slammed the heavy car door behind me. I rolled down the windows and stuck my head out the driver's side as I drove the fifteen miles back to Jackson—except it turned into twenty because the wind felt so amazing on my face that I didn't want the ride to end.

My detour took me to the Best Western Country Manor

Inn diner where I worked—my first official job—as a waitress alongside my cousin Ashley, the Shirley to my Laverne, who happened to be working the day shift.

I pushed through the door wearing a huge shit-eating grin.

"Hey! What are you doing here?" Ashley greeted me with a coffee pot in her hand, surprised to see me there when I didn't have to be.

I didn't know the answer to her question, and in that moment, I finally got the answer to *my* question. I giggled and whispered loudly, "I think I just got high."

"Of course you did," she said and shook her head, probably because she knew it was just the beginning.

I watched her pour coffee for a trio of farmers at the counter. I blinked and she was wiping down a booth on the other side of the room. I blinked again and she was coming out of the swinging doors from the kitchen with one of the big, frosty cinnamon rolls that the diner was famous for. I blinked and she set it in front of me, the frosting twinkling back at me. Ashley looked at me looking at the cinnamon bun and rolled her eyes, amused. I tore into it ravenously, and while I savored every sugary, delicious bite, I stopped dreaming about the future, and demanding that it come faster.

While I ate that cinnamon roll that seemed to sparkle, the present moment was magical enough.

SWEET SIXTEEN &
NEVER BEEN KISSED

I spent sixth period sniffing my new notebook instead of taking trigonometry notes on it. School had been back in session for only a week. Our supplies still smelled intoxicatingly fresh.

The year was 2000. Bill Clinton was putting the Monica Lewinsky scandal to bed. Y2K was now behind us. George W. Bush was just a twinkle of a punchline in America's eye—two months away from losing, yet somehow winning, his presidential race against Al Gore. Napster had made it not just possible—but almost impossible *not*—to steal music off the Internet at a snail's pace using a mouse with a novelty mousepad.

The month was September. My birthday month. I was sixteen, going on seventeen. I had just started eleventh grade. I was slowly but steadily recovering from a humiliating, humbling three-year awkward stage. A disastrous short, poofy pixie cut was just beginning to grow out. The black rectangular Lisa Loeb-inspired frames of my glasses—which had earned me nicknames like "lesbo" and "dyke" from some of my classmates—were ditched except when I truly needed them for nighttime driving. Eventually I ditched them altogether and forced my eyes to conform. Mind over matter was my personal mantra.

When I arrived home from cross-country practice that evening, my Uncle Steve was at the dinner table eating cheesecake from a pie dish with his bare hands.

Uncle Steve was my "sweatpants uncle," a Minnesotan Jeff Bridges straight out of *The Big Lebowski*, always with a hip-pack and his intrusive opinions. Whether you admired or abhorred it, he did whatever he wanted; he couldn't give a fuck about decorum, and that went double for authority. He was a Vietnam vet, and I can only imagine how being drafted into a losing war, a literal war, where your life was at stake would redraw your edges and send your innocence AWOL forevermore. It is only in my adulthood that I can properly appreciate him. Then, he was just an overgrown child to me.

"So how old are you, Courtney?" Uncle Steve asked from across the dining room table.

"I'm sixteen. My birthday's in a few weeks," I responded, angling to get a slice of the blueberry cheesecake my mom made for dessert.

"Sweet sixteen and never been kissed, huh Court?" he winked at me.

I winced, flabbergasted. How did he know?! How the hell did my oblivious sweatpants uncle know I had yet to properly French a dude?! Before I could manage to sputter out a reply, my eczema-cheeks flushed bright red—the world's worst poker player!

Uncle Steve chuckled to himself as he picked a hunk of cheesecake out of the ceramic dish with his bare talons and threw it back in his mouth, like a pelican. I stared at him, mouth agape, pissed on multiple levels.

Historically, Uncle Steve liked to tease and poke fun, but as I stewed, I realized there was nothing ill-natured in his comment. And there was that wink. He wasn't making fun of me—he thought I was in on the joke!

This made me feel even worse. He thought there was no way I was sixteen-going-on-seventeen and hadn't had so much as the tip of someone else's tongue in my mouth.

I peered into the decorative mirror behind Uncle Steve, deep in thought as he and my dad carried on their conversation. All I'd had was a measly peck nearish to my mouth, but definitely still on the cheek region, during a game of truth or dare on a class field trip. It was bestowed by a boy with the nickname "Pizza Face" who had acne so unruly that not even Accutane could rein it in. And though he was cute in a sweet nerd sort of way, I was not satisfied with a dare kiss on a school bus from Pizza Face as my first kiss. My lack of this milestone was excruciating.

Recall being sixteen. Get inside the enviably collagen-rich, baby-fat-trimmed skin of your teenage youth and let those outsized emotions come rushing back. Friggin' ouch, right?

I was already motivated, but now I was determined to have

my first kiss before my birthday. I was Kisserella, and I had to get my first official kiss by midnight before I turned seventeen, just a few weeks away. If I missed the deadline, I would be over the hill. I wasn't worried that other people would perceive me as a prude or undesirable—though having just gone through an unattractive phase, perhaps there was some of that too—so much as I was terrified that I would be forever lusting, lonely, watching all the action from the fringes. I didn't want to be the boring best friend character in a rom-com, I wanted to be the dazzling leading lady. And leading ladies get kissed. It didn't need to be perfect, it just needed to happen, and fast.

The start of the school year meant the first school dance of the fall, offering hopes of an intoxicating make-out session, even though my only buzz came from the hot chocolate I'd chugged while drawing on my eyebrows and covering my pink cheeks with foundation at home. There was a huge screen set up in the cafeteria. Britney Spears was all the rage. I danced along to her classic "Baby One More Time" schoolgirl video with a life-sized Britney on the screen.

While clumsily busting a move, I scouted out any potential dudes I could slow dance with, in hopes that pressing our bodies against each other would inspire some mouth-to-mouth action. But the only boy who truly gave me the urge was my long-time crush Zach Eldridge, and he already had a girlfriend.

The rest of them were like annoying cousins I'd been unable to separate myself from since elementary school. Some as far back as Gingerbread Nursery preschool. They probably felt the same way about me—like a sister who'd been correcting them and casually calling out their insecurities for years. It wasn't exactly a recipe for attraction. But it didn't matter. I could make my brain squint and forget their boring, blockheadedness. In fact, when Sixpence None the Richer's "Kiss Me" came on, all of those petty complaints melted away. I just wanted another set of lips on mine. I wanted to be sweet sixteen and kissed, dammit! The clock was ticking…

I weaved between awkwardly embracing couples and sweaty sandwich-style group dancing. I couldn't find an available target anywhere. Everyone was either busy or unfathomable.

There would be no romantic kiss this night. There was nothing. Not even the rogue boner popping into my leg that I got during a middle school dance, which was flattering at least.

That fall happened to be my friend's first semester at the University of Minnesota, Twin Cities. Travis, or Trav, as we called him, was two years older than me. His mom had been my dance teacher growing up. I gravitated towards him because he was also a theater kid. And while I thought it was pretty cool that he could play guitar as well as he did, we were strictly platonic.

It was getting uncomfortably close to my birthday and Uncle Steve's words reverberated through my head. "Sweet sixteen and never been kissed, huh Court?" What terrible fate would be sealed if my tongue remained unmolested by the stroke of midnight on my seventeenth birthday? Would I become a cat lady immediately, or would there be some sort of grace period? I didn't want to find out.

After doing *Hello, Dolly!* together in ninth grade, Trav and I formed a theater clique, which included Karissa and Matt Erickson, who'd helped me pop my stoner cherry the previous month. For two years, we were inseparable.

When Trav left for college, I didn't see it as the end of our friendship, but an exciting reason to stay in touch. He was going to be my lifeline to where I most wanted to be—the big city! It wasn't New York or LA, but I couldn't afford to be choosy at this point in my life. Minneapolis was good enough for me. I began to forge my way as a self-invited third roommate in his dorm room any weekend I was able to make up an excuse my parents would accept.

At that point, I'd never been drunk. I'd hardly drank, period. A half a beer, a few sips of wine, but never any hard liquor. I'd never even tried to get drunk. I'd smoked weed with Matt for the first time a month prior. Up to then, I'd been a "good girl" but I was ready to shed that skin.

I kicked my shoes off and lounged on Trav's futon, proclaiming, "I want to get shitcanned tonight." Whatever that meant, I was eager to find out.

Trav opened up his mini fridge and pulled out a bottle of

Southern Comfort—or "SoCo," as he kept calling it.

He filled up a row of shot glasses and cracked a Coke as a chaser. We cheersed and I only got half mine down before gagging at the syrupy flavor. Trav handed me the Coke and I took a big gulp and then finished my shot, alternating tiny sips of SoCo with swigs of pop. My throat burned, my brain fizzed, and warmth radiated throughout my body. We settled into our usual rhythm of impersonations and jokes. I wanted to hear all about Trav's freshman experience so far. What was the dorm like? Who were his friends? Did he feel like an adult since he didn't live at home anymore and could go to Chipotle at 11 p.m.?

After my second shot of SoCo, my awareness of the outside world began to dim. We moved down the hall and I met some of Trav's friends. There was one cute boy who played football for another nearby college, Concordia University in St. Paul. Really cute. He had a bad nickname—Dirty Paul—but his mischievous smile and football stud vibe more than made up for it. I gave him a sideways glance and puffed out my chest seductively. I could feel the SoCo tingling in my stomach now, and it was making me bold.

What I immediately loved about drinking was that I didn't need a plan. All my usual thinking had been getting in the way. With alcohol, I just had to take a couple glugs and next thing I knew I was giggling with Dirty Paul on someone else's top bunk.

He breathed on my neck like a steamy car window. I couldn't imagine anything more erotic. Then our mouths were enmeshed, and I was grabbing Dirty Paul's dick over his Concordia sweatpants. He reached under my Hollister faux vintage football shirt to feel up my boobs. It was on. Whatever I'd been waiting for, this was good enough. I looked over at an alarm clock on the precipice of midnight. I was sweet sixteen and kissed, dammit! I wanted to shout it into a megaphone at a school assembly. I had done it! And with a way hotter guy than I knew I was capable of.

We made out on that top bunk long and hard, not stopping for the rumblings down below. The sounds were loud and quiet at the same time as Dirty Paul licked my face clean like a mother dog. I faintly gleaned through the warbling that they were worried I would lose my virginity in a blackout. Frankly, that did not seem like an issue to me. I tossed my head back as Dirty Paul sucked on my neck, and all I could see were blurry colors and bright lights. If I kept my eyes open, I thought I might puke, so I squinted them shut and put my mouth to work, lapping up this beefy young man's salty, sour taste, my poisoned mind working overtime, mentally taking as many pictures as I could, holding onto Dirty Paul's dick for dear life until eventually a smudged mob of hands pulled me down and dragged me down the hall to Trav's room, where out-of-focus fingers rushed a trash can in front of my bobbing head and I promptly threw up—wiping the shit-eating grin off my face.

I was still clutching Dirty Paul's bandana when I fell asleep on Trav's futon. A memento from my first make-out sesh. A present just in time for my birthday. But instead of the souvenir, I would have preferred to kiss Dirty Paul all night long.

Two weekends later, I drove up to the Twin Cities for another visit. This time, I knew the ropes.

Unfortunately, Dirty Paul wasn't around when the party got started. But after a few shots loosened up the vibes, a different guy—Isaac—leaned in closer and closer until our arms were intertwined and he tickled my ear with his whisper, "Hey, wanna get out of here?" The hair on my arms stood up. I nodded yes and we snuck back to his room. Isaac was a put-together guy with a head of curly light brown hair and a pleasing face like an Adonis statue. Probably a better catch than Dirty Paul on paper, but he's the one who ignored phone calls from his girlfriend to whisk me to his dorm room to play house for the night, so maybe the wrong guy got the "dirty" moniker.

Anyway, Isaac was studying something serious: math, science, or architecture. He seemed like the kind of guy who could be *my* boyfriend, if I were a couple years older and he didn't have a girlfriend, but the cheating didn't seem like my problem. I was busy making my own mistakes, I didn't have time to judge this guy's. Plus, I was a co-conspirator to my own ends. I didn't care if Isaac was morally upright. I was just using him for experience. So I stayed all night, getting as much practice as possible.

As far as Trav knew, I was lost. Pacing his dorm room in the wee hours with me MIA, his mind began to race. A small-town girl in the middle of Minneapolis. Anything could happen. His mind quickly went to the worst-case scenario.

Around 7 a.m. the next morning, after Isaac and I slobbered all over each other until the sun came up, I found my way back to Trav's dorm room. By myself somehow. Isaac didn't have the balls to escort me.

I knocked on the door, and it opened immediately. Trav pulled me inside and hissed in my face, "Where were you? What the hell were you thinking?" It looked like the vein on his temple might pop.

"What's wrong?" I asked, confused. "I had a super fun night," I added with a smirk. Trav held the sides of my arms for a moment, struggling to reconcile his rage and relief.

I showered in the women's communal bathroom, scrubbing the spit off my neck, pretending I was a student. I fantasized that these were *my* dorm showers, and I was just taking a leisurely Saturday shower at home. I wasn't a student yet, but I finally felt like a woman might. *Sex and the City* was a cult hit, and I was Minnesota Carrie Bradshaw. Maybe I wasn't such a late bloomer after all—I'd just been waiting for the right moment to let my petals drop.

Trav and I went out to a Chinese restaurant nearby. He scowled at me as the egg rolls arrived. "I thought I was going to have to call your dad and tell him we found your body face down in the Mississippi River."

"Lucky for both of us, I'm right here," I said, shaking my egg roll at him before taking a big bite.

Trav was still salty with me, but I knew it was worth it. In two short weeks, I'd gone from "sweet sixteen and never been kissed" to a make-out maven. I had now been kissed by two separate gentlemen. Hard. All the way to second base and stealing toward third.

RAKED

"So… wanna go to prom?" Bryce asked, cornering me in the hallway outside of social studies class as I was closing my locker. A lineman on the football team, he towered over me as I turned toward him. I froze for a moment as stragglers breezed past us on their way to the next class. Bryce's eyes darted around like he was running a play.

I had wanted to go to prom, and not by myself or with one of my guy friends, but I had no idea who I would go with. The existing couples obviously paired off first. Then the active crushes. My crush Zach Eldridge already had a girlfriend, so he was out of the running. And I was running out of time.

"Uh… sure!" I finally replied, my voice squeaky. We hesitated for a beat.

"Okay, cool," Bryce said. We nodded at each other and went off in opposite directions.

This rushed interaction between classes was the perfect reflection of our mutual ambivalence about the pairing. But exciting, nonetheless. He wasn't the worst option—he was outgoing, I thought he would be fun, and most importantly, he asked.

I slipped onto my seat in statistics class just as the bell rang.

The year prior, my Uncle Tom died unexpectedly during surgery. This was my first big experience with grief. Our enormous family gathered at Grandma Betty's house for his wake and everyone in town brought food. A burgeoning binge-eater with a reckless teenage mindset, I ate my complicated feelings all week: bran muffins, scotcheroos, licorice, every kind of chip known to man. I hung out in Grandma Betty's kitchen, with my security banquet. The next time I stood on a scale, I was dismayed to find I'd gained more than ten pounds—I didn't even know that was possible!

When junior prom rolled around a few months later, I was still stuck in a body I didn't know or recognize. The extra weight felt unwieldy, strange to move around in. I was frantically experimenting for the antidote to shrink it back down to size:

fasting, eating only cereal, eating exactly half of my lunch. I wasn't just flirting with an eating disorder, it was already a full-on affair.

And how could it not be? Every magazine cover and diet inside reinforced rigid beauty standards that I bought into like an obedient sheep. I wanted to look hot in my black mini wrap dress from Express. The dress had a thin strap that cinched around my waist. It was a simple math problem—I was bigger than a clothes hanger or a mannequin or a supermodel, and so the dress didn't lay flat and sleek against my body as seemed to be most flattering. Determined to slim down, I was grasping for a miracle.

The problem was, as a binger, I wasn't very good at starving myself. And I was unable to make myself throw up, despite a valiant effort. I'd discovered a haphazard solution eighteen months prior—Ex-Lax—but it wasn't entirely reliable. Frankly, it made things worse, but it gave me a semblance of control when I felt most desperate. So after Bryce asked me to prom, and after I bought the dress, I also bought a fresh pack of chalky chocolate laxatives and choked nine of them down the night before the big day for a quick pre-prom cleanse.

My stomach stirred and gurgled from the laxatives as Bryce and I waited our turn in the Grand March lineup. The Grand March was our Midwestern version of a cotillion—a showcase of eighty-one couples decked out in their prom best, taking a promenade in front of family and friends and townspeople watching from the bleachers in the high school gym decorated with silver stars. The theme song was Eric Clapton's "Wonderful Tonight."

I froze when I looked at the Prom 2001 program and saw that we were bringing up the rear as couple number seventy-six. If I could make it down this hallway and through the march without shitting my dress, it would be a minor miracle.

I clenched my butt cheeks tight and clomped my heels, partly out of nervous excitement and partly to mask my bodily noises. Luckily, the hallway was abuzz with teenagers chatting and joking around. Bryce and I were reading each other's faces—was tonight a friend date only or was hooking up on the table?

Finally, the miracle was bestowed: We paraded in front of the crowd and let our moms take pictures without a mortifying accident. My body flooded with relief.

Afterward there was a dinner at the Best Western, where I picked at my plate and dared not eat anything aside from maybe a leaf of lettuce. I watched skeptically as a hypnotist provided post-dinner entertainment while friends at our table passed around a flask. Bryce leaned over and whispered, "Wanna get out of here?"

Minutes later, Bryce and I hopped in his car and drove country roads out to a senior classmate's farm for a bonfire afterparty where, after a few pulls of whiskey, the laxatives finally caught up with me and I found myself needing to take the craziest shit.

My eyes darted around, desperate for a solution. This was not a great location to relieve myself. There was only one toilet on the property. I tried not to clomp en route to the bathroom, making it just in time, but I majorly stunk it up in a way that only a laxative purge can. And worse, I clogged the toilet. *Oh shit.*

My bowels were relieved, but anxiety sank to the pit of my stomach when I pressed the handle and there was no flush. I did not want to be labeled the prom party's poop girl. I searched around for some spray to mask the stench, but came up empty-handed. I couldn't dawdle—I had to escape before someone saw me. I tiptoed out of the house and mingled chummily to give myself an alibi. A senior girl handed me a red cup, and I casually took a swig. Across the yard, I heard someone yell, "Who destroyed the bathroom?!" *Oh shit.*

Soon other partiers were giggling as they tried to solve the mystery. I bopped my head to the music and nonchalantly warmed my hands beside the bonfire, pretending this witch hunt had nothing to do with me. Bryce was mere paces away. He shot me a flirtatious smile and I bit my lower lip in return.

"Did you clog the toilet?" a classmate asked me, ineffectively suppressing a chuckle. "Someone said they saw you in the house," they explained within earshot of Bryce. *Oh shit!*

"It wasn't me," I protested, balling my fists in the front pockets of my hoodie. I wanted to clobber them for being so indiscreet about my indiscretion, extra vexed that it was a self-own—I'd set myself up for it by taking laxatives the night before. What the fuck was I doing? I didn't want to date Bryce, but I did want to get some action. Wasn't that the point of prom? Get dressed up and try to steal a few bases? I'd seen *American Pie*. Even "the band geek" gets laid.

Bryce ambled over. "Are you the party pooper?" he asked, laughing.

"No," I said emphatically. Though my red cheeks betrayed me.

Luckily, Bryce was horny enough to ignore the accusations. In under an hour, we had escaped the bonfire and were making out in the backseat of his car, swapping acrid alcohol spit.

We sucked each other's faces for a while, but I already had lots of make-out experience by this point and wanted to get a new milestone out of prom. Bryce was equally eager to go further—I reached down and his pants were already unzipped.

Soon his dick was staring me in the face. It was my first blowjob, but I'd read enough *Cosmo* articles to know that it was supposed to be more of a suck job than a blowjob. I confidently took his dick in my mouth, remembering to work the shaft. I gave him head for what felt like hours, drunkenly rotating around his cramped backseat, cycling through various positions trying to get comfortable. "Are you close?" I asked, gargling on his cock. "I think so," he said, squinting and biting his bottom lip. The longer it took, the harder I sucked. The most ambitious blowjob of my life.

There was no reciprocity. I don't think it was offered, but after becoming the destroyer of bathrooms, I was in no rush to expose my privates, and my thong stayed firmly in place.

By the time I crept up to my bedroom at 2 a.m., the corners of my mouth were raw.

Monday at school, Bryce and a group of boys were snickering in the back corner of psychology class.

"What's so funny?" I asked Karissa's boyfriend, on the edge of the group.

He leaned toward me and loudly whispered, "Bryce said you raked him." I had no idea what he meant, but I knew it wasn't good.

"Yeah, we hooked up," I shrugged. "What is he complaining about?"

Karissa's boyfriend pulled his lips back over his teeth and bobbed his head up and down with a biting motion like a psychotic PEZ dispenser. My jaw dropped and blood coursed through my body like a boiling stew. It had not even crossed my mind that I could be giving a bad blowjob, but I was annoyed that Bryce hadn't given me the appropriate adjustments in the moment. I was an actor, after all, I knew how to take a note!

Years later, I'd wish I shot back that maybe the problem was his whiskey dick. But I did not know better then, and I was mortified by the negative review (and the fact that there was a public review in the first place).

I passed Bryce at his locker. He nodded at me with a sheepish smile. My heart pounded as I blew past him, rolling my eyes.

After school that day, I was lying on the pole vault mat, looking up at the clouds during track practice, genuinely concerned about the blowjob dishonor that would surely follow me for the rest of my life. A gray cloud moved over the sun, and I sighed.

I imagined myself on the *Late Show* couch talking to David Letterman. Instead of asking me about my new movie, he said, "So I heard you have a funny story about your junior prom…"

I willed my cheeks not to flush under the hot studio lights. *I guess I have to own it*, I thought.

"How did you hear about that?" I replied archly. "Sounds like somebody kissed and told." I laughed Dave off in front of his studio audience and the millions of people watching at home.

LET'S RAIL

"Do you wanna rail?" Derek asked, his hand already up my white Abercrombie and Fitch long-sleeved V-neck, fiddling with my bra strap. The TV was on in the background of our basement make-out sesh and Derek's question was followed by a laugh line from *Friends*. But this was no laughing matter.

Yes, I wanted to rail. I had been strategizing this opportunity, this empty house, for weeks in the lead-up. For years I'd been getting messages from movies, women's magazines, and the rest of the culture that sex was spectacular—one of the best sensations on the planet. It was also inherently risky—perhaps part of its allure. I couldn't wait to be deflowered and find a piece of erotic pleasure for myself. I loved making out and, though relatively inexperienced, I took to it immediately and fancied myself a good kisser. I found dry humping quite a thrill; now I was ready to do that with unclothed genitals. My bases were loaded, and I was ready for the home run. Put me in, coach!

It was a Friday night, the beginning of Christmas break. Derek was still fully clothed and then some, wearing his winter coat—a big puffy FUBU (For Us By Us) jacket—inside, earnestly, as was fashionable for circa 2001 small-town white boys heavily influenced by hip-hop trends thanks to MTV and BET. You could live in Mountain Lake, Minnesota, and still style yourself like you came from Brooklyn, even though you'd never left the Midwest.

Derek was drenched in cologne—it drowned out every other competing smell. It wasn't Axe, it was something he was proud of. Probably Creed, which I later discovered was his favorite.

I see all the scenes, I smell it as if I were lying right there, but years later, I will struggle to remember what attracted me to him in the first place. I *was* attracted to him though—I must've been—because after I let out a little giggle at his phrasing, I said, "Yeah."

It all started with my attraction to a white Kangol visor. It was a stylish visor with its little kangaroo logo, and struck me as slightly more sophisticated than most of the farm boys with their Nike, No Fear, unironic Carhartt or Dickies, or, even more likely, generic clothes from Walmart or Target. And that handsome visor sat atop a handsome face, crowning a mop of perfectly symmetrical jet-black hair. At first, I thought I'd hit the jackpot. There were not a lot of dating options for a seventeen-year-old high school girl in Southwest Minnesota. Derek was as good as I was going to get.

Derek was ideal because he was from Mountain Lake, a neighboring town twenty-six miles away, so I didn't already know everything about him. I didn't want to waste any milestones on some boring local boy. I was planning to leave soon anyway, so there was no need to get attached to one of the few boys I actually thought was eligible. Aside from Derek's fashion choices, sinewy body, and attractive bowl cut (if that's even possible), all of which I liked, there was plenty of mystery on which I could map my desires. I didn't bother to vet his personality. How bad could it be?

Plus, the main reason that I liked him wasn't really about him at all, it was about me: I was restless. I was itchy. I was horny for experiences—it didn't matter so much which boy they were attached to.

I had wanted to lose my virginity before I even met Derek and I felt like I'd held up my end of the bargain. I had been a good girl; my life was a blur of extracurricular activities that were not euphemisms for sex. I wasn't willing to wait for marriage, like my parents and people at church wanted, but I had prudently waited until I was eighteen. Now I was free to gain some experience before I went off to college.

Intensely focused on my goals, I wanted to fuck without fucking up my future, so I thought through the calculus very carefully in preparation. Right after we went back to school for my senior year, I'd held a summit at the Burger King with my best friend Karissa—blonde, tan, and always laughing—and cousin Ashley—quiet, doe-eyed, and fast like a deer—to plot how we would get birth control, as we were all chomping at the bit to have our cherries popped. I drove thirty miles away to the Planned Parenthood in Fairmont and procured the Depo-Provera birth control shot (without my parents' permission) to avoid becoming a teen mom, an affliction I'd seen another cousin's ambitions succumb to a few years prior.

As soon as I got that shot, I was on the prowl. Karissa, who'd just started dating a guy from our grade, and I both felt that while we were destined to get the fuck out of this one-horse town, we would still make the most of our senior year. If you can't beat 'em, join 'em... at least until you can leave 'em.

This meant a lot of house parties after football games. On one such night, we stopped at Whoa n' Go—the truck stop up by I-90—to try to find someone to buy us some beer.

I spotted him in his white Kangol visor getting out of a car with a few other friends. He looked like the perfect mark. He was clearly older than us, but not by much.

"Hey, would you be down to grab some booze for us?" I asked, playing with a strand of hair.

"Aight," he said, without hesitation.

I gave him a twenty-dollar bill and he bought us a case of Bud Light. That was our meet-cute: mine and Derek's.

During the handoff, I thanked him with an invitation to the party at Karissa's house that night. His crew of guys was on their way to another party, so he couldn't come, but he asked for my number and we started texting. Old school texting—reliant only on the numerical keypad—was like swimming through molasses with your fingers. We weren't getting deep, but we were getting started.

A few weeks later, I went to a basketball game in Worthington with my mom. My dad was the coach. Derek might have been there to see his brother, or maybe I had mentioned my plans, but regardless, we sat on opposite sides of the court and watched each other more than the game. Not a word was spoken between us, but when I got home that night, I had fantasies about what that visor would do to me.

The Marquee bouncer squinted at my ID and back at me. There

was no doubt it belonged to me—it featured my school photo—but
there was also no doubt that it was fake. Karissa and I had ordered
them on the internet and they were ridiculous. The Common Loon
is Minnesota's state bird. Mine inexplicably had a turkey on it.

"Uhhh," the bouncer hesitated, shining his flashlight on my
ID.

Derek raised his eyebrows at me. I was squirming internally,
not wanting to ruin our first date.

"Here," I said, fishing out my school ID for the community
college where I was taking most of my classes and pressing it into
the bouncer's hand. "I also have this."

The bouncer scanned it briefly, shrugged, and waved us in.
Derek grabbed my hand and I tottered inside behind him before
the bouncer could change his mind.

The nightclub was next to a Hy-Vee just a few blocks from
a cornfield in another small town across the border in Iowa. Still,
going to the club for the first time felt so cosmopolitan.

Derek bought us beers. I took a sip of mine, grimaced, and
handed it back for him to finish. A shot girl in a short skirt and
tube top approached us. "Want a Jell-O shot?" she yelled over the
music. Feeling overdressed in my J. Crew top and jeans, I bought
a few and zealously threw them back. Derek took a swig out of
his bottle and leaned over and kissed me. I melted into a puddle.
We made out in his car afterward. I didn't want it to end, so I was
twenty minutes late for my curfew.

For our second date, I went over to his parents' house and we
watched TV on the futon in his family's computer room. Each
commercial break we moved closer and closer until we were dry
humping under a sleeping bag, completely oblivious to the show.

After that, things escalated on each of his visits home.

I was hesitant to give another blowjob after my first
attempt had been panned by the critics, so I had to coax myself into
it. I stopped by the grocery store on my way to his place and bought
a tub of whipped cream and a jar of cherries and made his cock
and balls into a sundae to psyche myself up for the performance. I'd
gotten some oral sex tips from a friend, so I felt ready for another

bite—or suck, rather—of the apple. Derek came quickly, which was validating. It was messy, but effective in getting over my fear.

By Thanksgiving, we were "in a relationship" and I was a confident cocksucker. We went to the movie theater in Spirit Lake to see the road trip thriller *Joy Ride* with Paul Walker, Leelee Sobieski, and Steve Zahn. For the first half of the movie, I grabbed Derek's dick over his jeans. Halfway through, he unzipped his pants and nudged me down to lick it. Eager to please and cross something new off my bucket list, I bent over and took his hardness in my mouth. We were in the fifth row of a nearly sold-out theater. The exhibitionism was exhilarating. I swallowed.

Afterward, I went to the bathroom and looked up from washing my hands to see my second-grade teacher's face in the mirror with her signature red cropped hair. Unbeknownst to me, she had been the shock of red in my periphery while I was giving Derek a beej. *Oops!* I rushed out without drying my hands, hoping she didn't see me. The whole situation went from bragging rights to cringeworthy real quick, but the silver lining was that I was racking up sex stories. It made me feel mature. I was ready for the real thing.

We'd been dating for three months when he said the magic words I'd been eagerly anticipating: "Do you wanna rail?"

The house was quiet. My parents and younger brothers were gone for a basketball tournament. I said, "Yeah," and we ran up the stairs from the basement to my room on the third floor. Shitty carpet, linoleum, hardwood, good carpet, shitty again, good again, then, after being briefly suspended in anticipation, we landed on my bed with a thud. Dark, except for the accidental candlelight—there was an electric candle aglow in each of the windows in Christmas vigil. Outside of my bedroom window, a star was brightly lit with string lights for the holiday.

"Do you have a condom?" I asked, like I was reading from the script of an after-school special.

Derek had a fresh pack of Magnums (ah, youthful

optimism) in hopes of this very scenario. I'd also purchased a pack
of Durex just in case. He rolled a condom over his dick. It fit like an
oversized sweatshirt, so he had to hold it in place. My lips tingled
from all the making out. I opened my legs. His eyes rolled back as
he entered me, tight as one of the attic's narrow crawl spaces.

The actual event took about thirty seconds—not that I
would've had time to get out my stopwatch. It was just two or
three pumps max, and then it was over. I wasn't expecting it to be
so quick and unromantic. The biggest build up for the smallest
payoff. I knew that couldn't be *good* sex for all the fuss people made
about it. But it didn't matter. Raised in a male-centric culture, my
concept of pleasure was more about notches on my bedpost than
actual orgasms for myself anyway. Having sex meant being let into
a special club, and I was euphoric to be in the land of the laid.

We went to a house party afterward. It was mostly older kids home
from college, but there were a few cool girls from my class circled
up in the dining room. I floated over to them and tried to act
casual, but couldn't resist telling them the news.

"You rode the train to Bonetown!" Angela Sterns exclaimed
as she gave me a high-five.

"How was it?" asked Hailey Hansen. Her eyebrows raised
playfully, thirsty for all the juicy details.

"Great," I said with a big smile and a shrug.

The details weren't as exciting as I'd hoped for. But I still
felt larger than life. After a lengthy delay, adulthood was coming
right on schedule.

Things were about to get interesting, I could feel it in the
chap of my lips.

GRAND MARCH

A lot had changed between junior and senior prom. I had a boyfriend, for one. And I was no longer a virgin, rapidly curating myself into the cool girl I wanted to be. Derek lived more than three hours away in St. Cloud, busy flunking out of college, but I convinced him to come back home for the weekend to escort me.

By then, I had my own little pipe and weed stash and got high at every opportunity. A few weekends before prom, I'd snuck up to St. Cloud to visit Derek and tried ecstasy for the first time. It was just half a roll and we spent the whole time in his dingy apartment, but still, it lived up to its name. I straddled him on the bed and gyrated with giddy elation. He put Vicks under my nose and told me to inhale. We traced each other's bodies with forks. It was a full-body sparkle—even my teeth were buzzed.

Derek suggested we should do more ecstasy again as soon as possible. I agreed. We decided that we'd participate in the Grand March for the sake of my poor, unknowing parents, but we would forgo the traditional after-prom activities, including dinner at Best Western. Why go to weak-ass prom when you can throw your own rave?

I danced around naked in front of the mirror, admiring my newly svelte figure thanks to my escalating Ex-Lax addiction and obsessive desire to be thin. (No, I did not learn my lesson from clogging the toilet the previous year, aside from not taking laxatives the night before prom.)

I slipped into a little black dress with a bikini-style neckline and tied the string around my neck. I twisted my bright blonde hair back into an updo. I looked like a sexy bobblehead.

I peeked out the window and watched Derek pull up in his white two-door Pontiac Grand Prix. "Do you want to come inside so my mom can take our picture?" I called out the front door.

He scrunched up his face. "Nah," he said, shaking his head.

"Do I look good?" he asked, stepping out in his car to twirl around, showing me the gray Men's Warehouse suit (that I paid for).

"You look great!" I gushed. "That's fine. We can take pics after Grand March."

I opened the passenger door for myself, moved empty plastic bags and pop bottles out of the way, and delicately slid on the dirty seat. "Here, this is for you." I handed him the boutonnière I bought for him.

"You're gonna have to help me put that on," he said, pulling out of the driveway.

Derek cruised into the high school parking lot with Incubus blasting. He was antsy to launch into the drug portion of the evening's festivities, so we took our tablets in the car before heading inside to wait for the ceremony, even though it was still light outside. Derek doled out half a roll for me for starters. He took a whole one. My teeth chattered in anticipation as Derek fished around for a warm soda to use as a chaser.

Once inside, we made jittery conversation and then begrudgingly separated. I was to enter the auditorium from the girls' side; his entrance was from the boys' side. Each couple was supposed to step out one at a time, meet in the middle as their names were called, and walk in front of the audience together.

I clopped forward a few steps at a time, whispering with the girls around me, until I was at the front of the line and it was our turn. At this point, the rolls had been in our systems for nearly an hour. I was starting to feel *smooooooth* and couldn't stop touching the fabric of my dress but my head was still in the game.

Green Day's "Time of Your Life" was playing when the girls' side chaperone signaled for me to go. I strutted through a balloon arch on my side, trying to move gracefully in my heels though I felt like a baby giraffe.

I stepped onto the basketball court, my pupils dilated like spaceships. I looked at the boys' entrance and giggled nervously. Derek was nowhere to be seen. My heels click-clacked as I teetered slowly toward the center, my bobblehead on a swivel, keeping watch for my MIA date.

Finally, a whole chorus later, Derek emerged.

Okay, phew! I stepped forward, relieved that I could see him. But after several steps toward me, he inexplicably did a U-turn and power walked back to the boys' entrance.

After a few more bars of the song, he reemerged at a zigzag. Then vanished again.

Once more he popped his head out of the boys' side with wild-eyed confusion.

"Derek," I hissed, gesturing for him to come. Despite dragging out every step, I arrived at the couples' photo mark alone. The MC called our names: "Derek Strommen and Courtney Kocak." I stood by myself under the bright spotlight with a crooked smile, fidgeting with the side of my dress.

No, Billie Joe Armstrong, I was not having the ti-iime of my life, but I was uncharacteristically content and chill thanks to the molly. There were a few laughs from the audience as I waited for Derek to catch up. Finally he was beside me. I looped my arm in his and gripped it tightly. The MC repeated our names. "Derek Strommen and Courtney Kocak." The cameras flashed.

We stood for a moment: two very high deer caught in headlights.

The theme of the prom was "Where You Want to Be," but I certainly wasn't where I wanted to be, stuck in Jackson.

After Derek's skittish performance, we let my mom take some pictures and then he drove us to his hometown. (I have no idea how—he could barely remember how to walk.)

I didn't take this final opportunity to hang out with my high school friends; we held our private rave on his turf, instead of mine. The couple other guys in attendance were his friends, burnout townies, spinning their wheels just like I was learning to do.

Prom was the one night I didn't even try to abide by a curfew. I took the other half of my roll and then a little bit more. Someone turned on the TV, but the only thing on was a jarring late-night infomercial for Girls Gone Wild. Over a bed of synthetic island beats, a man with an exaggerated voice shouted, "Warning: This contains adult content that is not suitable for children!"

"Turn it off," someone said. They fiddled with the stereo instead. I writhed around on the floor and made out with Derek as we listened to music until the wee hours of the morning. I felt like the most expansive version of myself—a vast, starry night sky— twinkling throughout my body.

When we roused again, it was the bright light of day and it was my turn to drive. Derek sprawled out in the passenger seat and was soon asleep. I sat up straight as a board, hands at ten and two on the steering wheel, and gazed ahead at the cornstalks swaying in the wind.

Mustering as much of my hazy, drained attention for the drive as I could, I had the bittersweet realization that my brain would never be the same. I felt exhilarated, ecstatic even, but different. I thought of the *Oprah* episode I'd seen about former club kids who had holes in their brains from doing too much ecstasy. I thought of the pores that were probably starting to form on my heretofore perfectly pure, undisturbed brain. I tried to reassure myself that a little texture was a good thing.

BORDER CROSSING

It took me less than six months to throw away my big dreams for a dude.

The prior summer I had toured Julliard, NYU, and Columbia in New York City. If I was going to college instead of straight into the entertainment industry, I was determined to go someplace "worth it." But as my mom and I sat through orientations and talk of steep tuitions, my mom got sticker shock and it rubbed off on me. I didn't know anything about how loans worked and what I would qualify for—or the value of a name-brand university's alumni network. All I heard was debt.

My plan B was a nationally noted BFA program in Missouri called Stephens College, which was an attractive option because I could graduate in two and a half years thanks to their summer theater programs. Stephens became even more attractive when I was offered a lot of scholarship money, so much that they called my mom to tell her they don't usually award that much to one student.

By the time I lost my virginity over Christmas break, the plan was in place for me to attend Stephens College and pursue my acting ambitions.

Derek was failing out at a state school, and I was getting recruitment brochures from Harvard. But the dopamine, serotonin, and norepinephrine receptors in my brain hijacked the plane and transported me to St. Cloud State University. It was a hostage situation. I wasn't in love with Derek because he deserved it. He wasn't trying to be a good student, a good boyfriend, or even a good person. My attraction to him wasn't earned in any way, it was an involuntary chemical reaction.

After I lost my V-card, the genie was out of the bottle. There were weekends we spent together the spring of my senior year where we fucked seven or eight times a day. We fucked each other raw. One time I gave him a hand job on a Bloomingdale's bench. We had sex in countless parking lots. We couldn't be bothered to wait for a bed. It was out of control horny rabbit shit.

More addictive than even drugs.

I was subconsciously in on the hijacking. There was a nugget of shame lodged deep in my cerebral cortex. I could hear my dad saying, "You know it was really important to me that your mom was a virgin." Whenever he'd said something like that growing up, I rolled my eyes and thought, *Okay, whatever, good for you* or *That's ridiculous, I'm not doing that*, but somehow I must have internalized this virginity standard. Somewhere lurking in the back of my head, I wondered, *Am I damaged goods? Am I supposed to marry my first? I guess I should give it a shot...*

As a grown woman, I will want to get in a time machine and go back to this girl I was in early 2002. I will want to shake her and scream, "Don't give it a shot! Break up with him now! Who cares if he's your first, he doesn't have to be your last!" But I'll be stuck in the same dimension my entire life, and in this dimension, I won't get advice from my future self. Instead, I'll redesign my whole life to try to make it work with my first boyfriend.

The same day I graduated high school, I followed Derek to St. Cloud for college.

My apartment was off-campus at 1 Rivercrest Drive, aptly named because a river ran behind the complex.

I toured it with Derek, who at that point had his own apartment north of town. A middle-aged female manager showed us the tiny one-bedroom—narrow kitchen to the left as we walked in the door, closet to the right, a few paces up was the bathroom, then the bedroom, and the rest of it was an all-purpose living room. Derek breezed past me and I smelled the cigarette stench emanating off his clothes. "There's no smoking in the common areas," the manager said with a forced smile. "No problem," I replied quickly. Derek's chain smoking made me self-conscious whenever we had to interact with actual adults.

I stood in the center of the living room, slowly rotating to take it all in. The apartment wasn't much, but it was just for me. I wasn't in New York or LA, but at least I had a place of my own.

My dreams had been downsized.

Derek didn't want to get a job, so he decided to grow shrooms. He got the idea from his hours on the Erowid forum and ordered a kit off the internet. He grew his first batch in his bedroom closet.

As the spores grew, so did Derek's anxiety and suspicions. Too many hours on paranoid message boards or his underlying mental health issues starting to make themselves known, it's hard to say. He'd had a bad trip at a festival a few weeks before I graduated (and cheated on me, but I wouldn't know that for another year or two). His personality grew more unpredictable, and it felt new and scary to be around.

Soon after I'd moved to St. Cloud, Derek's first batch of shrooms was ready to be tested. He wasn't sure if they were going to work, but of course we would be the guinea pigs. Midafternoon, we ordered cheeseburgers from the McDonald's drive-thru. In the parking lot, we each took off the top bun and buried strips of fresh shrooms in the ketchup, mustard, pickles, onions, and cheese to mask the taste—though it wasn't effective. "Oh wow," I said with a sour face after taking my first bite. "It tastes kind of like moldy dirt."

After McDonald's, we went to the park to play tennis while we were waiting for the shrooms to kick in. Tennis was the one semi-normal activity I'd convinced Derek to partake in. My parents would play all the time for fun, so I'd gotten into it too and then started playing with Derek because neither of us had money and there wasn't much else to do for free.

The tennis court was cracked and had a saggy net. Derek served ball after ball out of my racket's reach, sending me running back and forth across the court in my bright white terry cloth shorts.

All of a sudden the foreboding sky turned darker gray and began to cry. The balls were so green, their neon buzzing at me, there was no way I could get to them in time. "Derek, no—ha—please stop," I pleaded, out of breath, laughing uncontrollably. Chasing the glowing orbs had worked me into a tizzy.

The rain poured down harder and it was clear we were high, a state we had conjured yet not adequately prepared for.

Derek flipped from playful to paranoid, pelting the balls faster and demanding that I get to them in time. Finally he stopped and threw up his arms. "Are you tripping?" he shrieked, exasperated, the racket clattering to the ground.

Maniacal laughter rattled out of me like a jackhammer, and it was soon joined by tears, not sad exactly but stricken, the atmosphere and emotion causing my mascara and eyeliner to bleed down my face. I rubbed under my eyes and then my hands were black too. The fun and games were over.

"How are we supposed to get home?" Derek huffed hysterically.

I tried to slow my breathing until I could reply, "Maybe we should wait." I watched another couple scurry to their car on the other side of the park. "Or try to get a ride."

"No," Derek said. He grabbed my shoulders and guided me to his car, forcing me into the driver's seat. I took a dozen deep breaths and then peeled out onto the road, my tongue glued to my upper lip, concentrating like I was skipping into Double Dutch jump rope. Derek barked orders at me from the passenger seat, coaching me through the maze of streets that stood between us and our destination, though ultimately serving as yet another distraction I had to ignore.

I drove about two miles per hour, trying to stay locked into my tunnel vision. Each time we arrived at a red or green or yellow light it totally undid me. "What do the colors mean?!" I squealed.

But somehow we made it back to his apartment. Derek jumped out of the car and ran inside like he was fleeing the scene of a crime. I got out, took a few steps to survey my parking job, got back in and pulled up another foot and a half. I straightened out the wheel and slowly turned the key back in the ignition. With steady meditative breaths, I waited for the car to stop purring.

Soon after we got home, Derek's friends came over to play *Madden NFL 2002* on his PlayStation. I watched from his bed. Usually while they played, I tried to talk with them in their own language. I'd ask, "Why do you guys always pick Nashty?" (That was what they called Steve Nash, who played for the Dallas Mavericks.) "So the Mavs are the best team in the NBA?" They'd mostly ignore me. However, on this day, I was tripping, so they had a minor curiosity in the effect psilocybin would have on me as a first-timer.

"Are you feeling anything yet?" Derek's friend asked, looking away from the video game momentarily to study me.

I hadn't done any of my own research and we didn't have internet on our phones in those days, so I wasn't sure what to expect, but I felt fucking weird. My head felt like a balloon. I thought it might float away, so I had to walk slowly and intentionally to keep myself grounded.

I made my way out to Derek's deck and admired the view of the prison against the sunset. The smokestack looked wobbly. Someone said that's where Tim Allen, the comedian and actor who played the dad on *Home Improvement*, went to prison when he got busted for drug trafficking. I don't think this was actually the correct prison, but I felt a tinge blue—wistful for New York or LA. I was supposed to be out of Minnesota by then, chasing my dreams, trying to make it as an actor, like Tim Allen. How did I get stuck in St. Cloud? For a moment, it felt like I was in prison, but I didn't know how to get out.

Back on the bed, I sucked on a watermelon Blow Pop, which I enjoyed the shit out of, going to town until I'd gnawed it down to the gum. Before I knew it, the gum, while still on the stick, was in my hair. The sucker had jumped into my hair on its own volition… How rude!

I rolled out of the bed and felt my way to the bathroom to survey the damage. I fumbled around to turn the light on. I looked in the mirror and what struck me first was my DIY bleach blonde hair. Oh my, so blonde! It was electric, almost white. I admired my dye job and how I'd made myself look like a sparkling goddess or a mermaid, then I saw the red sucker, nestled in a snarl of hair behind my ear. Untangling it was out of the question, I would have to cut a chunk of my precious mermaid hair.

Then, out of nowhere, I saw every single vein coursing through my face. Red and blue slithering snakes. I peered closer and the snakes turned into spiders that quickly multiplied and infested the mirror. I had to get out of the bathroom. I had seen enough.

I switched off the light, the sucker still stuck in my hair.

The summer of 2002 there was a terrible weed drought in St. Cloud, so Derek, his friends, and I took a trip across the U.S./Canadian border to Winnipeg in search of cheaper, more plentiful greens. By then, I no longer had friends of my own.

We spent two nights in Winnipeg. The first night Derek wanted to hang out in the hotel room and play cards with one of the other weed-seekers in our caravan, so I just watched TV.

On our second and final night, I was enthusiastically dragged out to a strip club where I sat alongside the fellas. My first strip club experience, how fun! I was mesmerized by the neon thongs, shimmery tassels, eclectic tattoos, wild hair, and how the dancers managed to take off five layers of clothes when they didn't even start with one. They were sexual magicians, and I wanted to learn their art form.

Unique to Canadian strip clubs was that we got to flick loonies and toonies—one and two-dollar coins—at the dancers' torsos to tip them. I aimed between a dancer's belly button and the Superwoman emblem on the front of her thong. Then she wasn't wearing a thong anymore, and my throws got a little wilder. It was exciting to be included in the debauchery. Yes, I was far from my dreams, but it was still thrilling to engage in the spoils of adulthood.

The next morning, we ate a big breakfast at the hotel diner before splitting into two cars for the long drive back to St. Cloud. We had come all this way for the weed—it was hard to part with it. We hatched a plan that three of us would carry it back. When we checked out of the hotel, Derek and his barrel-chested friend of a friend each had a quarter taped around their upper thigh and I was crotching a small baggie of weed, less than an eighth, in my underwear.

I sat with Derek in the backseat of his buddy's car. Our accomplice, who we'd just met on this trip, was in the passenger seat.

As we approached the border, Derek got antsy. "Hey, you want to smoke this joint?"

"Now?" I replied. "I'm not sure this is the best time—"
Derek already had it lit and was taking a hit. I giggled nervously. He took another hit and passed it to me. I shrugged, accepted it,

inhaled, waited, and exhaled a cloud of smoke, which mingled with his, and our accomplice exclaimed, "Yo, WHAT are you doing?" He rolled down the windows, trying to air out the car a mere fifteen minutes before we had to go through customs.

When we pulled up to the checkpoint, I held my breath. A customs agent shared a laugh with his coworker, then gestured for our accomplice to roll down the window. The customs agent's face tightened almost immediately. Instead of sending us to the right, as he had been with the cars before us, he directed us to the left. Everyone in the car whispered a collective "Oh shit." I looked urgently to Derek; he sat stiff as a board with his stupid sunglasses on. I wanted to press pause on the whole situation—the car reeked like a skunk, of course they could smell it. What were we thinking?

A quartet of agents escorted us out of the car, patting us down, and asking stern questions. An inspection crew with dogs went through the car and pulled some items out of the trunk. I was separated from the guys and taken to another room with harsh fluorescent lighting for further questioning. "We're going to find it either way, so just tell me: do you have anything?" a female agent said, her eye contact sawing me in half.

"I have a baggie with a small nug in my—" I pointed down at my underwear.

I was instructed to retrieve the baggie, then immediately whisked in front of a gruff customs officer, who sat behind a desk flanked by an American flag and an armed agent. He looked me up and down, annoyed.

I felt incredibly stoned and oddly sober. My body felt like chilled Jell-O in the hard chair—I thought I would jiggle into a pile on the ground.

"Do these look familiar?" The officer set a nug jar, rolling papers, and other paraphernalia on the table in front of me. I confessed immediately, crying a monsoon.

"I was a National Merit Commended Scholar," I blubbered, my face streaked with mascara. "I'll never do it again," I promised.

"I'm supposed to get transport to take you down to the jail, but today is your lucky day. However, make no mistake, this WILL follow you anytime you enter and leave the country, so I recommend cleaning up your act."

I nodded emphatically. "I will… and I don't think I'll be coming back to Canada."

They let us off with a $500 fine each. I would end up paying Derek's portion after he demanded that it was all my fault, acquiescing to keep the peace, because getting him to pay for anything was nearly impossible. At one point I tried to separate our accounts, but once they were merged, the debts were both in my name. It would take me more than three years to pay off the $1,000 in tiny payments of $15 or $20 at a time, only payable in cashier's check or money order. I learned the lesson for both of us.

It was a very quiet ride home.

When Derek's lease was up, he moved into my apartment for a while. At first, I thought living together sounded adult and cool. Of course, he brought his shroom tank, though I was disappointed when it remained his singular attempt to contribute financially. I didn't understand why I was the only one working—overnight at Walmart, the counter at Leeann Chin, temping on an assembly line, even selling my plasma. Coming home with tired eyes, smelling like Chinese food, my hair matted down from my visor to see him shirtless, shouting at the TV screen, gleefully playing video games without a care in the world, I realized that living together was a raw deal—it just made it easier for him to mooch off me.

Derek living with me was always intended as a temporary situation for the summer, but he overstayed well into the fall.

On a crisp, snowy November night, we got into a super intense fight and Derek locked me out of my apartment with no coat. Shut out of my own apartment by an interloper. Not just my apartment, but the building itself.

"Let me in!" I pleaded, but Derek had already gone back upstairs.

I can't recall my contribution to the chaos. I don't think I knew even then, as I banged on the door, my teeth chattering. I don't remember being unreasonable. I was pretty chill, by nature and necessity, though running out of patience at the fact that I was paying for everything.

After I somehow got back in and we made up, Derek

wrote me an apology rap and performed it in the living room of my apartment. He cleared his throat and spat, "You know I'm corrupt as a thug, but please don't give up on our love." I wish I could quote more but it was so pathetic, I ripped up the paper and threw it away as soon as he went back to his video games. Perhaps it would have been touching if Derek were a skilled rapper, but my brow furrowed reflexively as I watched him in a horrifying moment of clarity: I was not only dating an asshole, but an idiot and, even worse, a bad artist.

After quite a bit of prodding, Derek moved into an apartment by the mall with his friend, who was nicer to me than he was. I would come over and watch them play video games. Because of Derek's growing paranoia, the shroom tank stayed behind at my place. At his new apartment, he quickly put a hole through the wall in a fit of rage. I stood frozen just a foot away from the chalky gash in the plaster.

Even during more tender times, his favorite pastime was a "game" where he tackled me over and over again, like I was a waifish defensive lineman with the bruises to match.

"Say 'hut, hut, hike!' and don't move early," he would instruct me.

"Hut, hut, hike?" I would repeat, obediently taking my licks, and he'd bulldoze me onto the bed. Only rarely would I voice dissent. It wasn't worth the argument. Sometimes he didn't even hide the hits in a game; he'd just hit me straight on. Once across my face knocked the bridge of my nose loose.

Derek didn't care about romance or foreplay or being nice or anything involving my pleasure, but we had to have sex whenever he wanted—something I typically enjoyed, but I didn't like the increasingly forced nature of these encounters—an expectation that would end in a fight if I didn't oblige.

One night we went to a house party and he introduced me to his friend, who'd recently been released from jail. We stood outside near the keg, me draped on Derek's arm.

His friend took a sip out of his red cup and smirked, "How

is she?"

Sheepishly, I looked at Derek. He glanced at me and then back at his friend. "She's a dead fish," he said. They both roared with laughter. My jaw dropped. Eventually my words came. "We have sex all the time, you've never said that!" I sputtered.

I was in St. Cloud to be with him and I'd spent much of my senior year distancing myself from friends and family, so there was no one to witness our dynamic and give me advice. My world had gotten small because he took up so much space in it.

That fall, in a paranoid panic, Derek threw his shroom tank, along with any hopes of making money, into the river behind my apartment, convinced that the DEA was after him.

I had complicated feelings about that shroom tank, including envy. Maybe being discarded would have been a relief.

The coldest I've ever felt was when I was nineteen, a freshman at St. Cloud State University, walking through the parking lot to my English Composition class. The winter wind was whipping me with sub-zero temperatures; the windchill was borderline unsafe—they would call off school the next day, which they rarely did. I thought I might freeze into a statue, and my bones were also frozen with the knowing that my life was all wrong. How did I get here: at this cold-ass school I didn't care to attend with a loser boyfriend who treated me like shit?

I ducked into the theater building to warm up. Reading the flyers on the wall, I knew I had taken a wrong turn, and I needed to find my way out of this most aggressively tedious and increasingly dangerous maze. I felt stupid for getting into this situation with Derek and for letting it get this bad.

In Comp class, we watched *A Simple Plan*, about two brothers who discover a mysterious plane crash and plot to steal the millions in cash they find alongside the dead pilot. We also watched the Gary Sinise and John Malkovich adaptation of *Of Mice and Men*. My wheels were turning—about the essay I had to write, yes. But also, about how I could hatch a plan of my own. An escape plan. There were holes in the walls of our respective apartments and the bridge of my nose was loose. I had to escape what my life had become.

I titled my essay "Jacob and Lennie: Lessons in Dependency." My main idea, underlined at the end of the first graf, was, "Though these characters play a very similar dependent role, each is vastly dissimilar in the cause of and the nature of, and greatly parallel in the meaningfulness of, the relationship with the man he is dependent on." On the next page, I characterized the brother relationship in *A Simple Plan*, pointing out that Jacob bases a lot of trust in Hank, who takes this trust for granted and sometimes abuses it. Ms. Wenz wrote in pencil at the end: "You might point out that although Lennie and Jacob were considered dependent, in the end, Jacob showed leadership when <u>he</u> made the decision that his life should end there."

I got an A—19 points out of 20—on the paper. Reading Ms. Wenz's comment, I realized how I could earn that missing point outside of class. Execute the escape plan, earn an A+.

That winter, I occasionally spent the night at my apartment on my own. During that rare alone time—when I wasn't in class, working one of my part-time gigs to support us, or with Derek—I would scheme about a future without him. I developed a nervous tic where I would play with my loose nasal bridge, moving the bone from side to side while deep in thought. I had watched *Sleeping with the Enemy* numerous times as a girl and wished I had her stack of money to escape. I didn't have that, but I did have some options. The most obvious one was that I could reapply to Stephens College.

I applied in secret. They didn't give me quite as much scholarship money the second time around, but they still gave me an affordable path to get back to plan B.

I executed the whole escape plan without telling Derek or any of his friends.

My parents helped move out of the Rivercrest Drive apartment in stealth mode. I put my cell phone on silent and ignored calls from Derek as we loaded up their van and a trailer behind it. They didn't hassle me too much for the details, careful not to upset me. They were eager to get me away from Derek by any means necessary, unimpressed by how he was treating me, even from the little they'd seen, and suspicious that he was unwell (confirmed over Christmas break when he made threatening middle-of-the-night phone calls, calling my dad a "little bitch" for refusing to put me on the line).

"I'll meet you back at home," I said, hugging them before they got in the van. I waved as they drove out of the parking lot and then I got in my Oldsmobile. Before I left town for good, I went over to Derek's new place—he got kicked out of the one by the mall for putting holes in the wall and was now living in a flophouse close to campus.

I skipped up to his bedroom and chatted casually, acting like I was saying goodbye for just a few days, and that I would see him over Christmas break. But I had an ulterior motive.

Derek had some topless photos of me that he refused to return despite several good-faith requests. I needed to steal them back.

I lay with him in his bottom bunk and outlined his dick over his jeans. He got hard immediately. "Quickie?" I asked. He was already taking off his pants. I lay like a dead fish, letting him thrust vigorously until he was done. He collapsed next to me on the bed. I patiently waited for a few minutes.

"Probably a good time for a shower. Wanna go first?" I suggested. When he was out of the room, I rushed to get my clothes back on and rooted around for the envelope of photos and the negatives. Jackpot! I secured them in my purse and swiftly made my way downstairs. The cum dripping in my thong didn't slow me down one bit.

Derek must've put it together when he heard me leaving because he chased after me in a towel as I rushed to my car, yelling, "You fucking slut. Those are mine!"

No, those were mine. I took a deep breath and shook my head in the rearview mirror.

I had lost myself with Derek and was in the process of finding myself again. Sometimes when you cross a border on your way home, you wind up getting detained. Pay the fine—just your own—and move on.

SMOTHERED, COVERED & CHUNKED

Soon after I got to Stephens College, I got a job at the Waffle House, an iconic restaurant famous for its comfort food and infamous for what belies its wholesome yellow, black, and white branding. The location I worked at was in a sketchy part of the outskirts of Columbia, near a motel my parents booked online and then, after arriving, were too afraid to stay at.

"It was rough," they said.

Honestly, I was surprised to see them prioritize their personal safety over a good deal.

Waffle House doesn't exist in my home state of Minnesota. Think IHOP or Denny's with a Southern accent. According to the Waffle House website, "In 1955, two Georgia neighbors opened up a restaurant that would change the world." I'm not so sure about that, but seventy years later, the Waffle House "system" has over 1,900 locations in 25 states and has become a pop culture icon, name-checked by rap superstars including Lil Wayne, Kanye West, and 2 Chainz.

The thing about Waffle House that is consistent across all 1,900-plus locations is that they're open twenty-four hours a day, seven days a week—that's what rappers and regular people love about them. So, when it comes to staffing, they need coverage for all three shifts. First shift in the morning, second shift in the afternoon, and third shift overnight when it turns into an asylum with unlimited refills. On weekends, I worked in the mornings, and occasionally I worked weekday afternoons, but mostly, I was a third-shift bitch.

My acting classmate, Wren, referred me for the job after an extensive job search wherein I'd applied to every job I was vaguely qualified for and sold my plasma to the point of passing out (on days I didn't get rejected for being anemic).

Ultimately, I got the job because I stopped by and talked to Frank one afternoon.

Frank was the franchise owner of this particular Waffle House. Frank liked me in a very fatherly way. Maybe father who'd like to fuck, but the feeling was mutual, and those were very minor undertones—almost undetectable. Any attraction was benign. He was happily married. He always had a playful grin and his face lit up like a Christmas tree when I talked about my future: going to LA, being an actress in the big city—like he knew, by the way I said it, that I was really going.

Frank also knew everything he knew about life, which was way more than I did, and his wry smile said, *Oh, baby girl, you are going to get rocked.* He was protective, too, and he gave me a job as a waitress.

Eventually, his son came to town and started working the grill. I developed a minor crush on him, too, though we probably said five words to each other in total. A father-son crush triangle between boss and coworkers—standard, I'm sure, with every Waffle House franchise.

Third shift was a blur of late-night drunks, frequent shouting, and fights. The patronage was that of any truck stop coffee shop or 24-hour diner but on steroids. Drunk people, hungover people, hungry people, people passing through, and people for whom this restaurant, this particular Waffle House location, was a central, often daily, part of their lives—the security guards, auto parts salesmen, retired couples without kids, and divorced dads with weekend custody; the Carls, Merles, Lindas, and Freds who returned to us like boomerangs.

I started at Waffle House in February, after transferring to Stephens in January. I was sort of a loner that first semester. Though I'd fled St. Cloud in secret to get away from Derek, I was still, somehow, dating him. That's a big part of why I had the job, so I could afford plane tickets and sexy clothes to go see him, and of course I always had to cover his broke-ass too.

I had been scared to break up with him in person, so I didn't do it with finality. After winter break, we stayed in sporadic contact. Perhaps it was the innate distance in our phone, text, and email communication that lulled me into a false sense of security. Only interacting with him in small doses allowed me to remember him with rose-colored glasses. And, of course, I was lonely. I had two non-theater friends I'd made during winter orientation, but it didn't seem like they were going to stay. It had been tough to break in with the theater kids at first. It was hard to make friends while trying to maintain an alluring mystique to mask an abusive relationship *and* working the overnight shift. I was exhausted and numb. I fit in perfectly at the Waffle House.

Working at the Waffle House meant learning a new language. The Waffle House is known for its unique ordering system, in which servers and sometimes even customers shout their orders out to the cooks behind the counter. I was expected to stand on the lighter, concrete-colored square next to the waffle irons and shout orders to the grill cooks, using a special shorthand. For example, if you wanted a popular dish such as hash browns—simply known as "browns"—made in the traditional fashion, i.e., spread out on the grill, I would scream "Browns! Scattered!" at the cook from the concrete-colored square. But that's a boring order. More than likely, you would want to dabble in the near-countless variations, like "Smothered!" meaning sautéed with onions, or "Covered!" with melted American cheese, or "Chunked!" with chunks of grilled hickory smoked ham, or maybe all three: "Smothered, Covered, Chunked!" And that's just the tip of the iceberg; they could also be "Capped!" with mushrooms, "Diced!" with tomatoes, "Peppered!" with jalapeno peppers, "Topped!" with chili, or "Served all the way!"—the full monty, for lovers of diarrhea.

DeeDee, my fellow waitress, trained me to yell, "Welcome to Waffle House!" or, at the very minimum, "Hello!" to every single person who entered the door.

DeeDee did meth. Visibly. It was crawling up her arms in red splotches and rotting her teeth. It infected her whole energy from her toes to the ends of her frizzy-ass orange hair. Everything was frazzled. I liked DeeDee for her straight-shootin' bluntness though there were definitely days she was easier to work with than others. I suspect on those days, she had a magic helper, a straightener named Meth. But she had kids and complicated relationships with her exes, and a trailer that always needed fixing in some way or another, so I didn't take her moods personally. Honestly, it's impressive she could ever muster the energy to be nice, even with the help of drugs.

DeeDee's hair was always winding up in the food. Waffle House has a hair policy for its employees. Hair is supposed to be clean and well-groomed, restrained, with no extreme hairstyles or colors, and no hats or head covers with the exception of a visor and a hairnet, when necessary. And a hairnet was necessary—a ponytail holder was not sufficient to restrain DeeDee's wild mane of long orange kinky hair. It looked like a lion's mane that had been electrocuted. After numerous complaints of browns with an unwanted ingredient for which we did not have a code word, DeeDee had to wear a hairnet every shift.

Another staple of the third shift was Hank or Trevor or whatever the fuck his name was who often worked as the main cook. He was in his forties, or maybe he was in his thirties and he just looked rough. Working third shift will age a person quick, and Hank or Trevor had been working there for years—our restaurant was fairly new, but Frank had poached him from another location.

Everyone who worked there chewed or smoked or had jacked-up teeth for some other reason. Even at my most tousled and unkempt, I looked like a fresh-faced suburban baby, on call for a Tommy Hilfiger ad, compared to the rest of the Waffle House crew.

Waffle House had a loose dress code for patrons, the only requirements were a shirt and shoes, rarely enforced. The chain attracts a certain kind of soul, a wandering discontent, who needs a home that will take them as they are, feed them, and scream "Hello!" in their face, no matter how weird. Waffle House won't ask questions. Or maybe we'll ask intrusive questions. But either way, it won't matter because we're not fucking narcs, okay? In those days, we were more likely to have our own questionable histories.

For the staff, the dress code was a lot stricter: A black polo shirt with the Waffle House logo, black pants (I wore yoga pants), Shoes for Crews slip-resistant footwear or some low-rent alternative that passed muster with the boss, a branded black Waffle

House visor, and a nametag, only occasionally with the correct name. A lot of times I was "Michelle" who worked there before me.

Still, our uniforms did not conceal the fact that most of us were barely hanging on.

One afternoon, a middle-aged guy from corporate came to audit our location. He looked up from his notebook as I topped off his coffee.

"Wow, you have all your teeth," he remarked, genuinely shocked to see me in uniform. "We need to put you on a billboard."

He and Frank had a good laugh.

I haven't worked at a Waffle House in almost two decades, yet I can't look away from the many weird news stories involving the Florida Man of restaurants. Most of them are so bizarre they almost read fake—like a 2017 viral video showing two female Waffle House employees in Alabama fighting with a spatula, plates, and other kitchen utensils over who would wash the dishes. Or Lana Del Rey in uniform taking orders at another Alabama Waffle House in July 2023. Or the time in 2017 when a Waffle House customer walked into a South Carolina location around 3 a.m. to find no staff in sight and an employee asleep in a booth. He promptly went behind the counter and grilled himself a double Texas bacon cheesesteak melt, and later returned to pay for the sandwich. After the story went viral, Waffle House management apologized and the district manager asked if he wanted to be a secret shopper.

In the Charleston, South Carolina, episode of his travel-foodie-culture show *Parts Unknown*, Anthony Bourdain made a late-night visit to the local Waffle House, which he proclaimed to be "marvelous—an irony-free zone where everything is beautiful and nothing hurts, where everybody, regardless of race, creed, color, or degree of inebriation, is welcomed—its warm yellow glow a beacon of hope and salvation, inviting the hungry, the lost, the seriously hammered all across the South to come inside. A place of safety and nourishment. It never closes; it is always faithful, always there for you." I'm a big Bourdain fan and to a certain extent, it's true, but that review is a bit twee for the number of times we had to call the cops.

Bourdain is right in that the Waffle House is a place of

refuge, though. They gave me a job when no one else wanted to. And my time at the Waffle House helped me clarify my sense of home.

My first spring in Columbia, I hadn't requested time off for Easter and hadn't really wanted it until the last minute when I couldn't fathom not going back to Jackson.

The restaurant was dead after the dinner rush. Frank was in his tiny office, reviewing credit card receipts. I stood in the doorway with my hands on my hips, begging him to reconsider. I was so homesick. One of the only times in my life. Maybe the first and last time I felt it so acutely.

"DeeDee said she could cover. It's been slow all day," I whined, throwing a minor fit in the break/mop/office area.

"No can do," he said, "We're already short-staffed tonight." He explicitly told me I had to finish my double shift.

I moped around until after he left and for a few hours after that.

Then, in the wee hours of the morning, after the overnight bar rush, I 86'd myself and drove the seven and a half hours to Minnesota fueled by 5-hour Energy and an assortment of questionable gas station uppers.

I rushed in breathless and dizzy to find my enormous family crowded in Grandma Betty's kitchen and dining room. Everyone had already eaten the main meal and was lounging around, grazing and loudly debating issues big and small. I remember how warm that house felt, smothered with familial love and mild hostility. I grabbed a plate and loaded it up with all of the familiar fixings.

I was always chasing the next crazy experience, but for once, I just wanted to be home.

PEEP SHOW, INTERRUPTED

I wore a baby blue paisley print dress with a white collar, tiny white Mary Janes, and a baby's breath crown atop my head. It was October 5, 1987, and I had just turned four. I was the flower girl for the high school Homecoming coronation. My mom was a teacher and I was quite cute at this stage with my curly lion's mane, so I imagine that's why I was selected as an attendant. Mason Crow, my first crush, was the crown bearer. We both had dirty blond hair and irrepressible smiles.

This was the first time I'd been in front of a big audience of more than just my fellow preschoolers' parents and I was elated. But I was not satisfied with getting attention just for being cute. I wanted to *perform*. As the ceremony dragged on, I lifted up the front of my dress to flash my little white briefs, a wink to the crowd. I got a dozen or so laughs and a buzz of whispers. They loved it! So did I.

So I flashed my panties again.

More laughs!

My mom gestured at me to stop, but I was too busy curtsying and preparing for my next well-timed flash to notice or care.

The next time I raised the hem of my dress with a giggle, I saw my mom out of the corner of my eye, down on her knees, begging me to stop. I could read her displeasure, though it was hard to square with the delighted audience in front of me, clearly amused by my show. I acknowledged her pleading scolds and reluctantly toned down my act, focusing on cheesing with my face instead. I got another scolding from my parents afterward, but it was a small price to pay for stealing the show.

The public flashing was new, but I'd always loved being naked. When I was a toddler, we lived in a duplex in Windom, where my mom taught special ed. As soon as we got home after daycare, I would immediately take off all my clothes and lay on the couch, completely comfortable like that, watching TV or talking to my mom. We didn't have many visitors, but even if my grandparents or aunt came over, I was not too shy to be naked in front of company. In fact, I would have a big meltdown when my mom would try to make me put on clothes.

After we moved to Jackson, it should have come as no surprise when I hoisted up my sundress and slowly rubbed the fabric back down along my body in the big bay window of our dining room at the Blue House. I was four or five years old by then. I was dancing to a slow, sexy song in my imagination. Pulling down a strap to expose my shoulder, throwing my head back seductively. I'd seen this recently in a movie or on TV. I can't remember what it was, but I knew what I was doing. I knew that it was naughty, but it felt so right.

Outside, a handful of neighborhood kids stood in a ring around the window with their mouths dropped into incredulous Os.

My mom rounded the corner with laundry and yanked me out of the window—busted just before the climax of my show.

"Courtney, what are you doing?!" she cried.

My first striptease.

Growing up with god-fearing parents and grandparents, I was taught that sex work—being a prostitute, hooker, stripper, or whore, as we commonly referred to it then, usually as the butt of a joke— was for broken people. Selling your body was shameful. It should only be done as a last resort. It wasn't wrong necessarily, but wasn't something that anyone we knew should ever want or ever choose.

That didn't stop me from being endlessly fascinated. My Grandpa Joe had the *Pretty Woman* VHS so I watched it in their basement during an early elementary sleepover. I don't remember watching in secret. Perhaps my uncle let me watch alongside him while babysitting. Or maybe it was just me, so caught up in the story, I forgot I was alone. Regardless, I loved it. How romantic, falling in love with your hot, rich john. I completely bought into the fairytale, as envious of Julia Roberts's character as I was of Julia Roberts herself.

In high school, I saw *Dancing at the Blue Iguana*, a movie about the complicated lives of strippers at a San Fernando Valley strip club, starring Daryl Hannah, Sandra Oh, and Jennifer Tilly (who'd also attended Stephens College). I wanted to live in that world.

I liked the idea of boys/men/people/whoever watching me. I wanted the attention. I wanted to be lusted after. I wanted to be the subject of sexual adoration—or perhaps the object, but there was a mutual objectification because I liked the idea of being shown that adoration with dollar bills even more than boners. I also just wanted to exist in that lurid world of heightened eroticism, so upfront about the sex part that money was changing hands. It seemed sexy, obviously, but also seedy and wild. I knew I wanted to be an actor. Maybe I could at least play a sex worker in a movie or a play.

During the summer after my freshman year at Stephens College, we put up Joyce Carol Oates's *I Stand Before You Naked*. It's a play of monologues, and I was cast as the ghost of the dancer/prostitute featured in the climactic monologue "Darling I'm Telling You." It was a meaty opportunity. My makeup included a black eye and bruises all over my body.

One day before rehearsal, I marched into the theater department lobby, pulled off my T-shirt, and let my jean shorts fall to the floor to demonstrate my dead hooker costume—a lacy bra and panty set with strappy heels—for the two older male professors who were directing the show. Their jaws dropped to the floor.

"It's been a long time…" one of them said.

They blushed and mumbled awkwardly amongst themselves for a few moments, like transformers that were running out of batteries.

After they collected themselves, the other one said, "I like it very much, but we don't want anyone to have a heart attack."

I agreed to add fishnets, a short skirt, and crop top.

The monologue played to my dramatic strengths and quickly became my favorite role to date. I thought maybe I could make a career out of playing the strumpet.

She starts out "oddly shy and girlish initially" but as
the monologue progresses, it becomes a seduction of the entire
audience, in this case, an audience filled with families and dads,
including my own.

Still, the audience was rapt; I had them on the edge of their
seats.

Still, the character winds up dead in the end, killed at the
hands of her john.

"ME watchin YOU watchin ME… what a laugh."

Oddly, I did not read this as a warning. I read it as a siren
song. How could I resist exploring the intersection of sex, money,
and power, even if it meant a little danger?

At twenty years old, danger wasn't tangible—it was more
like wish—inoculated against the fear of it by the invincibility of
youth. I had no firsthand evidence of consequences; they existed in
the ether of sensationalized *Dateline* news stories and B-movies far,
far away.

Wren, who got me the job at Waffle House, told me about a guy
who paid her a hundred bucks to kick him in the balls. Wren had
been unschooled—basically homeschooled without structure or
supervision—so she was a magnet for weirdos and always up to
something out there and fun.

"Oh my god, I wanna do that! Can you put me in touch?" I
begged her, instantly intrigued. I needed the money and it sounded
like a great opportunity to be professionally hot.

She passed on his number and we set a date. When the day
came, I pressed the tip of my tongue to my upper lip and studied
my closet with full concentration. How exciting to assemble a
suitably slutty ensemble! I went with all black, donning a miniskirt,
a '70s style half-tank, and, of course, heels. My dead hooker
costume, essentially, except for the bruises, which would be for him
this time.

We met up on campus, near the chapel, on a warm Friday
afternoon after class. I spotted him carrying a camera bag on his

shoulder and tilted my head, taking him in: dark hair, a small build, shortish height, wearing jeans and a black shirt, exuding a sort of beta energy I couldn't quite put my finger on. We'd just learned about cuckolds in the context of Restoration comedy—maybe that? Regardless, I wasn't scared.

We made small talk as he took his camera out of its case. I asked a few questions, first about the purposes of the video we would be shooting. He said it was for a website—a fetish site, though it was obviously a personal fetish, as well. I was happy to be of service, though a bit hesitant at first, particularly about how this would affect him physically. I wasn't worried about the one thing I probably should have been: the website. I wasn't worried about how it would affect my acting career or if my parents would stumble onto the site one day. It seemed like a fetish website existed in a far flung, vaulted corner of the internet, which felt like a much more fragmented, disconnected place at the time.

"Let's do a few warm-up kicks," he cajoled me, promising me it didn't hurt as bad as I thought it did. He informed me that there was a thriving community of dudes that were into ballbusting or bb or tamakeri (literally "ball kicking" in Japanese). *Whatever you're into*, I thought with a shrug.

We tried a few different locations—encountering stray students, professors, and a group of children walking in a line like baby ducks to their after-school program—before ultimately landing on the empty top level of a three-story parking garage in downtown Columbia. Then he started begging for it.

I took a deep breath and came at him fast, but reflexively held back my full force as I flicked my foot into his groin.

"Harder!" he demanded, squatting down like a baseball catcher.

I grimaced and wound up again.

"Harder! Harder! Again!" he begged, doubling over and cupping his junk.

Whatever he wants, I thought. I kicked his precious jewels over and over.

His reactions, which seemed exaggerated at first, began to seem more authentic. After thirty minutes, I was fully warmed up and got him good a handful of times, right in the 'nads, the point

of my shoe hitting his balls like a bull's-eye. So good that he gasped
and slumped over in pain. His face went from tan to white to red. It
took him several minutes to recover.

What can I say, I aimed to please. I wanted him to be a
satisfied customer of my newfound ballbusting skills.

By the end of our session, he staggered a little as he tried
to stand. I'd kicked him in the nutsack at least a hundred times in
under two hours. My instinct was to fawn and fuss, making sure
he was okay, but I knew that's not what he wanted, so I held back,
strutting around the parking lot as he collected himself instead. He
finally opened his wallet and forked over five twenty-dollar bills.
My eyes lit up. I flipped through the cash, recounting it in my hand.
A hundred bucks, all there. Easiest money I ever made. Beaming, I
feathered the bills over my palm before folding them in half.

Feeling celebratory after we parted, I drove through the
Hardee's drive-thru. "I'll take a large curly fries and Diet Coke,
please." The bag was hot. Impatient, craving instant gratification,
I did what I was prone to do: popped a searing spiral of potato
into my mouth, savoring its salty seasoning, even as it scorched my
tongue.

I wanted to kick him (or another guy) in the balls for
money as soon as possible. I can't remember why I didn't—maybe
he wanted a new girl each time or he didn't have the money, but
it was definitely something on his end because I totally would
have done it again. In fact, I would do it again today, right now, if
a stranger propositioned me or he somehow knocked on my door
from twenty years and several states away.

Sophomore year, Sydney, another one of my acting classmates, got a
job as a stripper at Club Vogue, on the Business Loop not far from
the Waffle House I'd worked at. Club Vogue had a sallow yellow
exterior that looked almost nicotine-stained, with a gravel parking
lot in the back. Inside was soiled and worn, sexiest when the
overhead lights went off, the specialty lights went on, and the place
took on a moody, cinematic allure.

Sydney would come to class in extravagant-looking
clothes that I now recognize as cheap fast fashion from places like

Charlotte Russe, but nonetheless, her style was campy and caught my eye. There was a dingy glamour to it all, a shabby chic. Plus, the money. I was on a substantial scholarship at a private school and my parents were covering the rest of my tuition each semester, but I had to take out loans for room and board and I had additional living expenses to cover. I felt a constant need for cash.

After a little gentle prodding, Sydney got me a job as a hostess at Club Vogue. Over the course of the next two weeks, I learned three things:

1) According to the door guy, even though I might think my ass was too tight for anal sex now, I just needed to look at the biggest shits I was taking. "Some of them are bigger than a dick, aren't they?"

2) My friend Sydney was the happiest stripper at this place. And that's really saying something because she seemed pretty depressed.

3) If I kept working at Club Vogue, it would be as a stripper, not a hostess. Part of my job as a hostess was to sell expensive non-alcoholic drinks no one wanted yet not get in the way of the dancers who were trying to sell these same guys lap dances. This proved nearly impossible and tips were the majority of my pay. Thus, the only way I would make any money was to be a dancer, the other employees and customers would remind me at every opportunity.

The pole, the music, the lingerie, the seediness, and the hyperintimate community of it all were compelling. Addicting, even. Leaning into one's sexuality and being rewarded with all those dollar bills at the end of a busy night. I was already selling my body—stripping seemed like a lot more fun than selling my plasma for money, and potentially a lot more profitable. Honestly, I was tempted. Very tempted.

But at Club Vogue, Sydney didn't make much more than I did at Waffle House most nights. I wanted to strip, but I wasn't sure how it would affect my career as an actress. Would it hurt my chances? In the early 2000s, people were rarely out about sex work. Sure, it was a topic of fascination, but it was still largely taboo. It worked out okay for Anna Nicole Smith—she had a new show on

TV—but she was also a laughingstock in a lot of ways. Stripping would be a risk that I couldn't be sure was worth it; I decided to play it safe.

I quit after just one pay period. Luckily, I'd been recruited to be a cocktail waitress at The Martini Bar by one of the door guys—not the anal aficionado, but a big 'roided up blond guy with a ponytail, a cross between Fabio and John Smith from Disney's *Pocahontas*.

I picked up my first and last paycheck from Club Vogue. On the way home, I swung through the drive-thru and got myself some curly fries. Their fresh-out-of-the-fryer smell wafted through the car, making my mouth water. But, for once in my life, I set the bag on the passenger seat to let them cool, waiting just long enough to make sure I didn't burn my tongue.

THE BLUE HOUSE

"I mean, I don't want to live in the dorms if I don't have to," I said as I changed into my character shoes in the lobby of the theater building with cast lists and rehearsal schedules on the corkboards lining the walls.

"Me neither," Zoe agreed. She tucked her weed pipe into a secret compartment of her purse.

"Well, I don't want to live with my parents!" Danielle scoffed dramatically.

We all laughed, five minutes from getting high.

"And maybe they don't want to live with me, because my dad sounded pretty excited about this rental."

I'd arrived at Stephens in the middle of freshman year, thus missing the fall orientation and initial clique forming. That first semester, I lived in a solo dorm and filled my free time with work. But we were now a month into the Summer Theatre Institute, all staying in the same dorm, and theater immersion had manufactured a closeness with my classmates and given me new friends.

Zoe had returned to school after a brief hiatus. She was sunny and self-deprecating, and we became fast friends.

Danielle and I had been circling one another and sussing each other out for months, but we didn't click until we started hanging out outside of class. She was a stunning young Michelle Pfeiffer lookalike. Her blonde pixie cut framed her Kewpie doll face atop a waifish frame draped in a vintage poncho, the epitome of shabby chic. Her dad was the chair of the theater department. "He showed me your tape. It was really good," she said approvingly, about the monologue I'd submitted for an acting scholarship.

It was easy for me to see her talent and magnetism, too. Danielle's voice was lower than you would expect and she laughed from a deep and honest place that reminded me that it was okay to stop wishing I was somewhere else for a while.

The Blue House was my second Blue House. The first had been my early childhood home on Park Street in Jackson, Minnesota. This Missouri Blue House was a classic two-story craftsman on Walnut Street, parallel to Broadway, which runs through the heart of downtown Columbia, just a block away from campus. Columbia is a college town, home to the University of Missouri's main campus and two private colleges, Columbia College and Stephens College.

The Blue House was shitty—with chipping blue paint and worn-out wooden floors—but we were excited to make it our home. On the front porch hung a rickety swing we almost never used except to smoke pot.

When we walked through the rooms together, I called the biggest room with a window facing Walnut Street, Danielle wanted the middle room, and Zoe took the little room in the back. I didn't want to feel guilty for my luxurious room choice, so I suggested we prorate the rent based on room size. I had to have a job anyway, so I could at least treat myself to a comfortable room.

My parents loaded up the van with two white and green dressers that my mom and Grandma Marge had painted for me. There was a matching mirror too, its frame lovingly spackled in the same color scheme, never imagining what that mirror would witness.

Our nightly ritual was sitting around in the "dining room"—the middle room downstairs on the main floor—and smoking stupid amounts of weed. The dining room was set up like a campfire. There was a round, low-to-the-ground faux wood coffee table in the center of the room and we had camping chairs and oversized pillows arranged in a circle around it. While passing pipes or joints, or taking turns on the gravity bong, we talked about acting. And oh god, did we love talking about acting! For however much weed we smoked, we talked about acting twice as much—famous actors we admired, the respective talent levels of our classmates, minutia of the theater productions we were involved with, and our lofty goals for the future. We loved talking about acting almost as much as we loved acting itself. We had only the foggiest idea what we were talking about, but we spoke with brazen confidence, delusion—

whatever you want to call it. The smoke haze above us was laced
with dreams.

We did internet searches for our favorite movie stars to
determine how old they were when they "made it." We wrote down
their ages in the quote book to make ourselves feel better, like
we had more time. The quote book was our collective notebook
with Cinderella on the cover, which served as a repository for the
funny things we said when we were high—things like my famous:
"If Angelina Jolie were the world, she would be the Mesozoic
Era" (obviously her correct geological era). It was usually just a
silly outlet for our self-important quotes and inside jokes, but the
notebook also functioned as a burn book.

Sometimes Danielle's boyfriend would play the guitar and
she would sing lead with the rest of us mumbling along. This was
during Jack Johnson's heyday, and we all loved Jason Mraz to what I
could already feel was an embarrassing degree.

In addition to being obsessed with acting, Zoe, Danielle, and I
had raging eating disorders in common. It was contagious really;
everyone was catching each other's ED like the flu. Danielle ate
one meal a day; she and her boyfriend ordered Gumby's Pizza
for dinner. I ate meals out of vending machines and went to bed
hungry and then ravaged the refrigerator, eating hard crusts out of
abandoned Gumby's boxes in the middle of the night.

All three of us had boyfriends and, somehow, within a few
months they made themselves roommates. Danielle's boyfriend,
boy Courtney, was a fellow theater student. Stephens College was
a women's college but it's hard to put on the classical theater canon
without men, so they accepted male "apprentices." These guys got
a hell of a deal: basically a full scholarship with lots of stage time,
plus a chance for the straight boys among them to be in high
demand for the first, and perhaps only, time in their lives. I liked
the apprentices, but I didn't want to date any of them.

Meanwhile, Derek was worming his way back into my
life. Occasional weekend trips to see each other had turned into
talk of him moving to Missouri to live with me. The dating pool
was pretty weak at Stephens and, unfortunately, so was my resolve.

Maybe I was bored romantically, sexually. Maybe I was still feeling internalized pressure to make it work with the first guy I'd had sex with. Maybe I didn't realize how lucky I was to have had a clean break.

After Christmas, Derek drove down to Columbia with me and moved into the Blue House—fittingly this was right after I'd had my wisdom teeth removed. Zoe's boyfriend, Levi, also joined us from Tennessee after the holidays.

Neither Derek nor Levi was attending school. Levi quickly found a job in a kitchen, but Derek dragged his feet. First, he put on a big show like he was going to attend the community college in Moberly, thirty minutes away, despite the fact that he'd flunked out of his last college. That lasted just a day or two, but he faked it for at least another week. I was going to school *and* working *and* paying for everything and it was getting annoying. Even at my worst, I had a sense of responsibility Derek just didn't possess, which made me a college kid on a budget paying for a plus one. I had worked at Waffle House until Christmas, then transferred my hospitality skills over to Chevys Fresh Mex. Yes, it was messy and sometimes demoralizing, but I wasn't too good for a restaurant job, I didn't understand why Derek thought he was. He certainly wasn't too good to spend the money I made at *my* restaurant job.

Finally, after much prodding, he got a job in a kitchen.

I went to Derek's employee party at the restaurant he worked at and had a rare come-to-Jesus moment—one of those crystalline experiences, like the rap, where I was fully aligned with my higher self and we were horrified that Derek was our boyfriend. The party was a fiasco. He was anxious and awkward and had no social skills with which to introduce me to his coworkers or bosses. But I was used to all that. It was miserable for some other reason I couldn't quite put my finger on. He was snippy and short with me, physically blocking my interactions with other people, probably because he was fucking or flirting with a coworker and didn't want me to find out. Regardless, the vibes were off. Way off. I stress ate my feelings, searching for a sense of equilibrium I could never achieve with him around.

In late August, Danielle got two kittens we were all obsessed with: Franny and Bianca.

In January, I went to the Central Missouri Humane Society, walked through the dog kennels, and adopted the cutest one: an adorable beagle-chihuahua. I wanted to name her after the supermodel Gisele, but it felt odd to call a dog that, so I went with Ellie instead. Already feeling trapped by my decision to let Derek move in, I was soothed to have this adorable cuddle buddy who I quickly fell in love with, though I didn't fully understand how to care for her. I took her to class with me. She rode along whenever I ran errands. I gave her licks of my Dairy Queen shakes. She sat in my lap or played with the kittens during our nightly stoner sessions.

In early spring, someone cut Danielle's kittens' whiskers. The suspects were Derek and Levi. There was no evidence except for Franny and Bianca's too-short whiskers and frequent bumping into things, but I felt guilty for inviting Derek into the house in the first place. The type of guy we'd suspect of mutilating innocent little kittens.

After spring break, someone scored some molly, which led to an impromptu rave. The kittens and Ellie looked on in confusion as the humans did ecstasy and hugged and danced and shouted, "I love you guys!" over the music, raging on well past dawn.

The next morning, I stumbled into work at Chevys Fresh Mex with bleary eyes. Running on candy necklace dust and Vicks VapoRub fumes, I proceeded to drag ass through the lunch shift instead of taking the nap my body was screaming for. Which didn't look good because a light lunch shift is kid stuff. I was already earning a bad reputation at Chevys. I *was* a bad waitress, especially that day.

"Oops, sorry ladies!" I shrieked, nearly spilling a tray of waters on a table from the Red Hat Society.

My eyes felt like shards of glass were in them. (Probably because that's what our ecstasy had been cut with.) I would have called in sick, but with my track record, I couldn't afford to flake. Plus, I needed the fifty bucks.

I rested my head on the metal sideboard in the kitchen and let my eyes drift shut. But every refried bean-splattered plate clanging against the expo line and each microwave ding was an electric shock to my fritzed-out nervous system. I tried to think about not puking, but that just made the urge come up stronger. I prayed for a miracle that would get me through my shift.

Just as I laid my arm down in some queso spillage on the sideboard, I felt a hand on my back. I jerked to attention. I forced my eyes to follow the hand back to its adjoining head and slowly I began to see that it belonged to Chase. Chase Kettering with the elfin baby blues and a devilish grin. Chase with a soccer player's taut body.

"You okay?" he drawled. "Savin' that queso for later?" he winked, pointing at my arm.

Chase, who you didn't even know you had a crush on until he opened his mouth and that Cape Girardeau Mason-Dixon twang came gushing out. He sounded like a Missouri Matthew McConaughey. Every time he spoke, it toppled me like an unexpected wave.

Chase was hot in the sort of way you start to think is hot if you stay in Missouri too long. Blond. Slightly lazy drawl when he spoke. Easy laugh. He loved to party but passed as more functional than most of his friends. He was unaffiliated but groomed to know the subtle difference in frat boy dress codes: flip-flop time vs. collared shirt time vs. fresh polo and hair gel time. Just kidding, it's always hair gel time. Chase played on his white boy privilege in an uncompetitive place. Quick to call a woman "sweetheart" but skittish when it came time to commit. It may sound like I didn't like him, but—I couldn't help it—I did.

I slumped against his shoulder. "Dude, I had the craziest night last night."

He laughed, his eyes dancing. "Looks like it," he said, raising his eyebrows.

Chase and I had trained together a few months prior. As things had become increasingly untenable with Derek, we were developing a work flirtation. He'd noticed my serving skills were even worse than usual after I'd fucked up my second order in under an hour and was struggling to balance the tray of drinks that had taken me fifteen minutes to prepare.

"Chase, how am I gonna get through this shift?" I cried, collapsing against the server station. "Seriously, should I go home sick? Brad's legit going to murder me if I get another order wrong,"

He drawled, "Well, you're a lucky girl because I got something that might help you out." He reached into his pocket, pulled out an orange circle, and bit it in half. He held up the remaining peach crescent in slow motion. Like a priest blessing a communion wafer. I didn't even know what it was, but I knew it was holy. "Here, take this," he said.

"What is it?" I asked as I poured myself a splash of Diet Coke from the soda fountain.

"Adderall. It'll get you through the shift. Just trust me."

I did trust him. Plus, my parents were special ed teachers and some of their students were prescribed Adderall, so I had a vague understanding of the drug's clinical applications. I figured if kids were taking it, it probably wouldn't kill me. Not to mention, I'd taken a double dose of ecstasy the night before. My body was a hedonistic temple at best.

I put half of the orange tab on my tongue, took a sip of Diet Coke, and threw my head back.

I delivered fresh tortillas to the Red Hat Society, then time started to pick up. First, it felt linear, then exponential. Double time, triple time. Suddenly, my body was no longer disjointed, but leading the charge. Thirty minutes later, I was zipping around the restaurant, refilling drinks, and bussing my coworkers' tables. The lunch shift had never known such fine service. My coworkers could barely recognize the proficient waitress in front of them. Irritation melted off of day manager Brad's face, leaving the beginnings of a smile. My chest felt warm and there was a tingle in my stomach that made me like Chase even more than I had before.

It was love at first dose.

At the end of the shift, Chase looked me over slyly as I organized my receipts to cash out. "Whoa, comeback of the year. I think you owe me a thank you for your best shift yet."

I looked up at him. "Oh, I'm definitely gonna thank you." I licked my lips. "But first you have to tell me how to get more."

One morning soon after, while I was getting ready for class, Derek lounged on the bed and lit up a cigarette.

"You can't smoke in the bedroom," I reminded him.

He already knew that, though, and hadn't paid any rent to have a say one way or another. Technically, he wasn't supposed to smoke cigs anywhere in the house—weed only was our rule.

"Oh, shut up," he said, making no move to put it out.

I picked up a Febreze bottle and sprayed around the room to diffuse the smoke smell. I circled to Derek's side of the bed and he lunged toward me, grabbing my arm with one hand and the bottle with the other.

"You're being an uptight bitch," he hissed. He sprayed Febreze on me point blank, twisting my arm tightly.

"Ow!" I screamed.

Derek opened the lid and dumped the remaining contents on me, all across my body, face, and hair.

"What the fuck are you doing?" I yelled.

He had hit and tackled me before, but for some reason, the Febreze was a bridge too far. I finally recognized his behavior for what it was: abuse.

Still shaking, I scurried to class, which I was late for, and afterward drove straight to the police station.

"Next!" an officer called out to the chaotic lobby of bright lights, ringing phones, restless bodies, and staticky walkie-talkies.

I approached the desk. "Hi, I'd like to report… um, abuse, I guess?" I said sheepishly.

"What kind of abuse?" the officer asked, squinting his eyes at me.

"My boyfriend doused me with Febreze this morning," I replied, my hair waxy and wavy from the incident.

"Febreze?" the officer said, turning down the volume on the scanner.

I nodded. "I know that sounds weird, but it's not the first time he's done stuff like this. I just… want it to stop."

I was assigned to another officer who guided me through filling out the paperwork for an ex parte—a civil restraining order—and sent me home with the document.

That night, I broke up with Derek. I thought if my words wouldn't get him to leave, surely the ex parte would. But he set up camp on the living room couch, refusing to respect me or the flimsy piece of paper that was supposed to protect me.

Nobody at the Blue House knew how to make him leave either. Derek would stay like cigarette smoke on the walls, and no amount of Febreze could remove him.

The rest of the school year was about survival. I lived alongside my enemy, and my mission was to extricate myself from a relationship with him and remain relatively unscathed. It was too late for the latter, but the former was mandatory.

We threw a couple house parties in our basement that spring—one before Derek and I broke up and one after—and everyone from the theater department came. Derek made his interest in Monica Rayburn and her ginormous boobs widely known and I was annoyed that he didn't even bother to hide it. What a scumbag. I wondered why I hadn't seen it before.

Whatever Derek was saying about or doing with other girls, he certainly didn't want me to move on.

"Who the fuck are you going to see?" he screamed as he jumped on the hood of my Oldsmobile Cutlass Ciera like he was auditioning for an Inmate of the Asylum in *Marat/Sade*.

I was leaving to meet Chase, who I'd started hooking up with soon after the Febreze incident.

"It's none of your fucking business! Get off the car, you psycho," I yelled back, not crazy enough to roll down the window. Being safe was more important than being heard.

Derek, stubbly and unkempt, crouched on the hood and pounded his fists against the windshield, but I kept inching out of the driveway until he finally jumped off and watched me drive away.

As I drove across town to Chase's house, I shook off the vision of Derek seething in my rearview mirror. Spending time with Chase was a perfect way to get over the perverted idea that Derek was my one and only.

After the spring semester came to an end, Danielle, Zoe, and I got ready to spend the summer at the Okoboji Summer Theatre in Iowa for our second summer program. In the sliver of time between school and summer stock, I was deeply depressed. But it was a manic depression, thanks to Adderall and the abusive ex-boyfriend downstairs on the couch. In fact, the Adderall and the abusive ex-boyfriend were related. I needed to feel like I was moving away from Derek fast, but he refused to go. Adderall helped me feel in motion at all times. My relationship with Adderall was new and fresh and good. My stomach tingled. My chest burned. It felt like being embraced by a warm body as I was learning to be alone again. My heart thumped harder than usual, and I felt vital and alive like never before. "Why would you ever not want to feel this way?" I thought (and occasionally said aloud), which should have been my first inkling that this habit would be hard to ditch.

The problem with speed is that it is an accelerant. So, if you don't know where you're going, you're going to get nowhere fast. On copious amounts of Adderall, I was a terrible captain; too delusional to see the destination clearly, too fucked up to steer properly. But I didn't care where I was going exactly. I only cared about getting away from Derek.

The horror of living in the Blue House reached a crescendo in late May. I could barely handle being there to take care of Ellie. Once I left her in her crate in the walk-in closet overnight because I was trying to avoid Derek and I didn't want her to get hurt. That night turned into a coke bender with Chase. She was whining when I got home the next morning. Probably had been for hours. I rushed to let her out but the guilt stayed—to this day, it's one of my deepest regrets. In the process of trying to leave an abusive relationship, I had become neglectful myself.

That June, I busted out of Columbia on a coke and sangria tailwind with Ellie in tow. I was happy that we were finally escaping the chaotic nightmare that Columbia had become. Derek still wouldn't leave the Blue House, and we had no choice but to let him and Levi stay behind.

After our summer theater season wrapped, Danielle, Zoe, and I planned to return and figure out a way to kick them out. Just us girls again—how it should have stayed from the start.

But in late summer, we got a call. We were being evicted. Derek and Levi had been partying like crazy, had trashed the place, and we all had to leave. We could pick up what we'd left in the closets when we got back to Columbia in late August, but we had to figure out another place to live.

Zoe and I moved into a dorm room together for our last semester that fall. Soon after we traded our tank tops for long sleeves, we got word that the Blue House was being torn down. That's how I finally got rid of Derek. With a bulldozer.

I drove by afterward, just to make sure it was gone.

THE BOJI MILE

After my third semester at Stephens, I dropped Ellie off with
my parents to live for the summer. They took her in a little
begrudgingly. They still had three kids at home to look after and
weren't big fans of pets.

None of our childhood pets lasted long. My rabbit froze
to death when winter came. A few outdoor cats stuck around until
they finally ran away or got lost. We never had a dog as kids, that
was considered too high-maintenance. Even hermit crabs and
betta fish eventually met untimely ends under our care. My parents
didn't want anything else they were responsible for keeping alive.
Humans only. But Ellie was such a cute little beagle-chihuahua—I
didn't think beagles could get any cuter, but a mini beagle? Despite
my mom's reservations about house pets, she was instantly smitten.
Ellie was a stand-in for her daughter at a time when she was feeling
increasingly disconnected.

From Jackson, I drove the country roads laced with fields
of corn and beans in full bloom down to Spirit Lake and then
to Okoboji, a resort area with five lakes. A big part of the reason
I chose Stephens College was because of the Okoboji Summer
Theatre, their summer stock theater in northwestern Iowa, twenty-
five miles from where I grew up, across the state line in Minnesota.

I had attended shows at OST throughout my childhood
and teenage years, as my acting dreams had been coming into focus.
For a couple summers in high school, after I got my driver's license,
I worked at a children's theater on the other side of the lake and
was in the audience for every play and musical the summer stock
theater put up. *All I Really Need to Know I Learned in Kindergarten.*
Neil Simon's *Last of the Red Hot Lovers. The Trip to Bountiful.*
Fiddler on the Roof. Dearly Departed. I never missed a show no
matter how obscure. I gossiped about the actors with a children's
theater castmate and fantasized about my future on that stage.

And then, all of a sudden after an interminably long wait,
it was my turn. I had spent so many hours dreaming of my time at
that theater, but now that it was about to become a reality, much of

the luster had worn off. That summer, we would put up a psychotic thirteen shows in nine weeks—not only serving as the core cast, but also the box office, set crew, costume crew, kitchen grunts, etc.

My casting was fine. Two mainstage shows and a children's theater show. The roles were decent, but only one of them was remotely juicy: Trudy in *Social Security*, a role originated by Joanna Gleason on Broadway, and I hammed it up. In *Social Security*, a swanky Manhattan art dealer couple's world is turned upside down when Trudy (my character) and her husband drop off the wife's mother for an impromptu stay while they go rescue their college-aged daughter from a threesome with two men (gasp!). Playing an aggressive prude gave me an outlet for my own pent-up frustrations.

Stephens College is a historic women's college, the second-oldest in the U.S. still in operation, but it was once dubbed a "famed finishing school for future mothers" and really showed its roots (and whole ass) with the way they hired roving bachelors in their late twenties through well into their forties to work for OST and scout for their future wives.

Not to mention, I never had to take a women's studies class the whole time I was at Stephens. Shouldn't that be *the* requirement of a women's college? But there was no feminist theory to guide me. Instead, I would keep learning about the patriarchy from life.

In addition to acting, we also had to crew the shows and the people who ran OST didn't believe in days off, so it was a grueling schedule and alcohol became a natural outlet for blowing off steam. I'm not usually much of a drinker, except for a few brief periods of my life, but drinking myself to sleep in the few hours we were allotted to unwind after frequently working sixteen-hour days felt like a necessary coping mechanism.

And I wasn't the only one drinking. My classmates and I drank redheaded sluts out of fish bowls at The Ritz. We sat in the front row at Zipper's Gentlemen's Club and did shots of cheap vodka. We ran around the theater property late at night, drunkenly streaking, and called it "the Boji Mile." One morning my black thong was tacked to the bulletin board next to the lost and found. During the Pig Roast, an annual cookout at OST, I was crowned with a black-brimmed hat with pig ears and a snout on it that said "Pork Prudess"—a joke inspired by my lust for streaking and lost thong.

I lived in a girls-only cabin with Danielle and Naomi, but we were determined to have a co-ed summer. Naomi was dating an older man, an alum of the apprentice program who was hired back to do set design and dropped vowels from his name as an artistic choice. Danielle was fucking one of our male apprentice friends who later came out as gay—a theater rite of passage. And I renewed interest in my hometown crush, Zach Eldridge.

The summer stock theater put me back in Jackson essentially, so I occasionally hung out with a group of guys I knew from high school, as a non-theater way to decompress. And as a way to see Zach, the only boy I grew up with who really got me hot and bothered. He had a laid-back magnetism and looked like a California surfer with a charming glint in his eye. I used to find him physically intimidating, but after two years of college, I had gotten hot myself. I finally felt like a viable match. I'd moved away to be an actress. Now I was the cool one.

It didn't take many nights of boozy revelry before Zach and I were bouncing away on my bottom bunk, not even realizing Naomi was home until she sighed loudly and rolled over to face the wall, which made us giggle uncontrollably. When we collapsed into an after-sex heap, I felt like I beat the final boss of a video game level I'd been trying to conquer since middle school.

The next morning, we dressed Zach up like a girl, in my sweater and floral scarf and Danielle's crutches (she got so drunk one night she broke her foot coming out of the cabin) and snuck him out.

A week or two later, after crewing the night's show, I changed into a vintage halter top and my favorite white jeans and took off to meet up with Zach and a couple other guys at a local bar that served underage kids. "Courtney, over here!" Zach howled when I arrived, already a few drinks in. We drank their specialty: vodka Red Bulls. After a couple rounds of those, Zach pointed out Latham Hancock, who arrived in a button-up shirt after selling cars at a dealership.

Latham was a few grades ahead of me in school and I was a late bloomer on the party scene, so we never ran in the same crew. But he was the son of a guy my dad ran marathons with and we'd been in art class together.

Latham joined our table, Zach and I singing along with the jam band and laughing at anything remotely funny. That night we'd gotten very drunk, blurry drunk, but I hadn't had more to drink than usual. It's one of the few times in my life I'd wonder if I had been drugged. My last memories are of us leaving the bar, fuzzy images of the gravel parking lot. Me, a stumbly mess who slurred, "I am *not* okay to drive." Neither was Zach. Latham wasn't drunk—at least not nearly as much as we were—so he gave us a ride back to his cabin. Both Zach and me. Perfect. I was hoping to go home with Zach again anyway.

I don't remember anything after the car ride, except wanting to go to sleep.

When I awoke the next morning, I was on a mattress on the unfinished hardwood floor next to Latham—not Zach—who was kissing me. Ew. My *not*-crush with his fucking disgusting corn breath was acting oddly post-coital. I shut my mouth and pulled my head away, but we were sharing a sleeping bag. It was a rude awakening.

"Did we have sex?" I asked, shutting one eye to the harsh sunlight.

"Yeah," he said, a smile spreading across his face.

What?! I pushed away for some space, trying to process the development. I'd never wanted to have sex with him, I knew that for sure.

"I was really drunk… I don't even remember getting here," I said, haltingly. I began running through mental tape from the night before, immediately questioning myself, even though my body told me I had not wanted this. I had been drinking more than usual this summer, but still, I was a lightweight. After four drinks, my absolute max, I passed out to a nonfunctional state. It wasn't ambiguous—I wasn't walking or talking in a blackout—I was asleep. If I was walking or talking, the memories always came back to me—in pieces, yes, but they always come back.

"I had a lot of fun," Latham said, breathing on me again. I shuddered. I definitely did not want to have sex with Latham. I was twenty and had only had sex with three other people. Derek, Chase, and, most recently, Zach. Choosing new partners wasn't something I took lightly. I hadn't even been kissing Latham that night—I had a *different* crush... and I had my period. It was towards the end, but I still had some light bleeding, so I'd worn a tampon that night. I'm not a fan of period sex anyway, and I couldn't believe I had voluntarily done that—especially on the first time, with someone I wasn't even into!

I got up and walked down the creaky hallway to the tiny bathroom to collect my thoughts and change my tampon, but there was no string. Weird. I didn't remember taking my tampon out the night before. That's another reason I was shocked when Latham said we had sex. I had a fear of sepsis, so I had never forgotten before and have never forgotten since. Other drunk nights I could at least piece together afterward, but this time the tape was blank. I was unnerved. Did I allow this to happen?

Whatever happened, I just wanted to get out of there, plus I had to work at the theater, so I asked Latham to give me a ride, still struggling to put the pieces together in my mind.

On the drive back, I shook my head involuntarily when I remembered science class.

It was a Monday. I was a sophomore in high school. Mr. Johnson was standing at the front of the room teaching science. Except he couldn't teach because the class was abuzz with gossip from a party at a classmate's house the weekend prior. The details came out in breathless fragments as sources corroborated that:

Bethany Haugen had been passed out.
Upstairs. Unconscious.
Then something happened.
With Latham Hancock.

"She got Hancocked!"

Hahahahahahahahahaha.

"Get it?—Got Hancocked."

Hahahahahahahahahaha.

So funny.

Because by "got Hancocked," they meant she was raped.

At lunch, I stole away from the theater to get the morning after pill for a sexual encounter I didn't even remember, though I tried to put the questions out of my mind.

Four days later, I started feeling sick. The whole morning felt off. During my set crew assignment, I could hardly hit the nails with my hammer. Everything went out of focus when I tried to stand up. It was a muggy ninety degrees, but I had the chills. My body felt heavy. I went to the bathroom and my pee was weird. Like a UTI but worse. It felt like my body was working against me whenever I tried to move, yet I couldn't be still.

I murmured "I don't feel well" to the Technical Director and stumbled back to our cabin. I got in the shower, but got right back out. Something was wrong. I was tired, but I couldn't lay down. I writhed on the bed trying to remember what I'd eaten recently. What could have poisoned me? Nothing was comfortable. I felt an inexplicable urge to push—what I imagine it feels like to have labor contractions. I thought maybe I was one of those women who doesn't know she's pregnant until she gives birth in the middle of her shift.

I hovered over the toilet and "delivered" what looked like a huge cyst, but it wasn't. It was a festering tampon that had grown into a disgusting coral reef of bodily fluids, tissue, and molten cotton.

My heart raced as I paced around the cabin, now knowing for sure what had happened that night with *not* my crush—I'd been date raped. He'd had sex with a passed out me, jamming my tampon up against my cervix, where it stayed, rotting like a ticking time bomb for days afterward.

I could've had Toxic Shock Syndrome and lost limbs, or even died, but I didn't go to the doctor, nor did I go to the police.

After my adrenaline crashed, I slept it off.

When Danielle got home from shop, I told her what happened.

Decades later, I would ask, "Hey, do you remember that weird thing that happened at Boji?" She would clasp my wrist and reply somberly, "Dude, how could I ever forget?"

The next weekend, Latham convinced me to get dinner. I agreed because I thought somehow it was my fault. I needed to figure it out. The restaurant was too empty to offer inspiration for our awkward conversation. After he ate and I picked at my food, we walked down the street to the same bar, which made my skin itch. I watched a bartender pour a vodka Red Bull and my breath caught in my throat. I wanted to get out of there and Latham wanted to do whatever I wanted to do, which made my skin itch even more. I turned around and ran into my much-older cousin ordering a beer. I shouted over the music, "Any chance you could track down some coke?"

While we waited, I watched the jam band intently, trying to ignore Latham. Soon my cousin came back with a baggie. Latham said we could go do it at his friend's nearby cabin—they would probably be there, but he had keys just in case. Eager to escape by any means necessary, I agreed.

When we got there, we were alone. We did lines off a mirror, one after another. Ironically, wanting to freeze time, I didn't take a break until my nostrils were stinging. Latham moved the mirror to the nightstand and put his arm around me. This time I was wide awake.

He leaned in for a kiss and I reflexively flinched. Undeterred, he opened his mouth and came at me, eyes closed. Soon his pants were off and he was poking near my vagina. My thighs buckled, but I hesitantly let it happen because I figured what the hell, it was already done. He thrust the tip inside me, and I couldn't accept anymore. Why was I letting this guy who raped me back inside of my body? I couldn't let it happen again.

"Stop. Stop. Stop." I said, pushing him off of me.

Then the words came spewing out of me: I tried to tell him

about the fucked-up thing he did to me—how I didn't agree to the first time, I was just trying to go to sleep, then waking up was such a shock, and the tampon as proof. I tried to explain that what he had done was unacceptable. It was a violation. I could have died. I even used the word rape. He furrowed his brow and argued, "But I gave you a ride…. But we went out on a date…" I tried to tell him that those things didn't mean "yes." He looked at me like he didn't believe me.

The next time I saw Latham, he'd invited me on his friend's boat. I don't know how he convinced me to come out. Perhaps I felt some pressure to continue talking with him until it made sense. On the boat, he was treating me like his girlfriend around strangers. I was attempting to bridge the dissonance of how violated I felt versus him pretending we were in a relationship.

"I want to show you something," Latham said. He opened a hatch to a private area of the boat. Immediately I felt claustrophobic. He closed his eyes and opened his cornhole for a kiss.

Inside I was screaming. I had to get off. Latham and the waves were making me sick. I knocked on the hatch and someone opened it from the other side. "Can we stop up here?" I said, quickly collecting my stuff. They pulled up to the dock and I didn't even wait for them to stop. Holding my heels in my hands, I jumped onto the wood and ran.

Up by the road, I got my bearings. I was at Arnolds Park Public Beach, across from The Ritz. I crossed the bridge and walked the mile and a half back to the theater, cutting my bare feet up in the process, but I didn't care. I was so happy to be free. That was the last night we hung out. I never answered another call from him.

The Weinstein story broke in 2017—more than thirteen years later—and opened the #MeToo floodgates. Watching Christine Blasey Ford testify against Brett Kavanaugh in 2018 had me shaking and livid for weeks. For a few triggering years, it became impossible not to think about how I had been raped.

I thought about how weird it was that I went to the doctor for a tetanus shot that same summer after a nail barely grazed my butt, but I couldn't fathom going after the tampon incident. I thought about how our culture incentivizes victims to stay silent. I thought about how victims have to be perfect to be deemed valid. What I thought about most was how routine this type of predation is. Guys like Latham are everywhere.

At the height of the #MeToo movement, an editor asked me to connect on LinkedIn. At first I didn't want to do it. It just seemed like such a square thing to do. Why do I need to join LinkedIn? I'm an artist, not a suit.

I swallowed whatever adolescent above-it-ness I had for the networking site and signed up. Three days and thirty-one contacts later, I got an email on my phone with the subject line: *Courtney, please add me to your LinkedIn network.* I shivered a small, work-appropriate quiver of anticipation at the thought of who I might reconnect with from my past.

Sitting cross-legged on my bed, I opened the email and saw Latham smirking back at me. Latham Hancock, Esquire, wanted to connect with me. Would I accept?

Suddenly any tinge of excitement dropped to the pit of my stomach and turned into a fiery cauldron of rage. The last time I saw that stupid smirk, I was crying and running away. Instantly I was twenty again. Twenty feels old when you're that age. No longer a teenager, you're legally an adult. But when I think of myself at twenty years old now, I almost melt from the tender, babyness of it all.

The timing of this LinkedIn request was strange. Had he been reading all this sexual assault news too and seeing glimpses of himself in these fallen predators? Maybe he was planning to apologize, or maybe he was hoping to use my acceptance of his request as absolution of any lingering doubts, or maybe it was just random (though I don't think we ever traded emails). Either way, I didn't want it. I didn't want to join his professional network, and I certainly didn't want to join his personal one. *No means no, Latham,* I thought. *Hell no.*

I knew how to say it, as I'd known even then, I knew it wasn't my fault, and I knew the problem was bigger than just Latham, but that's where I could draw a boundary. I was done here.

I summoned my twenty-year-old self, and together we pressed Ignore on the request and closed out of the screen.

MISS ADDERALL USA

Back at the dorms after finishing our season at Okoboji, Zoe and I had a tendency to stay up all night on Adderall, geeked out and sweating, our pupils as big as flying saucers. I wanted to feel like I was on a rollercoaster, even if I was sitting at my desk. We were "working," which meant sometimes cleaning the closet, sometimes sending regrettable emails, and sometimes coming up with cracked out schemes to advance our careers.

Jiggling my leg at my desk—Zoe doing an interpretive dance in the center of the tiny room—I looked up from my laptop to our pink mini TV. A news story about the latest Miss Minnesota USA winner had caught my ear. My eyes narrowed, watching. She was very pretty, but in an attainable small-town kind of way. She went to community college and wanted to be a newscaster or something. In some ways she seemed like a less ambitious version of myself. How hard could it be?

"Hey Zoe," I said slowly, eyes wide. "Should I enter the Miss Minnesota USA pageant?"

It was more than a light bulb went off—I felt like I'd stuck my finger in the socket. I thought entering the Miss Minnesota USA pageant was not just a good but a brilliant idea.

As in the Miss USA pageant system operated by the Miss Universe Organization, at the time co-owned by Donald Trump.

Of course, I watched the annual pageant on TV in awe as a child. I imagined myself cavorting around the host city with Miss Texas and Miss Pennsylvania like they did in the opening segments. However, I did not grow into a pageant girl. I wanted to be an actor, not a model. I didn't think beauty was my greatest strength. Up until this point, the thought of entering a beauty pageant would have been preposterous. Something I hadn't considered since adolescence. But I was high, and my mind was wide open.

"Zoe, don't you think that would help me break in?" I said, pitching her enthusiastically. "Like if I were Miss Minnesota, it would be way easier to get an agent and auditions when I get to Hollywood, right?"

"Actually… yeah!" she said her hands on her hips, her wild eyes matching her wide grin.

I was thinking that the validation of winning something would feel nice. I was thinking that if I could prove my ability to fit within the acceptable standards of hotness and presentability, it wouldn't just help my career, it would make my life easier. I was thinking that a sash, a crown, and a title would be irrefutable proof. To be the best at being the most beautiful? What could be better? I was high, but I was making a lot of sense.

During the month of October, in the wee hours of the night amid the restless chaos of our Tower Hall dorm room, I sat at my desk in preparation, tweaked out of my mind, dry eyes burning and sensitive to the fluorescent light, like a vampire trying to suck the blood out of this opportunity. I had a color printer and bought some card stock and résumé paper. I printed up photos of me and sponsorship invitations for businesses back home to donate to my pageant fund.

When I opened my mailbox a couple weeks later, I discovered a few hundred bucks and a handful of letters with well wishes. Honestly, super generous, though I'm surprised no one expressed concern. Nobody takes up pageanting at twenty-one unless they're on drugs, completely delusional, or already trapped in a bad marriage. And I easily fit two out of three.

I got a folder in the mail from Future Productions to help me prepare. As part of the Miss USA pageant's fifty-three-year tradition (it began in 1952 and I participated in 2004), all contestants would compete in three categories: swimsuit, evening gown, and interview competitions.

I attended a virtual workshop during which I furiously typed their words of wisdom like: "Be a fireball!!" "You have to 'Charge 'em up!'" "Give the judges a piece of you, and it must be believable." "Secret: Judges are human, too."

I drove down to Jefferson City in mid-November, a couple weeks before the competition, to buy an off-season clearance bikini for the swimsuit portion. Back in Columbia, I went to the mall and bought a sparkly red gown from DEB—the cheap prom emporium—for forty dollars.

I did not work out. I did not buy shapewear. I did not get a spray tan. I did not book a makeup artist. I didn't do any of the things I would at least attempt to do before a photo shoot today. Nor did I practice my answer to a single solitary interview question. I winged it.

Early Saturday morning on Thanksgiving weekend, I pulled up to the Radisson Riverfront Hotel on East Kellogg Boulevard in St. Paul in my Oldsmobile, hunting around for self-parking so I wouldn't have to pay for valet. My nipples hurt from the early winter cold, now acclimated to Missouri's milder weather. I staggered through the revolving door, heaving my big black suitcase behind me, juggling my purse, computer and toiletries bags, and the flimsy plastic DEB bag around my dress. My mouth dropped open as I gazed around the vast marble lobby of the hotel, spotting gorgeous girls with their mothers at the coffee bar and on the escalator and milling about everywhere in between. I felt my first tinge of uncertainty. The competition looked stiff. *Fake it till you make it*, I thought, sighing. I straightened my posture and pressed forward toward the check-in table.

I crept into the ballroom for orientation, immediately self-conscious that I was underdressed. We were instructed to come dressed in interview attire, but most of the girls looked airbrushed. Meanwhile my white shirt was wrinkled and my hair was still wet.

As soon as I learned there would be choreographed dance numbers, I knew I would have to pop pills to get through the weekend. I only had 30 milligrams, so I had to space it out, but had I the inventory, I would have taken much, much more.

There's one part I should have been naturally good at: the interviews and live questions. I would go on to host podcasts and interview people as part of my job. I do stand-up. I'm a pretty good talker. Definitely proficient. Instead, I totally fumbled this category because I didn't bother to prepare. I didn't consider any of the nineteen tips they gave us during the virtual workshop. I didn't practice ten questions with a tape recorder, looking into a mirror. I didn't record a video of myself doing a mock interview and watch it back first with my eyes closed and then with my eyes open. I didn't even journal on each possible question. I thought, *I know how to talk*. Wrong, bitch! Even though the preliminary interviews were conducted sitting down one-on-one with a judge, I couldn't string together a sentence, much less a compelling paragraph.

I immediately choked on hairspray as I entered the conference room serving as the dressing room for pageant finals on Sunday afternoon and knew I was out of my league. It was all spray tans, double-sided body tape, and dresses that cost way more than the one I'd bought off DEB's clearance rack. The rich, competitive girls had coaches, professional makeup artists, and hair stylists—some girls were rolling with an entourage five people deep. I coughed on the aerosols, tripped over the plastic bag covering my dress, righted myself, and searched for an empty mirror. Digging through my bag, I realized I'd forgotten to bring a comb. I had no chance.

I wish I'd put the pill bottle down long enough to ask myself, "Am I a pageant girl?"

The answer is no.

Not just a regular no, a resounding no.

I hate shopping for clothes. I wasn't particularly put together or concerned with visual presentation, and I certainly wasn't a girly girl. I hate not eating french fries. I never shave my legs. I rarely wear makeup. I wasn't glam, I didn't know how to do glam, and at that point, I wasn't sophisticated enough to hire professional help.

Looking at myself in that dressing room mirror, taking in the ultra-femme tableau behind me, I realized that when I saw that news clip back in the dorms, it didn't occur to me that this was a *beauty* pageant, not a *merit* pageant. They didn't care that I could act or get a high score on my SATs. They didn't care that I was scrappy or driven. In my spun out enthusiasm, I failed to process that we were there to bat our eyes under the male gaze and perform our femininity according to patriarchal ideas of how women should look and behave—certainly not my strong suit. Sure, I fancied myself a strumpet, but a strumpet on my own terms. Was that even possible? *Silly me*, I thought.

I stuck my tongue in my pill bottle and licked out the Adderall flakes before stepping into my spot in the backstage lineup. A producer said, "Go!" and we strutted onto the stage in a group of four and struck a pose. I thrust my hand on my hip and bobbed to the beat. The announcer roared, "Courtney Kocak. Miss Jackson USA!"

My parents had come up to watch with my Grandma Marge and Aunt Marcia. I can't imagine what was going through their heads. *Just look at our little girl up there, Miss Adderall USA!*

MODEL MAYHEM

I discovered the site ModelMayhem.com during my Adderall spring at the Blue House. I thought *headshots are expensive, this is a great way to get free headshots!*

Cross-legged on the bed with my Dell laptop in front of me and Ellie curled up on my lap, I signed up and filled out a profile. Requests from photographers based in St. Louis and Kansas City rolled in immediately using the acronym TFP, which stood for "trade for prints," meaning I would get a CD with the images for my portfolio. I was flattered by the easy attention. I guess I was meant to be a model after all.

By the next fall, I'd done several photo shoots. I thought I'd learned how to handle the creepy ones.

For some reason, I'd agreed to let this photographer pick me up, sight unseen. Just a few casual messages exchanged and there he was, pulling up to the Tower Hall dorms in his Mustang convertible.

I hopped in his hypermasculine sports car like a femme with a death wish, the whale tail of my black thong peeking out of my white low-rise jeans, a backpack of lingerie slung over my shoulder.

As we sped off, I remember thinking, *Am I the dumb girl in a horror film? The one who gets killed first. Maybe I should drive myself…*

But it was too late. He drove too fast. For ninety minutes all the way down to Lake of the Ozarks, I clutched the door, slid around in my seat, and said a prayer to who the fuck knows. The wind whipped through my hair as Van Halen and Def Leppard ripped through the speakers. The only upside was that the resounding din rendered conversation impossible.

He took his right hand off the wheel and rested it on the seat behind me, looking over with a maniacal smile like Jack Nicholson as the Joker. A bead of sweat dripped down his forehead.

Relieved to arrive in one piece, we entered his vacation condo (or maybe it was his friend's?) and my eyes landed on a trio of framed family photos, next to some decorative safari figurines—a spindly giraffe and a prowling lion. As I moved to check them out, he moved to block my path, "Okay, let's get started. I'm going to make us drinks. What do you want?"

An emergency alarm sounded in my mind. *Do not accept a drink from this man. Do not accept a drink from this man. Do not accept a drink from this man.*

"I don't really drink," I lied.

He drank his whiskey, his chest puffing out in his black T-shirt a little bit more with every sip. He took out his camera. *Flash!*

I posed on the bed. *Flash!*

He licked his lips. *Flash!*

We danced around like wild animals. The predator and the prey. Immediately locked in a frenetic tango. *Flash!*

I had the jitters of not having eaten much. Gnawing instinct, nibbling on my empty stomach. *Flash! Flash!*

I felt small on the bed. Skinny and splayed out. *Flash!*

Perfect prey for a bear. *Flash!*

Another whiskey. *Flash!* Another whiskey. *Flash!* His cheeks became pink. *Flash!*

He pushed me to do more. *Flash!* Nakeder. *Flash!* Now touch yourself.

"Um, I just want lingerie pics for my portfolio," I pushed back.

He didn't like that answer. "I guess you don't really want to be a model then."

He tossed the camera on the chair. A *flash!* of fear.

Another whiskey.

He said he had a gun. Or a knife. Or there was a knife in his hand. Something scary.

I ran away from him.

I locked myself in the spare room. Trapping myself for my own safety.

I called Zoe in hushed tones, "Hey, can you come get me literally right now?"

He pounded on the door. "Hey, what are you doing in there?"

"I'm headed out the door right now," she said from all the way back in Columbia.

He pounded louder and louder. "You better come out here, you little bitch. We're not fucking done."

I felt very far from home. Waiting for Zoe. Waiting for the photographer to wear himself out.

Ninety minutes later, Zoe texted me that she was outside. The condo was eerily quiet. I opened the door a crack and saw the photographer slumped over. I grabbed the straps of my backpack, took a deep breath, and snuck out as stealthily as I could. Closing the passenger door to Zoe's baby blue Honda Civic, I exhaled a sigh of relief and she drove us to the safety of our dorm room.

In my frantic escape, I left my drug purse behind, a pouch of weed and Adderall.

After the photographer came to in the morning, he called me and left a roaring voicemail, pissed that I had left. Safe and sound back in Columbia, I felt secure enough to return the call and arrange for him to leave my dope pouch under the welcome mat, so I could go back and get it when he wasn't home. He was a dick about it, but whatever, I wanted my pills. He obliged I think because he wanted us to still be cool.

He wouldn't send me the pics from that night though. I wanted them on principle. I wanted to see if it looked how it felt.

A year later, in the kitchen of my apartment in St. Louis, I got a phone call from an unknown number. Looking for work, I answered.

It was a private investigator. I paced the linoleum and he asked me, "Can you tell me about the photo shoot you did in Lake of the Ozarks?"

I stopped in my tracks. "How do you know about this?"

He asked me if the "photographer" tried to hurt me.

"How did you get my number?"

He told me the photographer's wife—soon to be ex-wife—found out about our "photo shoot" gone wrong, that it wasn't the first time. "You could help stop him," the investigator pressed.

"I don't want to be involved," I said, and pressed END on my cell phone.

My mind was steady, but racing. He didn't *actually* hurt me. But he *almost* did. I wasn't about to get dragged into a marital dispute, cross this crazy son-of-a-bitch, and make myself a target again. I was not the linchpin to this man's demise (though I hoped that he would meet it very soon).

How would I explain why I was there in the first place? "Well, you see, Honorable Judge Whoever-the-Fuck, I went against the wisdom of every Lifetime movie I'd ever seen and allowed a creepy stranger with a camera to whisk me off to a remote lake home because I was building my portfolio for a modeling career I will likely never have... At least he chose a deserving victim, am I right, Judge?"

That was perhaps my biggest hesitation: I felt dumb, but not like a victim.

How many women decide not to speak up because they feel like idiots? Because of the near-certainty they'll be treated like idiots?

How many men are telling on themselves by treating women like idiots when they *don't* assume that every man they meet is a potential rapist/murderer?

I thought, *Maybe the girl from the horror film wasn't dumb, but I still don't want to end up dead.*

I got more calls from the private investigator, though I tried not to answer them. When I accidentally did, I said, "I don't want to talk about this."

Then I began getting calls from a St. Louis police detective too. One of them mentioned something about testifying in a child custody case.

I thought, *These aren't free headshots.* "Please don't call me again," I said, hanging up the phone with finality.

I deleted my Model Mayhem account, relieved.

A few years later, when I moved to LA, I would sign up again.

I could really use some free headshots, I thought.

We would meet at this new photographer's condo near the beach in Marina del Rey. The saltwater would splash against my silk dress. The waves would slice at my nipples, leaving them raw. He would want more, less, nakeder. "How about you just take off your top?" he would suggest. Afterward I would have to hound him to get the photos for my portfolio. He would use my likeness to promote his friend's business. I wouldn't get paid. He would want to grab a drink, crash on my couch, do another photo shoot at a hotel.

What's the definition of insanity again?

1311 NASTY FRAT

I had the world figured out when I lived at 1311 Nasty Frat. The address was actually on Windsor Street, it wasn't a real frat, I didn't technically live there, and I didn't know jack shit. But everything else about that sentence is true.

I was a stowaway at 1311 Nasty Frat, otherwise known as Windsor Castle, with Zoe. It was fall semester, our final semester, and we officially resided in the Tower Hall dorms on campus, but between photo shoots and preparing for my pageant, we often needed to escape our drug den for another, more spacious drug den.

1311 Nasty Frat was a brown two-story Craftsman with a wraparound front porch. The house was almost quaint if you didn't know what was going on inside. It was a purgatory on my way to "real life" after college, which I was about to graduate from in a matter of months. While I was studying to become an actress, Nasty Frat was a seedy underbelly of regular people who weren't driven by big dreams. Their lack of ambition was perplexing; I labeled everyone not consumed by their creativity as muggles in the pejorative. But one day I would act out this sort of ordinary debauchery on the screen, I figured. This was more than a diversion, it was research. I have been an investigative journalist long before I was aware. Plus, the guys at Nasty Frat were our friends.

We became affiliated with the gentlemen of Nasty Frat through the bistro I worked at, which I think was just called The Bistro. I became a hostess at The Bistro after coming back from summer stock theater. I got the job on the recommendation of a buddy I knew through Chase. By this point, aside from my parents helping with tuition, I had to pay my own way. So this was one of the myriad jobs I juggled during my final semester before graduation.

In addition to my hostess duties, I spent a lot of time at work stealing glances at Joe Love. Joe Love was a bartender with pretty blue eyes and a roguish grin, and at twenty-one I could've fallen in love with him based on his name and looks alone. We started fucking and for a week or two, I thought I had.

But Joe Love didn't love me back. He was happy to have sex with me a handful of times, but he soon became restless. He had other girls he wanted to bang and parties to attend and beers to drink. He couldn't be tied down.

So his roommates became Zoe's and my platonic boyfriends instead. Goose, K-Dog, Ben, and Nick Vroman.

Goose had mousy brown hair and always wore a dirty white tee and worked at Chili's in the kitchen. He also played in a band, but a lot of times heroin got in the way of his other extracurriculars. When you're eating out, you rarely think about the odds that the guy making your food is a heroin addict. The chances are actually pretty high. Goose was one of those heroin-addict line cooks, but Zoe and I loved him the most of all the Nasty Frat brothers. Goose had puppy dog eyes and a lazy lisp. He was sweet, but slightly devious, always down to do or talk about anything at any time, except when he needed to get high again.

Goose would do heroin in the basement with a dirty spoon. Zoe would go down and keep him company. I only went down a couple times. I didn't like to watch, it made me dizzy. My memories of it are clips: cement basement wall, graffiti, spoon, me looking away.

Goose had been doing heroin since he was sixteen. It was a family tradition passed down from his father, the elder heroin addict. Unfortunately, Goose's dad was now dead.

One time, Zoe and I went with Goose to school to visit his mom for lunch. I was floored to learn that his mom was a teacher. *My* parents were teachers. We opened our milk cartons across from this prim woman and tried to make small talk that didn't involve drugs.

When I wasn't wearing my gray Bistro T-shirt and khakis with my thong poking out, I was wearing my off-duty uniform: lingerie as a shirt and low-rise jeans with my thong poking out. Occasionally a head scarf as a shirt. That's what I wore to the elementary school to meet Goose's mom. She probably thought I did heroin with Goose, but I never did. My addiction was much more socially acceptable.

K-Dog was another chef and substance abuser. He lived upstairs in 1311 Nasty Frat, kitty-corner across from Joe Love, with a fuck-ton of hedgehogs. Seriously, he had at least five little spikeballs under his care at all times. He liked rockabilly, whiskey, drinking pretty much all the time, those fucking hedgehogs, Zoe, and me. Despite his prickly exterior, K-Dog was shockingly sweet.

But sweet K-Dog was an alcoholic. I probably would've fucked K-Dog—Keith—if I thought he could keep it up for me. Keith would have loved me back, but he didn't love himself, just the caricature that had been superimposed on top of whatever trauma he was running from.

Then there was Ben, a big guy, full carnivore. He managed a local Buffalo Wild Wings franchise. He was nice and had a good sense of humor, but he was very obsessed with meat—eating it, hunting it, skinning it on the porch. I was in one of my vegetarian eras, so that's probably part of the reason we didn't have a deeper connection.

Nick Vroman was the most functional member of the household. He was also a bartender at The Bistro. He was training to become a masseuse. Sometimes he would practice on Zoe and me, but it was hard to relax with the amount of Adderall I was taking at the time. Nick Vroman liked the cheap rent and the Lost Boys-style camaraderie of the Nasty Frat, but he spent a lot of time rolling his eyes at the chaos that surrounded him.

This was the golden age of Napster and the Nasty Frat bros pirated every song you could possibly want to listen to. Red Hot Chili Peppers' "Under the Bridge." O.A.R.'s "That Was a Crazy Game of Poker." Dispatch's "The General." 311's "Love Song." Modest

Mouse's "Ocean Breathes Salty." The White Stripes' "Seven Nation Army." Everything.

Their bathroom was fucking feral—what was supposed to be white porcelain was now grimy and gray, there was a fuzzy coat of beard and pubic hair, and it was rarely stocked with toilet paper. I usually held it as long as I possibly could when I was over and definitely went home when I was due for a shower.

Back at the dorms, I stayed up around the clock, making binders. One was for my self-created independent study course, "Nonprofits and Arts Education," an elaborate excuse to get the last three theater credits I needed to graduate early. I turned in a gorgeous and comprehensive binder with a detailed accounting of my many failures as a children's theater intern—having to find a sub for my class, failing to get the hand props in time, sleeping through a performance, etc. The only thing I was good at was sending long emails making excuses for what I'd fucked up, which provided content for my binder. A polished turd of a project. Effectively, a total waste. Somehow I got an A. It should have been titled "Advanced Bullshitting."

When I actually went to class that last semester, I felt like I was entering the portal to another dimension. I took Advanced Acting I and II, but it was disorienting to try to perform Shakespeare so fucking high. My mind was racing with half thoughts and bizarre hypotheticals. Not the ideal headspace for textual analysis. I'd rather play the fool and drink cheap Boone's Farm wine. So I made it part of the scene. Thank god for the infantile cell phone technology of my youth; there is no photographic proof.

My other official class was a senior acting seminar called "Nuts and Bolts: Acting as a Business" with a seventy-year-old professor who taught us about call-in services, an industry antique from his era in New York City, long since out of use. The professor had a delightful personality, but none of it was relevant. I felt wholly unprepared for what was next.

Had I gone to NYU, I would have been forced into some

sort of seriousness. Or at least my extracurriculars would have been more industry-appropriate. But it was too late.

So after class, every week or so I would drive to St. Louis or Kansas City for photo shoots, promotional modeling gigs, and to audition for anything and everything—no-budget independent films, cheesy industrial videos, even hair shows—praying I could at least get a commercial or industrial film so I wouldn't have to go to LA with nothing on my résumé except theater.

I busied myself by rustling up any casting notice that had a morsel of potential. I should have read more books and worked more hours at a steady, boring job to save money to follow through with my tenuous plan to move to LA in January, but that was antithetical to my philosophy at the time.

Somehow, I already felt over the hill. The pressure felt real; the message I got was that for both actresses and women, younger equals more valuable. The irony is, if I'd slowed down and been more strategic, I'd have gotten further ahead in the long run. But you already know that's not who I am—or, at least, it wasn't who I was at that time.

Every feature film opportunity garnered excitement, but it didn't take long for a trend to emerge: the "director" was typically an older guy in his forties. I was twenty, about to turn twenty-one. The director would want to take lots of time getting to know his star, talking ad nauseam about method acting and camera angles, which I ate right up. One director in particular wanted to meet up on a regular basis, professing to take the process very seriously. After a quasi-romantic meeting at Dave & Buster's, I realized the "role" he was casting most urgently was that of his girlfriend. It was time to start looking for another debut.

One afternoon, I staggered to our dorm room from Nasty Frat. I'd been up for something like thirty-six hours, taking extended-release Adderall after extended-release Adderall. I was incapable of functioning, yet couldn't go to sleep. I lay on the bottom bunk and watched equations and philosophical arguments materialize on the ceiling, layer after layer like *A Beautiful Mind*, until the puzzle was complete and I threw my head back and smiled up at heaven with a satisfied smirk. I thought I had the whole world figured out. I also felt like maybe I would die. Maybe I was hallucinating. Or maybe enlightenment feels like a sort of death—a death of your stupider self, perhaps.

When I wasn't a junkie hanging out with other junkies, I was an undercover junkie among the normies. Seating tables and expediting plates of spin dip, teaching theater to children, flirting with what my future would look like after I jumped through one last set of hoops. In the meantime, my out-of-town auditioning finally paid off. I'd managed to book one of the lead roles in an independent film—and this one actually seemed legit. In two days, I would start rehearsal.

The first day of the rest of my life.

And in my new life, I would be a successful actress.

Maybe, for a split second, I did have it all figured out.

February 6, 2005—one of my last days at 1311 Nasty Frat—I was watching the Super Bowl like a normie. It was Super Bowl XXXIX, the New England Patriots vs. the Philadelphia Eagles. The Nasty Frat brothers had cleaned up just enough to host a party, so there were extra people in football jerseys milling around the ground floor.

Zoe and I painted numbers on our tits like they were jerseys and flashed whenever the Eagles scored a goal or anyone at the party yelled, "Flash! Flash!" Great party trick if you're a young woman seeking attention during a sporting event.

Nick Vroman raised his eyebrows at me, "I'm making edibles."

I had smoked copious amounts of marijuana over the past four or five of my twenty-one years, but I had not yet let my digestive tract get in on the fun. I hadn't eaten any food that day, so I entered the situation starving.

"Are the brownies ready?" I pestered Nick.

"Give me fifteen minutes," he said with a laugh.

"Are they ready now?" I pressed ten minutes later.

"Here," he said, slicing through a pan of brownies with curling wisps of heat coming off the top. "Fresh out the oven. But go slow, they're strong," he warned, handing me a paper plate.

I had one brownie. Didn't feel anything. So I went back for seconds. Then thirds. The brownies were delicious. I could barely taste the weed.

"Zoe, do you feel anything?" I said, bobbing my knee up and down impatiently.

"Not yet," she giggled. Zoe always giggled. She was a fun best friend. Whip smart, but equally reckless. She had blonde baby-fine angelic curls. She also dressed like a trailer park slut—my favorite brand of fashion.

"They better not be regular-ass brownies," I said, eyeing the tray.

Fuck it, either way I was gonna eat one more. Even more than I wanted to get high, I was hungry. There wasn't a lot of food in the house, plus Adderall and my eating disorder; sometimes I got ravenous in my body's quest to stay alive.

I gobbled the brownie, which brought my body count to four pot brownies in a row *bam bam bam bam.* I fidgeted on the couch, watching the game and waiting for my brownies to kick in. I waited and I waited and I waitttteeeddd untillll everything turned to slow-mo—like watching a replay, but for the whole game.

A whistle blew on the TV and the guys said, "Flash! Flash!" But we couldn't flash anymore. We had melted into the couch. We were stuck in the quicksand of its upholstery. Zoe could just as well have been in Alaska. I had my heavy mind and my heavy body and everything that existed outside of that was blurry.

I stayed like that for twenty-six hours.

Then, I somehow drove to St. Louis.

When I arrived, I face-planted on the bed and stayed there for another thirteen hours.

Then I woke up, bleary-eyed, and ready for my new life to begin.

INTERMISSION 1

This is where the plot thickens. The midpoint of my coming of age.

This is where the path diverges. I had been on an intelligible road. Preschool, elementary, middle school, high school, college, and—then I was in the weeds, hacking my way through.

I didn't know anyone else who was a successful, full-time artist. Sure, I knew some local hobbyists growing up, who got their rocks off on the community theater stage. But they had real jobs to sustain them and families to care for and no knowledge of "the industry." I knew some professors at college, but they were as much teachers as artists. They offered me no blueprint for a lifestyle ripe with risk—or if they did, I failed to see it.

This is where rehearsal ends and real life begins. I thought I knew the script for the second act, but I would discover it was constantly being rewritten, sometimes as an act of my own sabotage, sometimes intentionally or coincidentally by others, and only rarely for my benefit. Unlike most plays I'd been in, I did not have the advantage of scene study, rehearsal, or even learning my blocking. None of the lines I had memorized would be relevant, not for pursuing my dream nor for existing as an adult. I would have to improvise.

This is where the fear sets in. Maybe not then, but looking back. I dread going down to the basement to dredge up those old scrapbooks and letters and journals that will tell me who I really was. I hope time has shorn off some of the rough edges, as it is wont to do. To make our former selves bearable from within our current skin.

This reckoning that is so necessary to finishing, to filling in the gaps, seems so hard. Maybe all of this was harder than I ever acknowledged when it was happening.

Even though part of me wants to bury the past in the

woods, or, better yet, light it on fire and let it burn to ash, never to be heard from again, a bigger part of me can't resist playing in the mud, telling jokes at my own expense, compulsively digging up the bodies of my former selves from where they are buried. The ones I had to lay to rest to become this still-flawed-but-more-evolved person on today's side of the story. Even though my cheeks are hot, the core of me doesn't want to be disembodied from the past. I don't want to tell a crooked narrative. I want to love all the hers as they were. Even the rotten bits.

This is where the dream—the only dream I'd ever known: to be an actress—turns into a nightmare. Where the stage manager yells, "Places!" And as soon as I say, "Thank you, places," I realize I'm unprepared to go back out there. The more I know about life, the less I want to play pretend. I don't know my lines, I don't even know the plot, and maybe I don't belong on the stage anymore, but it's too late, or too early, to bow out now.

THE POISONED COURT

When I first saw the listing for *The Poisoned Court*, on one of
the audition boards I checked daily during my last semester at
Stephens, I felt imposter syndrome.

Sitting at my desk in our dorm room, I bit my lip nervously
as I clicked through the highly stylized test photography. *The
Poisoned Court* was a Lucrezia Borgia-inspired independent film
that aspired to be gothic, grunge, and high fashion. I yearned to
fit into the aesthetic. Most of the sorceresses in the test photos
were scantily clad, but I wasn't opposed to some tasteful nudity. I
immediately began typing out an email to the director, attaching
my acting résumé and a few photos.

Two days later I got a response. The director loved my photos.
They were shooting for twenty-eight days, starting shortly after
my graduation. Most of the roles were still open—if I wanted to
audition in person or send him a tape, he would love to talk.

I submitted an audition tape and then met the director in person at
a McDonald's off of I-70 in suburban St. Louis on my way home
for Thanksgiving. I'd stayed up the night before on Adderall, sewing
a babyish sundress out of a thrift store find. He took a picture of me
wearing it on a patch of grass in the parking lot.

"A little to your left," he said, gesturing me away from
an overflowing dumpster. The stench of grease and trash wafted
through the air, but I felt like a movie star. In the photo, I looked
like a pouty brat.

At a booth inside, the director informed me, "I was
considering someone else for the role, but I'm looking for more of
an actress. You're good," he said, casting me on the spot.

The director and I both had big dreams. It was clear from
his flashy gold coat and our brief conversation that he wanted this
to be his breakout just as much as I wanted it to be mine.

The role was posted as a SAG Modified Low Budget contract, meaning I would be Taft-Hartley'd—granting me entry into the Screen Actors Guild union—and earning something like $250 a day. This would be the nest egg that would get me to LA.

And oh, did I need it. I had only a hundred bucks to my name at any given time with a creeping balance on my credit card. Now, there was hope on the horizon. I was going to be in a real movie—a feature film! I thought maybe it would go to Sundance. Could even win an Oscar. At the very least, it would help launch my career. It would be something for my reel, and I'd be in the union. Everyone has to start somewhere. Jennifer Aniston did *Leprechaun* and went on to make a million dollars an episode for *Friends*. *The Poisoned Court* would be my start.

A few weeks later, I met the director at a studio on Grand Boulevard in downtown St. Louis for a fitting. Even trying on musty second-hand clothes felt like a glamorous thing to do.

I unbuttoned my jeans and slid into a pair of camo pants. I pulled my henley over my head and replaced it with a cream cut-off tank. I adjusted the waistband, then put my hand on my hip and turned toward the director with an apathetic intensity so incongruent I'd only seen it on the faces of models. He got down on his knees to snap a picture of me.

The director rocked back on his heels to admire the image, then looked at the costume designer and smiled, "She's perfect, right?"

I thought the director was perfect too. He was kinda hot and seemed cool and unpredictable in a punk rock kind of way. He was older and had a family, but that only made him hotter. Maybe I had a little daddy complex with him; he was going to rescue me. Finally, my Guffman.

I ripped off the cream tank top and draped a faux fur jacket over my shoulders—very Marla from *Fight Club*. I didn't care about changing in front of him, I didn't even ask about a dressing room. I loved to get naked, but it was also for show. With my lack of boundaries, I was saying: I'm a cool girl, I'm a chill babe, I'm down for whatever. I casually opened the front edge of the jacket for a topless pose. *Flash, flash.*

I enjoyed the idea of being his muse. There is something terribly complicated about being an attractive young woman under the watchful eye of every older man you meet. Leering from professors, bank managers, even doctors. The constant attention is intoxicating and gross, and it feels like a damned if you do, damned if you don't source of fleeting power in this patriarchal world. I had to use it. The game was fucked up through no fault of my own. I still had to play it. How else was I supposed to get where I wanted to go?

I played as best I could, alternating tough and hard-talking with naive and demure. It was an effective recipe for getting older men's attention, but sometimes I tired of my own shtick and rolled my eyes—at me, at them, at the whole hopeless dance.

After my initial housing in St. Louis fell through, I'd been squatting with Zoe at 1311 Nasty Frat in Columbia. With just a couple months until filming, they needed me around for pre-production. I visited their production office a couple times, and on one visit, I revealed my housing quandary. The director and one of the producers, Bill, who was big, warm, and an eternal problem-solver (a great set of producer traits) found me a temporary place to stay through another producer, Rocco, who generously let me live in his rental property during filming.

"Meet me in Dogtown at 1," Rocco said.

On my way to the address, I drove my clunker through streets of modest homes bordered by industrial warehouses.

"It's called a shotgun house," Rocco explained as he gave me a quick tour and handed over the keys.

It was the first time I'd heard the term shotgun house, which meant a narrow house with rooms in a row so you could open the front door and shoot a bullet straight through. A name that didn't inspire feelings of safety.

Amid a confetti of snow flurries, I moved into the shotgun house with Zoe, for whom I'd secured a small acting role and production assistant gig on *The Poisoned Court*. We schlepped Rubbermaid totes, cardboard boxes, and milk crates full of our shit in several trips from our cars to the house.

We cleaned and organized in an Adderall haze, setting up the first room as our living room, surrounding the coffee table with decorative pillows and Zoe's portable camping chairs. The middle room was our bedroom with a full bed left behind by the previous tenant. The back room was the kitchen, which had a rusty stove and cockroach infestation. We only used it to collect trash.

Filming was pushed back from the initial estimate, so I had gotten a couple of restaurant jobs to tide me over. Chase hooked me up with a hostess gig at a tapas restaurant in Clayton, and then I picked up a serving job at Syberg's, a family-friendly sports bar and grill. Meanwhile, the director was pressuring me to lose weight. I was already thin, but underweight was his preferred aesthetic (and the industry standard).

In a group email, he asked: "How's the diet?"

With the extra pressure, anxiety, and excitement, I found myself constantly sneaking back to the prep area at Syberg's where I would binge on pretzel bites and house salad with their famous white cheese, which was problematic because shooting was just around the corner. I looked down at my distended belly in horror—I was sabotaging my feature film debut! So I dramatically quit both jobs during service on two separate nights in the same week.

"I'm sorry, I don't feel good. I can't do this," I said breathlessly to the Syberg's manager in the middle of a busy service.

Confused, the manager replied, "Are you sick or are you quitting?"

The answer was both, but I just cried, "I'm acting in a feature film next week!" as I handed her my apron and chaotic order pad filled with indecipherable scribbles.

I thought financial relief would come when I finally got my paycheck for the movie, but at the last minute, as I was presented with my contract, the director told me that it wouldn't be SAG Modified Low Budget after all. Instead of $250 a day and an invitation to join the Screen Actors Guild, I would make $2,000 for the three weeks of shooting (and there was no additional compensation for pickups or ADR in Los Angeles).

"What? I thought it was SAG this whole time," I said, shocked, but the director had already moved on to putting out his next fire.

Producer Bill stepped in to reassure me. "You're one of the leads," he said. "This movie is gonna be so good for your career."

I was supposed to shave my head during one of the scenes, and I was initially down to do it, but when they reneged on the contract at the last minute, I reneged on losing my hair. With a shaved head, I'd only be cast as an anarchist or the antichrist—and that would cost me a couple years of potential work. It was a bad business move. I tried to pull the director aside and talk to him about cheating that scene with a wig, but he was so busy I don't think he understood that I was firm on not shaving my head.

Or perhaps we were both engaged in our own wishful thinking.

Rehearsals began a week before filming. I met the two other leads—an actress in her thirties from Los Angeles, who seemed to find my naïveté annoying in the way of wasted youth, and Mateo, an actor in his late twenties from Montréal, with whom I had a very real spark. I could barely look him in the eye during our first rehearsal together, but he was adamant about getting to know me. We hung out after hours, taking field trips around St. Louis. Walking the grounds at Forest Park. Dining at the Union Station Hooters. Sometimes Zoe joined us. I was drawn to his brooding, poetic nature and bohemian style. He drank matcha tea before it was cool. He burned me an Interpol CD. He often pulled out his journal to take notes. I wondered if he was writing anything about me.

Mateo was "on a break" from his partner. I didn't see that as a red flag, but an opportunity. He did too. He was staying at an Extended Stay east of St. Louis. I drove over to his hotel room to rehearse with him the night before filming. We ran our lines and then had trouble saying goodbye at the door. He extended his arm and lured me back in with a kiss. Before I knew it, I was fucking my costar—number one and two on the call sheet. I wondered how many times that'd happened in the history of filmmaking.

The next day, we moved to a small town two hours outside of St. Louis. Mateo and I each had a room at the local bed and breakfast, across the hall from the other lead, while Zoe and the rest of the cast and crew stayed at the Days Inn. The B&B was on a sprawling property, which contained an abandoned hospital that was rumored to be haunted and doubled as many of our shooting locations.

I used my room for storage only. Instead, I slept with Mateo in the honeymoon suite with its romantic claw-foot tub. Sometimes we would bathe together.

Late at night, we snuck downstairs to the big kitchen to devour homemade bread. Even at room temperature, the bread was divine. We would make out between bites.

For a few fleeting weeks, the honeymoon suite felt like a warm bath.

Aside from my budding showmance and the thrill of starring in a movie, however bad, *The Poisoned Court* was, for me, a dystopian nightmare of an independent film in both plot and execution. It was shot on 35mm film, now rendered a relic of the past by digital technology. The first day of shooting fittingly took place at a morgue. One of my first lines was "I don't know if I'm poison or the cure" (not exactly Shakespeare, but satisfyingly edgy). It was, however, a legit, professional production with a budget of almost $500K and I wanted the best for it—after all, it was to be my feature film debut.

When I first got the DVD, I watched the movie over and over again, picking out scenes for my reel, pinching myself that I was finally a real actress. Returning to it again recently was a truly painful experience. My Adderall-infused performance wasn't actually the worst part. Sure, my performance was a little uneven, but how could I have made sense of that script, even sober?

From the beginning, I found the script unwieldy—ever-changing as a document and too comprehensive a tale to follow all the character backstories and shifting alliances. Watching the film with the distance of decades, it struck me as meandering and tonally jarring. Thematically, I found it shallow and trite: loyalty is a game of chess; bloodlines are poisoned by ambition; daughters are pawns in the games of fathers and brothers. As a meditation on power, it was patriarchal corruption masquerading behind rosary beads, with sex and marriage as weapons of state. And, of course, the woman at the center was either evil, a dumb bitch, or both.

One night after we wrapped, I kissed Mateo and wished him a relaxing bath. I stopped on my way out of town to fuel up on gas and Diet Mountain Dew before driving four hours to Columbia, my bloodshot eyes growing blearier by the mile. I sang Jack Johnson, Ashtani, Alanis Morissette, and Stevie Nicks to stay awake.

When I got there, I texted my hookup and traded all the dollars to my name for her Adderall prescription. A full bottle. I shook it and smiled. I popped a capsule into my mouth and chased it with warm DMD. Then I turned around and drove back. I had to stop to refuel at a creepily quiet backwoods gas station in the middle of the night. The sun was coming up when I pulled into the B&B. Mateo was already on set. I collapsed on the bed in the honeymoon suite, waking up hot and sweaty to a loud rap on the door, "Courtney! You're needed on set."

Then all of a sudden it was over. On the last day of shooting, the crew held the film—the literal film—hostage because nobody had been paid. *The Poisoned Court* ended in mutiny.

Mateo and I took a road trip to Chicago with Zoe, postponing our goodbye. We kept talking for a week or two after he went back to Canada, but then he cut me off cold turkey. I was devastated that he went back to his girlfriend and even more devastated that he wouldn't answer my calls. I also felt like an idiot—was this his plan the whole time? It was so close to the plot of the movie. How could I not see it coming?

Mateo came back to shoot pickups and gave me a handwritten letter full of excuses. His sweet nothings were all the more insulting because they'd been written in cursive. When he disappeared again for good, my heart sputtered like a rusty trumpet.

But that wasn't the biggest grief that came from *The Poisoned Court*.

I loved executive producer Bill. He told me that my use of profanity sounded poetic, and he accurately guessed that I would never be good at having a real job—I would be an artist for life.

One night, I had an insane UTI from fucking Mateo too much while we were playing house in the honeymoon suite. Bill got his doctor girlfriend to write me a prescription for Cipro.

I flew to LA for ADR, to re-record some of my dialogue, and Bill offered to give me career advice on my next steps. I felt understood by him, we had a mutual appreciation, and he wanted to help me—qualities that were so rare to me at that time. We made plans to speak again.

But that conversation would never happen.

Instead, I would get a phone call from another *Poisoned Court* producer.

"Bill had a heart attack. He's dead."

HOW NOT TO MAKE IT IN HOLLYWOOD, PART 1

I was at Carney's Express Limited, not to get a hot dog, but to make it in Hollywood.

Carney's was a bright yellow train on the Sunset Strip. But it wasn't going anywhere. It was a stationary freight car-slash-hot dog stand flanked by Godzilla-sized billboards and bougie hotels. That's where the producer suggested we should meet.

I was there to see about a movie. In from out of town. It was my first time in Los Angeles. I flew in from St. Louis on a now-defunct airline called American West. The ticket cost $119, which I'd charged to Bill Me Later. I was a twenty-one-year-old actress, ready for her big break. The LA equivalent of the star-to-be in *Annie*, naively rolling into the big city with "Three bucks, two bags, one meeeee!" As if my five-year plan were based on a punchline in a musical.

I was doing figure eights in and through and out and around the restaurant-train, trying to identify a producer I'd never seen before in my life.

The producer had emailed me one blurry photo the size of a thimble, so I wasn't really sure what I was looking for. Or how old he was.

I, on the other hand, looked like a homeless hooker hunting for my next trick as I crisscrossed Carney's dining car with my red lace bra poking through my cropped wife-beater, matching red tanga peeking out the top of my ripped white jeans, dragging a suitcase with my whole life behind me. But I was much more innocent than I appeared.

It was a late April Monday. Not a particularly warm day, but after a dozen laps pulling my giant rolly suitcase around Carney's, I was sweating through my tank top.

This was not the version of Hollywood the movies had prepared me for. I thought they were giving out sitcoms at the airport, like that line in *Swingers*.

When I'd landed at LAX a few hours prior, no one was there to meet me with a little sign that said "Kocak." Instead, I heaved my oversized black suitcase off the baggage claim belt and dragged it out to the arrivals curb, greeted by nothing but the smoggy midday air. I staggered along a row of honking taxis in a daze. I'd been dreaming about LA my whole life. Apparently, LA had not been dreaming about me.

"How much?" I asked one of the taxi drivers. "Depends where you're going," he said, blowing smoke out of the side of his mouth. He shrugged. "Forty-five plus." I ran a frantic ledger in my mind. My debit card was dangerously close to zero. I'd already spent $15 on soda and a snack at the St. Louis airport. My only choice was to catch the cheapest shuttle I could find and endure at least a handful of stops before being dumped off near Carney's in West Hollywood, a disorienting tour afforded only by the grace of my credit card with a $500 limit and the mensch shuttle driver who took pity on me.

It was then I became acutely aware: There was no safety net, I was gambling with every chip on the table, and all the clichés about small-town fools getting duped in the big city were well-earned. The realization hit me like jumping out of a plane and getting slapped by a wall of wind.

Yet my optimism was undeterred. This day was going to be big for my career!

On this day, I was finally going to meet the producer I'd been emailing with, who was in pre-production on a found-footage horror film called *The Unmarked Cabin*. Due to my diligent emailing, I was up for/maybe had already landed(?) one of the main roles in the ensemble. I'd found the casting notice on Mandy.com, a nationwide job board for actors and crew, like Craigslist for indie filmmakers.

When I'd replied to the listing, I was beginning to overstay my welcome in the shotgun house owned by Rocco, one of the producers on *The Poisoned Court*. Filming had wrapped two months prior, and I had no idea what my next move was. Every submission felt high stakes.

A few emails into our exchange, the producer had requested bikini or topless pics, indicating they were actually for the director and he was merely a good samaritan passing them on.

"I think he's looking for girls with big tits since they are going to be naked," he explained.

I read the email sitting on my knees at the coffee table in the shotgun house. I was scraping resin out of my pipe. I couldn't afford new weed. Zoe had taken off for her mom's. The house felt empty without her and her camping chairs. I had to get out of there. I took a hit and a scraggly wisp of smoke vanished in front of me.

I immediately replied with the thirstiest photos on my computer.

The producer slipped "You can be my snow bunny :-))" into an email he'd sent about a Mammoth Mountain location scout and offered to let me stay with him in LA sight unseen.

Still, this independent film seemed like a totally legit showbiz opportunity. He'd sent me his bio and the director had a feature film credit on IMDb. What more could I ask for?

I booked my flight. Because I didn't detect any funny business, there was no reason to tell anyone that I was going on this trip, especially not my parents back in Minnesota. *I'll just surprise them when I come back a famous movie star*, I thought. *It will be more fun that way!*

While I waited for the producer, I called my college friend Tatum, a regular visitor to the Blue House. A year older, she had moved to LA after graduation.

"What's up, girrrl?" I purred into my Cingular Wireless cell phone, trying to sound cool and casual about the fact that I was in LA for the first time *ever* and my game plan with the producer was off to a rocky start. Tatum was my plan B couch to crash on and literally the only person close to me who I knew in all of Southern California. There were a few random, tangential people I knew *of*—a guy my dad golfed with once who lived somewhere in or near

LA, my great-aunt used to live in Palm Springs (two hours away)
though I was pretty sure she'd moved to Tucson, a few famous
Stephens College alums, etc. I suddenly realized that none of those
were real leads. I didn't have contact info for any of them. And even
if I did, what would I say?

Tatum was my only hope.

The problem was I forgot to give her a heads up about my
trip.

"Oh, you're already here?!" she said, stunned. "I have to
babysit for my boss after work tonight, but maybe we could meet
up tomorrow night?"

My throat caught. "No worries, let's talk then!" I replied
casually.

I hung up the phone and my eyes glazed over imagining
the twenty-eight hours I would have to survive in the meantime. I
was on an impossibly tight budget, so I couldn't really afford to eat
and a hotel was out of the question. My stomach growled. I kicked
pebbles and continued to wait for the producer.

The afternoon sun had already moved the shady spot to the other
side of the parking lot when the producer finally showed up, in a
grubby gray T-shirt, shoulders hunched and head down.

"Courtney?" he said gruffly. "What have you been up to?"

"Uh, I've just been here since I called you... three hours
ago."

"Sorry, I had some errands to do," he said unapologetically.

But it didn't matter. At that point, I was ecstatic that I was
not going to have to sell my body for a hotel room.

The producer helped me with my smaller bag as he led
me to his apartment a block away. I lugged my big suitcase as fast
as I could to keep up and finally got a good glimpse of him. He
had to be in his sixties, looking a little bit like Larry David with
his tousled gray horseshoe surrounding his bald head, but before
Larry David made that look charming. And this guy didn't have
the playful eyes of Larry David. He had the spotty eye contact of a
serial killer that occasionally concentrated into a stone-cold stare.
The sight of him made me shiver. We turned onto Sweetzer, and for

the first time, I started to wonder if this was a casting for a horror movie or a real-life murder.

He bitched about the neighbor lady's cat as we headed up the stairs to his apartment. Once inside his studio, the murd-o-meter in my head beeped wildly. The whole place was covered in a sticky, dusty film coating stacks of books and scripts and piles of other crap. There was an odd smell. It was nice to set down my suitcase, but I grimaced as I took in his hoarder's nest.

When he asked if I was hungry, I clobbered him with a, "Yes! What's nearby?" even though I didn't have a budget for meals.

He said he knew the perfect spot and we headed out, walking downhill in a zigzag until we got to Santa Monica Boulevard. The blocks of colorful West Hollywood cottages and apartment buildings lulled me back into my fantasy. This was Wonderland, this was Oz, this was where dreams came true, nothing bad was going to happen here. (Never mind the reference to two terrifying fairy tales.)

We sat down at the counter at French Market, where it was clear he was a regular. As he introduced me to a male server, it was also clear that he brought me here to show me off. "This one's on me!" he declared loudly, so I tolerated the whole charade. "I like the soup du jour," he said, looking at the menu over my shoulder. "Hey, Chris, what's the soup today?" he called out. Across the room, Chris looked over, annoyed, in the middle of taking another order.

All of the producer's interactions with the waitstaff were soured with rudeness. I could tell he was on his best behavior trying to impress me, but unfortunately, his best wasn't very good. He curtly demanded refills. Forced the servers to listen to lengthy updates about his movie project. I clocked several eye rolls, suppressed snickers, and muttered retorts. I could tell they all hated him.

I finally panged with long overdue desperation—inside, I was grasping around like I couldn't get my parachute to open. I made lingering eye contact with Chris, who looked about my age, maybe five years older, as we got up to leave after our soup. I wished he could take me back to his place at the end of his shift and teach me everything he knew about how to make it in Hollywood, instead of whatever lay ahead of me this evening. I wished I could send him some sort of signal that I needed help.

The sun set as we walked back along Santa Monica Boulevard, which reminded me of the lyrics to Sheryl Crow's "All I Wanna Do," where she has fun until the sun comes up over this very street! So I sang that song in my head, trying to think happy, non-serial killer thoughts as I nodded along to whatever inane thing the producer had just told me.

All of a sudden I heard *RRRRTT!*

I looked up and made eye contact with Donald Faison of *Clueless* fame, his silver Hummer coming to an abrupt stop, mere inches from hitting me. His face went from laughing-to-panicked in the split second it took him to brake. I couldn't believe my luck—I almost got hit by Donald Faison! I was just grateful to recognize someone for a minute.

I'd already known Donald Faison for a long time at that point. *Clueless* was a huge movie the year I was in sixth grade. A teen comedy about a rich girl with cool friends and great fashion set in LA with a campy plotline and catchy one-liners? You're totally buggin' if you think I didn't watch the movie and subsequent TV show a million times. *As if!*

Donald and his lady-friend passenger sat in stunned silence as the producer and I cleared the front of his vehicle. Relief washed over his face when I smiled and waved. But my heart panged as they turned out of the parking lot and left me alone with the producer again. I wished Donald Faison did hit me, to rescue me from this situation.

We got back to the apartment fully intact, and I watched the producer move his messy piles around to make space for me.

"I just sleep on the couch," he said when he saw me scanning the studio for a bed. "But you can have it tonight."

"Unless you want to share?" he asked hopefully.

I choked on nervous laughter.

"I don't think there's room," I said, gingerly sitting on the couch, careful to avoid the groove of his body imprint.

Exhausted from the travel and constant risk assessment, I covered myself with a flimsy blanket I'd gotten on the plane and tried not to get psyched out about spending the night. The producer creeped me out and his filthy place was the stuff of nightmares, but I didn't have the money to be picky.

He took his sweat-stained pillow and a blanket over to the floor near the fridge. His loud panting told me he really wished he was on the couch too. I was doing my best to ignore it, and then I heard, "Hey… are you okay over there?"

I pretended to be asleep and he tried again.

"Hey… I was just wondering if there's any room on the couch?"

"No." I said firmly.

I only pray when it's a fucking emergency, and I prayed to God that I didn't die that night. I thrashed my head against the yellow-stained, mite-ridden pillow at the thought of it. It was so trite it hurt. I was dog tired but remained alert for hours before finally succumbing to sleep.

The next day, my skin felt covered in the same dusty, sticky film as the rest of his apartment, but I was too scared to strip down for a shower before we headed out for errands. I quietly watched him move months of junk mail out of his front seat to make room for me. We stopped by his office on the CBS Radford lot, where he had a contentious exchange with the director, who did not seem to recognize me from my sexy pics or even know who I was, period.

"Get her the audition info, I guess," the director said with a shrug. It seemed like maybe I was not a shoo-in for the role as I'd been led to believe.

The producer went from highly annoying to unbearable as we ran another errand to his post office box in Burbank. "I can't get this crick out of my shoulder," he complained, grasping at it futilely, shooting me a pleading glance like I should rub it. I ignored his plea and looked out the window at the quaint shops we passed on Magnolia. LA was a lot different than I'd expected in almost every way.

I waited for the right moment to gently, softly, not directly, but in a roundabout way, maybe possibly ask about my potential casting.

He bristled and said, "Everyone hates me today." He stared me dead in the eyes.

My increasing apprehension made me uncharacteristically kind and accommodating. "What are you talking about? Everyone thinks you're great!"

Back at his apartment, I said, "I'm gonna make a quick call."

I went outside to call Tatum. The fresh air hit me like a cleanse. I looked up, squinting at the palm trees, and took a deep breath. I dialed Tatum, and this time when she answered, I dropped the pretense.

"Okay, so I don't really know this guy," I began.

"I'll be there by eight," she reassured me when I finished.

Back inside, I told the producer I was going to hang out with my friend for the night. I didn't tell him I was never coming back.

At 7:47, I was waiting outside when Tatum rounded the corner. I ran across Sweetzer with my luggage skittering behind me as she pulled over and rescued me from my big break.

SEEKING: MODEL 4 MASSAGE

After I returned from Los Angeles and packed up my things from Rocco's shotgun house, I moved to Chicago. I have never been poor like I was in Chicago. When I first arrived, I lived in a parking lot at the edge of the city. For thirty-six hours, I was homeless. After sleeping in my car overnight, I begged my frugal, disapproving parents to help me out with a security deposit for a tiny studio apartment on Belmont.

My studio apartment wasn't really livable. It didn't have a bed. I only spent one night there. I had another sort of home base: mostly I stayed with a guy a couple years older than me named Sam.

I knew Sam because four months prior, I'd responded to his Craigslist ad and modeled for Bong Girls, his T-shirt startup. A Bong Girls T-shirt had been featured in the movie *Van Wilder* with Ryan Reynolds, so the business seemed destined for success. Somehow, inexplicably, this was part of my genuine effort to get my "career" off the ground. Zoe was always down for whatever, so we drove from St. Louis to Chicago for the photo shoot. By day, we tied the samples in knots to expose our midriffs and pouted at the camera of a Columbia College photography student. By night, we drank PBRs at a dive bar with Sam.

Shortly before I'd left for California, Zoe had gone home to visit her mom in the Ozarks and stayed. When I got back, I was best-friendless and Rocco was nudging me out of his shotgun house. With nothing keeping me in St. Louis, I moved to Chicago and started hanging out with Sam all the time.

We weren't fucking, yet I was essentially living at his Lincoln Park apartment rent-free. Sam had a crush on me and was eager to welcome me into his daily life, but I was too immature to understand the allure of dating a sweet nerd with a receding hairline. That would come later. At this point, I fancied myself a lover of bad boys and my heart was still smarting from Mateo.

I could not find a steady job that would cover all my bills, and I was starting to feel weird about my relationship with Sam, my only friend in Chicago. Sam kept a tab at the Mayan Palace, the Mexican restaurant downstairs from his apartment, and we had the daily habit of ordering chips and guac and tamarind margaritas. But I couldn't have my non-boyfriend paying for everything, not when I had the audacity to tell him the sound of his chewing made me sick.

A few months later, my parents came to visit. Amid all the hustle and bustle of city life, they were out of their element.

Every time we would pass a homeless person, my mom would mutter, "Oh, that's so sad."

I was already impervious to stepping over bodies to get where I needed to go. I was sympathetic, but I had my own struggles.

But it was unlike anything she'd seen up to that point. When they got back home, she mailed me a card with forty dollars and said half of it was for me, and I was supposed to hand the other half out to homeless people.

I wanted to call her and scream, "YOU HAVE NO IDEA HOW CLOSE I AM TO BEING A HOMELESS PERSON!"

Of course I pocketed the whole forty dollars.

I tried to get a job at the Baskin-Robbins across from Sam's apartment. The owner was a Middle Eastern man who seemed to take a shine to me the few times Sam and I went there for ice cream.

"I saw your sign on the door. You're hiring for the overnight shift?" I inquired, taking a lick of my Rocky Road waffle cone.

"Come back for an interview tomorrow at 4:30," he told me.

When I came back for the interview, he took me to a sit-down restaurant. "Oh wow, the menu is embossed," I said, leaning forward with my elbows on the table. I was feeling conspicuous, wearing the same white low-rise jeans I'd been wearing all week and a spaghetti-strap tank top. A server in a crisp white shirt and black vest came over to talk us through the wine list. "I don't drink," the Baskin-Robbins owner said dryly and waved her away. It seemed like a weird spot for an interview, but I didn't realize it was a date until our entrées came—a very specifically cooked fish dish for him, mac and cheese for me—and he was asking me to be his second wife. I didn't get the full story of what happened with his first wife, but I was not interested in taking her place.

"I have high expectations for a wife," he said. "Probably not as much independence as you're used to, but you would never, ever have to worry about money."

"The thing is, I really like my freedom. Also, it feels a little premature to be talking marriage," I said, laughing lightly. "What I really need right now is a job."

"I would not want my wife to have a job like that," he said, grimacing.

"Yeah, but I would just be your best, most trustworthy, and reliable employee. I worked third shift at the Waffle House, I'm a pro," I said, opening my hands like Vanna White revealing a brand new bedroom set.

"I watch my employees on the security cameras. It's a tough job. Not right for you," he insisted.

"Okay... but I need money, my nights are free, and I'm a hard worker," I countered.

He set down his knife and fork, perplexed—he'd already offered me a solution.

I sighed and took a big cheesy bite.

He didn't move forward with my application.

I was out of money and growing increasingly desperate. All day I lounged on Sam's couch with my laptop burning my thighs, scrolling through Craigslist and applying to literally everything, including gigs with headlines like: SEEKING: MODEL 4 MASSAGE.

An "Old Town professional" was looking for a hot young woman to come over to his home and give him a "private massage" for an hour. I knew enough to know that regular massage jobs required a license, but I didn't have time for all that—I needed money and I needed it now. I responded to the ad with a few suggestive pics from my Model Mayhem photo shoots.

Can you come over tonight? he replied almost immediately.

I pursed my lips, considering my nonexistent options. A minute later, I typed out *Yes, I'm available* and pressed send.

I dressed up in my matching red lace tanga and bra with a wife-beater and miniskirt. Usually, I hated primping, but getting ready at Sam's apartment was fun. Sam was the perfect non-boyfriend, ordering us our favorite snack while I did my hair and makeup. He was a concerned friend of the "are you sure you want to do this?" variety, but not judgy. His half-brother had an actress girlfriend named Kitten who was always up to weird shit, so he wasn't as shocked as most guys probably would've been.

When I was done, Sam watched me check myself out in the mirror, adjusted his baseball cap, and nodded approvingly, "You look hot."

I took one last look and said, "Okay, I guess it's time."

Sam helped me as I teetered down his back steps in heels and drove me to my client's townhouse. The street was lined with well-manicured trees and expensive cars. It looked like people were making good money in Old Town. Sam stopped in front of the address. "Are you sure you wanna do this?" he asked.

"I'll be fine," I said matter-of-factly, unfastening my seatbelt.

My client greeted me at the door in a mostly unbuttoned linen shirt and basketball shorts.

"Hi!" I chirped and then just stood there for a second, unsure of the standard private massage protocol.

He nervously sucked in the air, taking in his first impressions.

I waited patiently, nipping out in the crisp night air, well aware that looking was part of what he was paying for.

"Come on in," he said, finally making eye contact.

He was younger than I expected, but still at least fifteen to twenty years older than me. In his late thirties, maybe forty. He was about 5'10". Heavyset with a big paunch. Dark and hirsute, he was balding at the crown of his head. Though he was barely wearing any clothes, he gave off an air of the kind of guy who lived in a suit—wearing it for power the way some women wore makeup.

I crossed the threshold and gazed around his dimly lit place. It was modern and minimal, the shadows of sleek furniture suggesting luxurious taste and disposable income.

"Get comfortable," he said, escorting me to the massage table in the middle of the living room. "I'll get the music."

Soon Norah Jones's syrupy voice was dripping out of his speakers. The inviting way she sang "Come Away With Me" caught me off guard, completely at odds with the scenario unfolding before me.

"Her voice… Pandora is no substitute for seeing her live," my client gushed, returning in just a towel after dimming the lights.

Norah's biggest fanboy handed me a bottle of body oil and lay down on the table. I squirted the greasy liquid onto his hairy back and pressed my hands into it, shuddering at the feel. I hated how sloppy my hands felt. But I took a deep breath and steeled myself against any unpleasant corporeal sensations. People do things they don't want to do for work all the time. Why was I special? I needed money, and he needed a woman's touch; it was a fair trade.

There was no chemistry, but I imagine sex work is not just easier, but exhilarating when there is. Then you have the best job in the world. But it's not ideal when your growling belly is the most desirous part of you. As the album played, each new song brought me momentary relief—it meant another four minutes had passed.

Norah crooned about feeling as empty as a drum.

Shut up, Norah, I thought. Listening to her was the best part of my experience, yet I wished I could be her in this scenario—getting paid to do something I actually love, my art only occasionally the backdrop to misery I didn't have to actively participate in.

"You know, usually when I get a massage, the girl will touch my dick," my client said, gesturing at his penis and pitching me the idea like it would knock my socks off, not something I was actively trying to avoid.

"Oh really?" I said hesitantly. "That wasn't in the email." I needed this guy's money, but I didn't want to have to touch his dick for it.

I tried to massage around his groin area without touching it directly. But it wasn't enough. He encouraged me again, and I held his soft cock in my hand for a minute and gently squeezed the shaft a few times. I grimaced at the thought of giving him a hand job to completion. I would need to mentally prepare.

"Maybe I could do more next time…" I offered enthusiastically, returning the sales pitch.

He bought it! The idea of a next time got him to let up on the HJ pressure. "You're an actress, right? I have a really good job in the business side of the entertainment industry. Every July, I'm on a yacht with Robert De Niro. You could be my date. I'll buy you a new dress," he said as I ran my fingers up and down his furry back and tried not to gag.

I imagined meeting Robert De Niro under those circumstances—on my client's arm trying to explain our relationship—and squinted at the wall clock, counting down to the end of the hour.

Sam was waiting outside when the hour was up.

"Are you hungry?" he asked.

I was starving and, more importantly, not ready to go home yet, so he drove us to Clarke's 24-hour diner on Belmont, one of our regular haunts. They had an awesome jukebox, and the fellow patrons were courteous enough to avoid Norah Jones during our meal.

As soon as we sat down in our booth, I jumped up and went to the bathroom to wash the oily, sticky residue off my hands.

Back at the table, I counted my stack—$150 total, seven twenties and one ten. I felt powerful and weak at the same time. I was on cloud nine, planning to pick up the check for the first time in a long time. But I knew I didn't want to try to psych myself up to massage around that guy's dick again. Or even his hairy back. And I didn't want to give him a hand job like he really wanted. Or to be his trophy "girlfriend" on a yacht with Robert De Niro. That wasn't how I wanted to meet De Niro. I wanted to be on a movie set with him or meet him at an awards show afterparty with an actual boyfriend.

I liked the idea of sex work, but ultimately, I didn't want

to ruin sex for myself. I didn't want to test my boundaries or overcomplicate my romantic life. And even though I was poor, I got more promotional modeling work soon after and a gig as the door girl at Le Passage. I had the privilege to go with my gut. But there was a curious comfort in knowing that if I ever needed money badly enough again, I'd know how to get it.

When the waitress brought the check, I grinned slyly at Sam and flicked two twenties off the top of my stack to pay. A great jam came on the jukebox. I bobbed my head, licked my finger, and counted my remaining bills, relaxed to finally have a little cushion. Sam studied me with a quizzical awe as I tucked my wallet in my purse and exhaled deeply.

Basking in the momentary relief, I leaned back in the booth and let myself enjoy the last fry.

THE DREGS OF SUMMER

The reason I moved to Chicago in the first place was to act in an independent film. The assistant director from *The Poisoned Court* was also working on *The Dregs of Summer* and he recommended me. So I went in for an audition.

The sides included a sex scene. Thus, I wasn't totally shocked when, after a run-through of the dialogue, someone said, "Can we take your top off for this next one?"

"Yeah, let's put this on its feet," another agreed.

I peeled off my baby blue Hollister three-quarter sleeve shirt and straddled my potential costar. I brazenly delivered my lines as we dry humped the carpet of a West Side office with a video camera rolling. The nudity and simulated sex were explicitly expected to secure the role. You know, just so the director and producers could confirm that everything was as it should be on my twenty-one-year-old body. In some ways, it makes sense—of course they would need to see the goods. But I was growing weary of this typecasting. Why couldn't I play someone who wore clothes the whole movie?

Soon after, I nabbed the part. Yes, my character had some don't-give-a-fuck energy that I was adept at playing, but of course, I also booked the role because of my willingness to get naked. This would be my second film, and I'd now been to LA, so I had a slightly more realistic idea of what it would take to make it. Money, basically. How I was going to make extra money while working for a contractually obligated one dollar (that I was never paid) was beyond me, but that was the assignment. I couldn't turn down another film credit, more scenes for my reel, and a chance to do my favorite thing.

The shooting schedule kept getting moved back, so I applied to dozens of Craigslist ads every day, doing everything I could to

try and make a buck: I worked the door at Le Passage nightclub.
I sampled Bear Naked granola during in-store promos at Whole
Foods. I gave away free shit on the Navy Pier. I worked a brand
ambassador gig for a sports conference where O.J. Simpson
made an appearance. I spent days making a binder to apply for a
marketing position at a Gold Coast hair salon, outlining Strengths,
Weaknesses, Opportunities, and Threats in my SWOT analysis
of the business—and then didn't get the job. During Tech Week,
I handed out free shit for Motorola on a Segway in Millennium
Park. I even interviewed for an escort service called Rent-a-Date
Chicago, but after my Craigslist massage, I decided against it.

I couldn't commit to a normal job until filming was over,
and the logic was that I would make decent enough money from
these random gigs, so I would be available to audition and take
acting jobs whenever they came up. In theory, it worked. But in
practice, it very much didn't. Chasing down these one-off jobs was
a lot of work, so I had three jobs—trying to find acting jobs, trying
to find random jobs, and working the jobs themselves. It was bad
math, but it took me a long time to figure out my error.

I loved and hated Chicago, this big, bustling city of skyscrapers and
high-rises right next to a giant, placid lake. The L-train thundered
around the city and rattled the anxieties loose in my body. It made
my jaw stiff. When I didn't have money, which was all the time, I
felt claustrophobic everywhere except near the shore. So many tall
buildings that held things I couldn't afford, so few places where
I felt like I could breathe. I didn't have a parking spot, so I kept
getting tickets. Anytime I managed to save a hundred dollars, I
would immediately get another parking ticket.

I walked down Michigan Avenue, alongside the fancy
shops of The Magnificent Mile, wishing I could afford to truly live
in this city. I didn't need Gucci or Chanel, but just to pay my rent
and buy dinner without all the jitters.

When I got home that night, I peeled another parking
ticket off my windshield, put a CD in my Discman, and drove the
city top to bottom to soothe myself.

The summer of 2005 was a quintessentially Chi-town summer. After the snow evaporated and the city heated up, al fresco dining took over the streets. Kanye West's *The College Dropout* and Common's *Be* were the soundtrack of the city. The summer had a rhythm that felt fresh and new. *Late Registration* came out in late August: the cherry on top of a summer of iconic earworms and sampled beats. I was nursing a broken heart and couldn't bear to consider Sam as anything other than a friend. Still, there was a fleeting sexiness to this place where I could not get comfortable and knew I wouldn't stay.

As I tried to get my bearings, I was constantly getting lost. I typically have a good sense of direction, but some of the streets would intersect at a diagonal and split three ways, so it was harder to learn than a traditional grid. Sometimes this disconnect from distance, time, and location would have consequences, like being late for an interview, which made my problems even worse.

When I didn't have work, I helped Sam with his T-shirt business, accompanying him on meetings with potential stores and manufacturers in lingerie tops and kitten heels. I sewed labels into Bong Girls shirts and stole Sam's Adderall, which felt like fair payment for a tedious job. When he ran out ahead of schedule and confronted me about it, I drove three and a half hours to East Lansing, Michigan, to meet up with his fraternity brother's ex-girlfriend and buy her prescription in the middle of the night.

Sometimes Sam and I hung out with one of his frat brothers from college and his frat brother's older girlfriend. They were both in tech sales and she owned a condo in the trendy part of Bucktown. We had absolutely nothing in common. I can't even imagine what we talked about, aside from the gorgeous, sunny weather. Sam and I mostly just watched them tease each other and get in petty fights. I never say anything in my memories of those interactions. I wonder if I said anything in real time.

During a heat wave, Sam's dad, who owned a chain of massage parlors and lived in a penthouse on Wilshire Boulevard, came to visit from LA with his much younger girlfriend. They met at a sugar baby party. She went to UCLA, barely older than me.

Maybe twenty-three?

Sam and I tagged along everywhere they went while they were in town. When his dad took his girlfriend shopping, I tried to identify the choreography of how she coaxed him into buying her something expensive, taking it in like a sociology class.

Even though Sam's friend and his girlfriend fought all the time and Sam's dad and his sugar baby didn't have a relationship based on love, there was something contagious about being around these unlikely couples. Sam was infected first. I could feel him calculating how he could make a move on me without upsetting our status quo. I started to get curious too, even flirting with the idea that I would stay in Chicago, but he was my rock and it was terrifying to ponder dating my only friend in town.

One night we went to Bucktown and there was something romantic in the air. Visiting a wine store, stopping by a friend's party, and teasing each other at a bar, we both felt it. The warm summer night air twinkled. There was a force field between us that buzzed.

On our way home, after a few drinks, Sam finally worked up the courage to kiss me while we were waiting on a platform for the L. I wanted it to happen, but when it did, my lips went numb. I watched from across the platform with my arms crossed. We went home and sank onto his bed, for the first time as lovers. I hovered above us, watching him fuck me missionary style.

I woke up to my fear: the aftermath of not being impressed.

"It's not always good the first time," Sam implored. "Please give me another chance."

But much to his dismay, I immediately put him back in the friend zone. Luckily, we didn't have too much time to obsess about it. *The Dregs of Summer* was finally ready for action.

The film was about a crew of lifeguards, so we shot in large part on North Avenue Beach. It was an ensemble piece with four main leads—I was number six on the call sheet. One of the leads was the son of a C-list actor, part of a comedy dynasty. While he was marginally charming, he was mostly making his way based on the family name. Still, I took a liking to him, perhaps because he was to be my love interest in the film.

After being in the majority of scenes for *The Poisoned Court*, it was disappointing to have only a handful of scenes with dialogue in *The Dregs of Summer*. Still, I was building my reel, which was important to my acting career, and I couldn't do it on my own. This was pre-smartphone, pre-TikTok, pre-Instagram even. These independent films were shot on film—every minute cost money, and I knew how hard that was to come by.

While I was excited to finally start shooting, I'd gained ten pounds in the waiting period, making the nudity of my required sex scene more anxiety-inducing, which inspired me to further eat my feelings. It was a vicious cycle. But that didn't stop the son of the C-list actor from flirting with me. Despite my failed showmance with Mateo, I was in love with the idea of falling in love on set, so I slept with him. For him, I think it was practice for our scene, but that just made me want him more.

This new development didn't sit well with Sam. It was one thing that I wouldn't fuck him when I wasn't fucking anyone else, quite another when there was competition in the picture. After a round of tamarind margaritas from the Mayan Palace, Sam and I got in a fight. Both of us were unable to express our desires and intentions as well as we wanted, and worse, they weren't aligned. My instinct was to flee. I got on the L headed south with no plan. Drunk and crying and confused and happy to be alive and royally fucked all at the same time.

I went home-home, to my actual apartment, and spent the only night of my whole tenancy there. But I couldn't sleep. The next day, I would be shooting my sex scene for *The Dregs of Summer* at a cabin off the lake—and I didn't look or feel how I wanted to, nor did I know where I stood with my costar-with-benefits… or Sam.

As the shoot went on, I felt more and more desperate—for money, for love, for an inkling of how I should proceed. In between scenes at North Avenue Beach, I paced back and forth on the sand, mentally calculating my lost wages from acting in the film. The night we shot the big sex scene, I anxiously raided craft services. When my costar-with-benefits was out with another girl, I called and confronted him about why he didn't want to be my boyfriend. On location at a house, I lounged on a bed with one of my female costars and had long talks about the entertainment industry and our typecasting as I pondered my escape to LA.

To clear my head when I needed time away from Sam, away from hustling to make money, away from the movie, I would drive. Just me in my Chevy Corsica cruising Lake Shore Drive, going from Sam's apartment in Lincoln Park to my studio in Lake View, all the way up to Evanston, all the way down to Kanye's old hood on the South Side. Driving along the edge of the city, blasting Kanye or Common or Paul Wall, singing along to "Drive Slow" on repeat, gearing up for my next move, whatever that would be.

Then, I got a Get Out of Jail Free card. An audition with Productions Plus to be an auto show presenter. The pay was not just livable but cushy by my standards at the time, and I could be based in any major city, including Chicago or LA—an opportunity to solve at least one of my problems.

I read over the script a few times in preparation and wore my favorite top: a pretty blue tank that brought out my eyes, but the lace was ripping along my bust. Intimidatingly, my audition was with the director in her slick pantsuit. At first, I could tell she was skeptical. But after I read for her, she cocked her head and gave me a once-over.

Maybe there was something salvageable to this trainwreck.

She gave me a few notes. After the next take, she was thoroughly impressed. "Buy a new shirt for the callback tomorrow," she said. It was pretty much in the can, she told me, I just needed sign-off from the car manufacturer.

I was thrilled! I needed a job, and now I almost had a really good one.

The callback was the next day at 10 a.m. Then I got the call sheet for *The Dregs of Summer*. I was to be on set, all day, to say one line. I tried to finagle another call time, another audition time, anything to make it work. But alas, the audition times were limited and the producers wouldn't budge. Despite the fact that I wasn't getting paid, I spent the next day sitting around in holding, trying to avoid my costar-with-benefits, waiting to say my one line until late afternoon, unable to make the audition that would change my life.

By then it was clear that there was no reason to stay in Chicago. No boyfriend, no permanent job, no prospects for anything good—I even felt out of sorts at the Common concert Sam took me to as a going-away present. After *The Dregs of Summer* wrapped, I would leave for LA. By early August, I would be gone, en route for Hollywood once more—credit cards pushed to their limits, sleeping in my car, and continuing to tempt fate's more dangerous inclinations along the way.

GIRL GONE WILD

Cameraman: When a girl gets wild, what does that mean?
Girl: It means she shows her titties.

I'd been in LA for three weeks when I got the gig selling T-shirts on the Girls Gone Wild tour. I'd grown up with their infomercials on late-night TV.

"Warning: This contains adult content that is not suitable for children!" is how the infomercials began. That should have been my first clue that this was a job unlike the other promotional modeling gigs I had experience with. The thing is: the infomercials looked kind of fun.

Full of white smiles, the girls, always attractive and laughing, would flash the camera—*Spring break, wooooo!*—but there was no porn on late-night TV, not even boobs, just playful pop-up censors. I didn't want to do any naked stuff myself, not on camera—by 21, I'd already done my fair share of nudity for photo shoots and the independent films I'd acted in. But those girls looked cool. Maybe we could all be friends? Co-eds dancing around to lighthearted steel drum music. I mean, what sounds more innocuous and carefree than a freaking marimba?

I had no idea what I was in for.

It was 2005, and I had graduated from college eight months prior. The job wasn't part of my original plan to be an actress, but that was the problem—I was twenty-one; I didn't have a plan. But I did have a dream, and that inspired the trek west. I thought Hollywood would be clamoring to meet me, a budding starlet. Unfortunately, no one had gotten word I was coming. No one seemed to care.

I was financially ill-prepared for the move, as was my tendency. Three hundred dollars on my debit card and dwindling by the day. Zero savings. Anxiously waiting on freelance checks for work I'd done before I left Chicago. Midwestern parents who got sugar-coated updates and would not react kindly to a phone call asking for money. The looming threat of hand-to-mouth poverty was becoming the basis of my decision-making. I genuinely did not have a home; I couldn't keep crashing on my friend's futon forever, especially without money to buy groceries. This kept me awake late at night, in the living room of Tatum's tiny Van Nuys apartment, scouring Craigslist for jobs.

Amid the dire tedium of a door-to-door temp gig in the blistering Inland Empire heat—repeating over and over: "Hi, I'm here on behalf of Staples, and I just wanted to stop by to drop off ten dollars in Easy Bucks to make things a little *easier* for your business."—I got a call from Girls Gone Wild. I'd responded to their Craigslist ad seeking a "Merch Girl" the night prior, and they wanted to meet with me about my submission. I didn't even have to think about it, I already knew the answer when I'd attached my résumé and hit send.

Did I want to party and travel for work? Yes, I did.

Did I want a gig that didn't require me to drive to the Inland Empire and nearly sweat to death while going door-to-door handing out unwanted coupons? Yes, I did.

Did I want to stop overstaying my welcome on my friend's futon? Yes. Yes, I did.

I told my boss for the Staples promo that I wasn't feeling well and sped down to the GGW office in a gleaming corporate building on Cloverfield in Santa Monica for an interview with one of the head honchos, which felt an awful lot like this:

Him: *Hi, I used to be VP of Online Jizz at Hustler and now I'm here at GGW in charge of the Hand Job Infomercial silo. I make a looootta money doing this. I wear hair gel. You can trust me.*

Me: (sucking in my stomach)

Him: *So basically the most important part of your job is to make the girls feel comfortable enough to get wild. If a girl's waiting and you're on the bus, get her a drink. Really just having another girl around makes everyone more comfortable.*

Me: (laughing at whatever he said)

Him: *And you're cool with working in Canada without a work permit? Because we don't really have time to get that straightened out.*

Me: *Oh yeah. Totally, totally cool.*

I would have said anything to get a job. Any job.

But this wasn't just any job—Girls Gone Wild was a pop culture phenomenon and I was a fun, sexual person. It wasn't acting, but as far as civilian work went, this was a dream job.

And it worked. I was hired on the spot. They wanted me to board a flight to Vancouver the next day. So I packed up a wad of clothes and got on the plane. I was broke, and I could not wrap my not-yet-fully-developed brain around how to get started in LA, so I felt like running away. Running away on a party bus seemed like the best-case scenario, an exciting change of pace and a chance to get my shit together and catch up on my credit card payments while I didn't have to pay rent. However, I hadn't considered the consequences of where I was running.

At twenty-one, I thought I was a badass, made of metal. I'd taken college classes in high school and Adderall in college and graduated a year and a half early. I'd fucked a handful of dudes, done a handful of drugs, and worked in a strip club and third shift at the Waffle House—what could you possibly show me that I hadn't already seen?

Anytime you ask yourself that question, you need to brace yourself because you are about to see some shit that will rock your tender little world.

Going through customs in Vancouver, the agent found it suspicious that a young woman was "vacationing" by herself with only a tenuous idea of her own plans. He looked me up in the system and found my prior offense.

Flustered, I tried to explain myself: "It was just weed—I mean, I shouldn't have done it, but not like it was coke or something—and I've been paying my fine—only $300 left—and I would never do it again."

"I'm going to swab your bags," the agent informed me,

rubbing a small disposable cloth across my suitcase.

"No problem," I replied nonchalantly, trying to keep my face as straight as possible.

He ran the swab through a machine and furrowed his brow, "There are traces of acid."

I shook my head emphatically. "No-no-no, that's not possible. I've literally never done acid. Other stuff, yes. Never acid. I swear to you," I said, holding up my hand like I was swearing on a Bible.

His face looked torn—he probably should have pursued this further, but he was too nice, too Canadian. "Enjoy your trip," he said, gesturing toward the exit.

I couldn't believe my luck. I hastily gathered up my luggage and rushed to get a taxi.

I gave the taxi driver an address for a seemingly random intersection. Greeting us when we got there was the outrageously branded bus. "Whoa, the Girls Gone Wild bus," the driver said with wide-eyes.

"Are you one of the girls?" he asked, scanning my body through the rearview mirror.

"Not exactly," I said, forcing a smile.

The taxi driver wanted a tour of the bus. I trailed behind him, meeting the crew: a producer, a few cameramen, and our bus driver, Bo.

Then, in an attempt to live up to the hype my first night on the job, I squeezed into some GGW short-shorts, my rumpus poised to rip the ass-seam with one wrong move.

I teetered into the nightclub on the heels of one of our cameramen and was instantly greeted with a crude display of idolatry that I would see replicated time and again throughout the tour. A fortysomething man with a beer gut came running up to us, dragging behind him a woman in her third trimester. He was a huge fan of Girls Gone Wild. His greatest wish was to gain access to the infamous bus. Begging for an invitation, he dropped to his knees in front of the cameraman and simulated fingering and oral sex on his fully pregnant wife.

He looked directly into the camera and raved, "She's wonderful. She even lets me fuck her in the ass!"

This guy was going to be someone's dad? I didn't recognize *this* from the infomercial.

In my early twenties, I still saw the world in black and white. I was just beginning to notice the insidious gray permeating every frame. I was just figuring out that you could be both a creepy weirdo *and* a dad.

In fact, I would meet a lot of guys from the "creepy dad" demographic on this tour, traveling from town to town like porn carnies. Sometimes we got mobbed by them when we were stopped in the parking lot of, say, a Walmart just to pick up supplies. It shocked me how quickly fathers with their kids, and even moms, went feral, begging, willing to do anything for a hat. I saw a wide spectrum of responses to the brand from locals in the towns we visited. Some would have given almost anything to get on the bus, but others were offended and considered its mere presence in their streets obscene.

On Vancouver Island, while we were across the street eating at a restaurant, someone graffitied "PORNOGRAPHERS" on the bus in black Sharpie. We spotted it walking back to the bus, sucking on spearmint hard candies.

"Pornographers," Bo read the tag out loud with a scowl. "Not subtle are we? Now I gotta figure out how to get this shit off."

I was taken aback. I still hadn't seen the videos at this point, but it was clear that they contained more than just flashing.

Victoria was a beautiful city with statuesque brick buildings and downtown streets lined with charming little shops. We'd taken a ferry to get there, our garish bus tucked underneath. At that point, I'd been on the tour for just a couple of days, I'd only worked one club event, and I was already torn between loving the landscape and being grateful for this opportunity to travel when I was in debt and dodging calls from my credit card company, and being sickened by the feeling that I was in on this ruse. I was part of this exploitative porn company. I was shilling for the patriarchy. I was a bad feminist.

On the surface, my job was really simple. All I had to do was sell
Girls Gone Wild-branded merch—booty shorts, tank tops, and
thongs—to the drunken masses at the "parties" we threw at bars
and nightclubs. However, it was not that simple. First of all, drunk
people are assholes, and plenty of men asked me to flash them
to get them to buy a T-shirt. And despite what the infomercials
might lead one to believe, the Girls Gone Wild crew wasn't actually
showing up and throwing the best parties ever. We would park
the bus outside a bar, much to the chagrin of conservative (or just
smart?) locals. Most of the time, the parties were just a regular
night out at the bar, dashing overhyped expectations. It was rarely
the fun and exciting atmosphere that I'd been envisioning when I
replied to the Craigslist ad, and people who attended the events
often seemed similarly underwhelmed. Then there was the fact that
I was the only girl with the crew traveling from city to city—odd
for a brand predicated on topless women.

The biggest issue was more insidious, though it didn't take
me long to figure out: the business model was rigged. Bars paid to
have Girls Gone Wild show up at their venue, and the producers
and camera guys used those events to scout for hot girls to film
for *GGW* DVDs, which could cost up to $29.99. These featured
way more than just tits, including scenes of solo masturbation
and girl-on-girl porn. In a typical entertainment employment
scenario, the girls—the face, the tits, and the *product* of this porn
company—would have been called "talent," and they would have
been paid. (These days, OnlyFans creators get eighty percent of the
subscription revenue they bring in.) But in this case, they weren't
treated as talent, and they certainly weren't paid as talent. Famously,
girls would sign model releases in exchange for nothing more than
a branded T-shirt.

In an episode of the documentary series *Rich and Shameless*,
a former video editor for *Girls Gone Wild* said, "Every hot chick in
the place wanted to get on camera." Maybe that was true at certain
spring break beach locations, at fever pitches of especially raucous
parties, but most of the time, instead of girls lining up, begging to
show their boobs, what I saw looked more like coercion.

On one of my first nights, as the party was winding down, I saw a drunk girl on the bus encouraged to jiggle her tits and say "Hi, Daddy!" to the camera. For free, I already knew. I felt the sudden urge to escape—or at least to get some space from the poor drunk girls who thought they were going out for a fun night of partying and instead wound up on explicit footage that would follow them around for years to come.

I escaped with a sweet local boy, who drove me to perhaps the most romantic Pacific Ocean lookout in all of Vancouver Island. We smoked weed and flirted, and he tried to kiss me, but I just couldn't do it. Almost immediately, the constant exposure to Girls Gone Wild's depressing brand of sexual exploitation dressed up like liberated exhibitionism left me feeling divorced from my sexuality.

At a club in Red Deer, Alberta, the next province over, I was determined to crawl out of my mind and try to relax and have a good time. I scored some ecstasy from a local while the cameramen were simultaneously making a score: a threesome scene featuring a Kirsten Dunst lookalike, a professional stripper—who wore a wig, got paid $300, and cried afterward while she told us her life story— and their friend. The stripper who got paid was a unicorn. She was literally the only girl who I know got paid, and it was only because she was already in the industry and knew the ropes. That almost never happened.

Exploiting girls was part of the business model—lawyer Lisa Cervantes told *Rich and Shameless* about a client of hers who alleged that she was filmed in public and used in a *Girls Gone Wild* video without providing consent. The company refused to take down the content. Cervantes also stated that on a P&L statement from 2003 that she found, Mantra Films paid their legal team $198,000, while only $3,000 went to pay talent. Also on *Rich and Shameless*, a former employee said that at one point, he suggested the girls get paid as a show of good faith. He recalled Girls Gone Wild CEO Joe Francis laughing and responding, "You're fucking crazy."

There was another girl in Red Deer, who earlier that night had quizzed me about my life in Hollywood while I poured her a drink. "I bet it's really nice," she said, eyes wide. "How often do you see famous people?"

Later, she masturbated for the camera and had sex with the weasely-est camera guy. She seemed to think it might be her ticket out of town—or just made her feel like that for one night—and it made me sad to imagine girls thinking that this could in any way be their big break. I knew what it felt like to want to escape your reality. I also knew what it felt like to take the wrong ticket out of town.

As everything wound down in the wee hours of the morning, I had seen enough. I'd scored four capsules of pure MDMA from a local. I gave one of the rolls to the producer in charge of the bus, dedicated to the brand, but an otherwise nice guy who I was trying to befriend. It was his first time doing ecstasy. He took his capsule and then went to party with the rest of the crew. He invited me to join, but I wasn't in the mood.

Occasionally we'd get hotel rooms, but just as often we were crammed together on the bus, sleeping in our tiny bunks. This was a bunk night, so I went back to mine, popped one of my rolls, closed my eyes, and tried to become one with the hum of the bus.

But the usual crutches I leaned on—sex and drugs—weren't working as well as they used to.

The next morning, when I woke up, I rubbed my groggy eyes, pulled back the curtain, and rolled out of my bus bunk. The rest of the crew was already up. On the big screen TV in the bus's kitchen/dining room/lounge, we watched tape of the women from the previous night like highly competitive NFL coaches reviewing the big game. All I heard was a full account of what was wrong with the women on a physical, sexual, and sometimes mental/emotional level. Apparently, the friend's soft body and bad skin weren't up to *Girls Gone Wild* standards, so the cameramen were instructed to "Shoot around her!" Someone else had "beef curtains." I tried not to listen to the rest. The real life behind those bright, bouncy infomercials was bleak.

How do you incentivize shooting really great footage of hot chicks playing with their labia or eating out their best friends without getting paid? By giving the cameramen bonuses for shooting those scenes. They wanted to go home with as much money as possible, so all they did was scout for pussy. Most dinner conversations involved numerically rating every eligible female within their field of vision. Who these guys rated—judged as hot or not—and who they didn't and why rang in my head like a steady bell. I would buy a bag of tortilla chips and a jar of queso and try to crunch at a volume loud enough to drown it out.

I felt for the male Girls Gone Wild crew members too. They were primarily film majors just trying to make some money and advance their dream careers, like me. A few of them were great and made it possible for me to last as long as I did on the tour. The problem was that all of us were working on a project with a flawed premise—and it didn't bring out our best behavior.

I don't know what I expected, but it wasn't this. Girls Gone Wild was an empire that our economy had supported, elevated to the status of a cultural institution. It spawned from a *Banned from Television* blooper show, the demented brainchild of an up-and-coming Hollywood bro named Joe Francis, inspired by a clip of spring breakers getting arrested for going topless. In a stroke of pre-social media savvy, Francis bought a glut of late-night TV airtime, sometimes featuring celebrities like Snoop Dogg and former *Real World* castmates (our first reality TV stars). I'd grown up with Girls Gone Wild infomercials full of fun, flashing co-eds and so had the rest of my generation. It was a frequent pop culture reference, used even by serious people like politician John Kerry, socially sanctioned in a way that made it seem safer and less predatory than it actually was. Before experiencing it firsthand, I'd been blinded by the same glimmer as the girls we would shoot on the road.

The booker quit in the midst of our Canadian tour and the gigs began to dry up. We flew out of the Toronto airport. After another tense exchange with a customs agent, I landed in Raleigh-Durham and joined another tour traversing the Southeast United States.

In St. Louis, about a month into the tour, we finally threw a party that resembled anything from the infomercials. It was an epic party in a huge warehouse that was packed to the brim. There were actually hot girls—hot people in general—in attendance. Under the dim, pulsing nightclub lighting, it appeared everyone was having a blast.

The police came at the end of the night to shut it down, and we took off with a handful of girls on the bus. An eighteen-year-old mom, four weeks postpartum, hooked up with a cameraman because her baby's father was in jail for something meth-related. She felt lonely, she told me. Hanging out on the bus was a good distraction. Of course, they documented her low point on camera: strumming her body so acutely in need of healing, in between passing mentions of the wreckage in her life. This struck me as a low point of my own.

The weeks seemed to stretch on forever—a chaotic collection of moments that made me question who I was. I tried to buy Adderall to speed up the time and concentrated less and less on making the girls feel comfortable. It seemed like every time I tried, the conversations revealed something tragic about their lives. It became glaringly obvious that I wasn't the sort of wild woman cut out for this job, and my feeling like an outsider became constant.

I lasted about seven weeks. It ended with a conversation in Muscle Shoals, Alabama—or maybe it was somewhere in northern Florida. I always forget that I've been to those states. What I remember is the muggy, oppressive heat. Feeling stifled, trapped, stuck—unable to see more than six feet in front of me. Being so fucking done, but also so desperately poor that I was worried that they would make me buy my own plane ticket.

The producer wasn't surprised when I kicked pebbles in the parking lot and told him, "I'm so sorry, but I've gotta get out of here." He seemed to know it was coming, welcomed it even, perhaps would've fired me soon. "It's pretty clear you're not happy," he said. He didn't even make me work the last night.

I left the tour with what felt like the weight of the world on my shoulders and a cloud over my head; I felt dirty and guilty. My presence had been tacit approval and made me a traitor to the other women—the silent kind, the kind you thought you could trust. I should've said, "*Run!*" but instead, I said, "Would you like something to drink?"

My flight landed safely back in LA on my twenty-second birthday, but I couldn't stay. Danielle had taken up residence on the futon where I had been crashing. It was fine; at this point, I didn't think I could handle another round of trying to "make it."

I wound up briefly back in Chicago, then made my way to St. Louis, where I found a cheap place to put myself back together. I got an eight-dollar-an-hour job at a dry cleaner's where they treated me a lot like the dirty laundry, and honestly, that's how I felt.

Two years later, I would make it back to LA—older, wiser, yet still struggling to find the proper words to categorize my Girls Gone Wild experience. It would still be a full decade before #MeToo. I had to wait for the world to shift.

Today, Girls Gone Wild, as we knew it, is out of business. Founder Joe Francis was convicted of tax evasion, bribery, false imprisonment, assault causing great bodily injury, dissuading a witness, and record-keeping violations. He pleaded no contest to child abuse and prostitution. Throughout Girls Gone Wild's years of operation, the charges stacked up as he lost his ability to wriggle free from the consequences until, ultimately, in 2015, he decided his best option was to flee the United States—becoming a fugitive from justice—and hole up at Casa Aramara, his twelve-bedroom seaside estate in Punta Mita, Mexico—a sprawling property of more than 40,000 square feet—long associated with celebrity guests like Jennifer Aniston, Eva Longoria, Paris Hilton, and the Kardashian clan; where Mario Lopez got married and Kim and Kanye honeymooned. And with outstanding warrants still waiting for him back home, he's at risk of being arrested if he steps foot on U.S. soil.

I can't tell if he's completely socially ostracized these days, but according to his Instagram, it seems like it. The bulk of his

729K following on IG appears to be either bots or the most basic, unevolved people on the planet. It's a far cry from his days as a media darling. He posts about the Kardashians, but they don't reply to his comments. Kim went from defending Joe on camera to publicly non-responsive. The only celebrity friend who I've seen comment on his posts is Mario Lopez.

But he's not just a pariah because of the sins of Girls Gone Wild. In the *Rich and Shameless* doc, there was a recording made by his partner Abbey Wilson at his house on August 1, 2020. In it, she whimpers, "You're killing me." "I hope you fucking die!" he retorts, which is followed by guttural screams.

Eight years prior, Abbey had won the Girls Gone Wild Search for the Hottest Girl in America contest. Her unofficial prize was becoming the mother of Joe's twin daughters, conceived through IVF with genetic screening specifically to select for girls.

At present, Joe is estranged from Abbey and his daughters, who seem to be in hiding from him, amid a nightmare domestic abuse and custody situation. His private island now looks like a private hell. Perhaps eventually, there are consequences to a business model based on young women, some allegedly underage, making potentially life-altering decisions while inebriated—and not only for the young women involved.

In 2005, I sold T-shirts on the Girls Wild tour across Canada and the U.S., and all I got were a few lousy T-shirts, a handful of thongs, and two pairs of boy-cut briefs I still have to this day. Oh yeah, and an indelible experience that changed my worldview forever.

But that doesn't mean I didn't get sick with the same cultural distortion as everyone else. After I got off the tour, even my language was infected in the way that I talked about women. For example, if I were to describe a pretty, curvaceous Latina woman, I might say, "She's a poor man's Salma Hayek." Like, *what?*

Sometimes I wonder how my life would have turned out if I'd never taken that job. Looking back, it feels like a fork in the road. In my quest to be an actress at any cost, I discovered the underbelly, and it fucked me up. The structure and equality I thought I knew of the world did not exist. There were so many cracks in the architecture; it was flawed by design. I felt unchaste by the knowing.

I was learning there weren't Madonnas and whores; there were women and shitty societal constructs about how they should be. And companies like Girls Gone Wild, perpetuating narrow beauty standards and profiting from taking advantage of (mostly) women. I wasn't against porn or sex work; I was against men making money by separating women from their worth, taking advantage and taking away their agency, and doing it all while they were drunk, just trying to have a good time. I had been called a feminist before, even called myself that, but after this, I knew that it was true.

While all that was bubbling below the surface, I began to rethink what it really meant to be a girl gone wild. Girls gone wild aren't under the thumb of a man with a private island, a substance abuse problem, and an American Express Black Card, I mused. The girls caught in the crosshairs of Girls Gone Wild trying to make an easy buck weren't girls gone wild, they were girls done wrong.

When girls really go wild, it's not in ways that can be easily manipulated or monetized by others. When girls really go wild, it's not spring break or a cross-country party bus tour—it's a homecoming. They return to themselves, and they are done with the system that oppresses them. They are done with the rules, done with the lies, done with the bullshit. They are done with the damned if you do and damned if you don't—if they're damned either way, they're going to do it their way and that doesn't look like flashing a camera so some douchebag can become a millionaire at their expense. They return to themselves, and it threatens the patriarchy.

Sometimes it takes a while to find that wild and unleash it, but when they do, it's powerful. They're called witches, banshees, bitches. They evoke fear. They won't shut up. "They must be stopped!" When girls really go wild, nothing's ever quite the same.

HOLLYWOOD CLEANERS

After the nightmare of Girls Gone Wild I couldn't get a job. I don't know if it was the job market or my polluted energy, but the only place that would hire me was Hollywood Cleaners. To add insult to injury, I wasn't in Hollywood anymore.

The day after I landed back in LA, I took off to visit Sam. After a few days in Chicago, Sam told me I couldn't stay with him indefinitely. It was fair, he wasn't looking for a live-in friend, and our attempt at dating hadn't worked out so well. I'd missed him while I was gone, but I wasn't ready to be his girlfriend and his feelings were hurt by my hesitation.

No part of me wanted to regroup in Jackson, perhaps a wiser choice than anything else on the table. But that would have meant living with my parents and working in Okoboji—since summer was over, so was the high season and thus the opportunity to make decent money. Maybe subconsciously I didn't want to run into Latham. Or think about him ever again. So I decided to head to Missouri.

In St. Louis, I reconnected with the craft services guy from *The Poisoned Court* and it just so happened he needed a third roommate. Our other roommate had recently moved back to St. Louis from New Orleans after Hurricane Katrina. We lived in a University City three-bedroom and we were all three in the midst of emotional chaos.

I gave a half-hearted attempt at quitting Adderall. I could tell the dosage I had become accustomed to was tearing up my insides—a few times I shit blood, which was of slight concern. But mostly I was quitting because I couldn't afford it, because I couldn't, for the life of me, find a regular job. But not taking Adderall made me feel like a slug, mentally and physically, which made it even harder to find a job.

Finally, I got a callback for Hollywood Cleaners. They would pay me minimum wage.

I could barely pay my rent. I was too sad to do anything but work at my terrible job and then go home and go on the internet and eat fast food. I'd gained ten pounds on the Girls Gone Wild tour and then ten more in St. Louis, ballooning to my heaviest weight, completely uncomfortable in my body. In retrospect, I think it was a defense mechanism. I had been raped twice the year before, had my heart broken, and felt alternately confused and used in my romantic life. I felt so wildly out-of-my skin uneasy with the power dynamics on Girls Gone Wild. It was a living hell to go out to dinner with my coworkers, constantly rating women. Perhaps I gained weight in an attempt to desexualize myself.

I didn't even have money to show for my Girls Gone Wild experience. According to my 1099, I only made $2,120. I must have been making $300 a week? And I'd rung up a huge phone bill of over $1,000 in Canada talking to Sam—I didn't think long-distance could possibly be *that* expensive. The bill was sent to my parents' house and my dad spent hours on the phone with Cingular Wireless trying to talk them down.

I went to the mall and bought new, bigger khaki pants to work a promotion. I went from store to store searching for the most flattering size that would still fit me. The brand manager took a group photo during the promotion, and I made a stink, forbidding them to post it anywhere. "I need to protect my likeness," I said crossly, my cheeks stinging.

I was humiliated by the weight gain and all the mistakes I'd made in the nine months since I'd graduated from college. But I was too miserable to fix it, if I even knew how. I was also too miserable to drive home for Thanksgiving or Christmas. "We'd really like to have you," my mom said gently on the phone. "You're always welcome back home." But I didn't want to face my lean, athletic family who'd warned me incessantly that I probably wouldn't make it.

"Just look at the stats," I could hear my dad say.

As the snow began to melt, I walked up the slushy sidewalk after work one early spring day and saw paperwork posted on the door: NOTICE OF EVICTION. Apparently I'd been paying the craft services guy, but he hadn't been paying the rent.

"So what happened?" I asked, irritated, when he got home.

He shrugged. "Looks like we have to be out by the end of the month," he said unapologetically.

Finally, there was no choice but to go back to Jackson. I knew it wasn't going to feel like home anymore. Nowhere felt like home.

Luckily, I wouldn't have to stay long. Ashley offered to let me move in with her and her boyfriend in River Falls, Wisconsin— forty-five minutes from Minneapolis/St. Paul, close enough to a metropolitan area to function. I could work in the Twin Cities as I tried to get my life back on track.

I gathered a few Rubbermaid tubs' worth of possessions and drove back to my parents' house. I was excited to see Ellie. I hoped once I found my footing, she could live with me again.

My cell phone rang somewhere in Iowa.

"Courtney, can you pull over?" my mom said.

"What's wrong?" I said.

"Oh," she whimpered, sounding like a wounded animal.

"Tell me now," I said firmly.

Ellie had been hit by a car. They were taking her to the vet. They didn't know if she was going to make it. I drove as fast as I could, tears streaming down my face. I wanted to see her again. I wanted another chance to be a better dog mom. "I'm almost home!" I implored the empty seat.

My mom called again a few hours later. There was nothing the vet could do. When they got home, they held her outside on the steps until she turned cold. They would wait until I got home to bury her. I was inconsolable for days.

My dad said she took a bullet for me. Saved me from an accident on my drive home. He's so rational except when he says crazy woo-woo stuff like that.

I couldn't help but wonder if maybe she did. My furry guardian angel. Giving me another chance to try to get it right.

DEAR DEREK

Dear Derek,

I'm reaching out because I had your abortion. Obviously not recently; we haven't spoken in over a decade. I did try to tell you before it happened, but you never called me back. So for a long time, I didn't think you deserved to know. But now I think you don't deserve *not* to know.

I had your abortion because I'd already fallen from God. I never believed to begin with, but then I met you, who became my first boyfriend, and traced the thick scars on your chest and your back, and maybe I needed it too much or was looking too hard or seeing what I wanted to see, but: you felt saved to me. It felt like someone let you live even though you'd already been sentenced to die. Like someone fairy godmothered your teenage lung cancer and said, *Here, you can go now. You only need one and a half lungs to have a wonderful life. Go in peace, child.*

You were the closest I'd felt to religion.

But there isn't a god, right?

You started chain-smoking Marlboro Reds, and then Lights and Ultra Lights, but still sometimes Kools. You failed out of college (twice) and were shitty to your parents and couldn't keep a job and fried your brain and struggled to find a morsel of gumption or a tiny will to thrive. Wasted.

Today, I consider myself agnostic at best.

I had your abortion because I kept seeing that woman from the parking lot outside your St. Cloud apartment in my sleep. The woman who yelled at you to "Stop it! Leave her alone!" as you shoved me. As you degraded me. The woman who yelled at me that I didn't have to put up with it—that no matter who I was, I deserved better.

I had your abortion because that's how we celebrated my nineteenth birthday. (Not to mention, you smushed my cake.)

I had your abortion because you were a loose cannon. Always. The whole time I knew you. And people like that don't just stop.

I had your abortion because in every iteration of "us," I got further and further from "me."

I had your abortion because you followed me down to Missouri and poured Febreze on me when I asked you to stop smoking in my room. I had to file a civil restraining order and you still wouldn't leave.

I had your abortion because you jumped on the hood of my Oldsmobile like a Ken Kesey psycho when I finally broke up with you and tried to move on.

I had your abortion because, a couple years later, I moved back to Minnesota. I needed a temporary refuge to get my shit together, but I was followed by a faint ringing in my ears, a constant reminder that I wasn't pursuing my dreams, my friends were elsewhere, I was wasting time. Then you texted while I was sitting next to my mom in the pew at St. Paul's Cathedral.

"Who are you texting?" she asked.

"Nobody," I replied.

My family kissed me goodbye and wished me a happy twenty-third birthday! "We're so glad you're closer," they said. "We're so glad you're safe!"

You came over later, your face as puffy as your coat, and I thought, *Wow… he's let himself go.*

You told me you were doing well now. "I'm a professional poker player," you told me. (Which I guess meant that you still played online poker in your underwear all day, but now I was to take it seriously.)

"We should go out to eat," I suggested, and you begrudgingly drove us through the McDonald's drive-thru. The value meal sank into my gut like an anchor—before I became more cautious about where I let those drop.

That night you broke my fifteen-month sex drought, and for a few hours, I felt the loneliness subside. A welcome distraction from (and confirmation of) the fact that I was off course.

I had your abortion because you had a girlfriend who wasn't me. Though that didn't stop you from sleeping with me several times before you let me in on that little detail.

A month later, we were still fucking each other for old times' sake. That night with your dick in a raincoat. The next morning, we woke up side-by-side. I nuzzled your neck and whispered, "How 'bout some morning sex?"

You were down to fuck, but not to put on a condom.

"Okay fine, please pull out," said the idiot.

But you were too sleepy and you came too hard and some of you stayed inside me. Too much of you stayed inside me.

After you left, I cleaned up the sticky condom from the night before and stripped my sheets. But Tide can't wash everything clean. I calculated my cycle and thought I was probably safe, yet still decided, better Plan B than be sorry!

I went home for Thanksgiving a few weeks later. I sat on the toilet in my childhood home and wondered why my period was a brown-speckled joke. *Where is my bright red flood of a period?* the naïf mused. *Why does it feel like I'm underwater?* I navigated my old stomping grounds like a vessel submerged. Governed by a different, heavier gravity than the rest of my family.

My parents asked what was going on with me.

"I'm just tired," I answered, sincerely believing that was true.

Back in the Twin Cities, I sat in traffic on the way to one of my housecleaning gigs and suddenly a white-hot light bulb went off in my head. *Ah-ha!* My brain finally solved the equation. I called my boss, and said no cleaning today. "It's an emergency," I said.

I sat in a clusterfuck of traffic working my way across town to Planned Parenthood, seething envy for my fellow drivers' more innocuous commutes. I spent the whole drive trying to convince myself, *Hey, I don't know for sure either!*

Once I got there, I pushed through the barrage of protesters screaming, "Don't kill your baby! Choose life instead!" and I waited and waited. Then the receptionist called my name and I peed in a cup, and I waited and waited.

They finally called my name and I went into a room the size of a broom closet and fluorescent lights pulsed down on me. The harried nurse's assistant sat down, took a deep breath, and said in her softest, most soothing timbre: "You are pregnant."

My eyes bulged and the lights throbbed and warbled and my mouth formed a silent *NO* and my shaky hand splayed over my chest to keep my heart from falling out.

Soon after that is when I called you. *Ring ring. Ring ring.* No answer. *Beep.*

My unsteady voice spurted, *Hey I know this is random but it's REALLY IMPORTANT and I can't leave it on this message but again it's really important and I really need you to call me back as soon as you get this.*

Do you remember that message?

Afterward, I went home, curled up in the fetal position, and cried and cried. I did MSN.com searches, stared off into space, and cried and cried. I threw away all my weed and loose pills, plastered on a fake smile to work a liquor promotion, and cried in the bathroom. All the while, I tried to wrap my mind around having this baby. I tried to conceive of having our baby. I tried to conceive of myself swelling up with your spawn inside me. I tried to conceive of not being able to see my toes or recognize my life, everything mangled beyond recognition. I let it all swirl around in my head and my body for a few sober days, until I had induced more nausea than any bout of morning sickness ever could.

But still, I tried to picture someone who was half you and half me. With my round face and your lying eyes. I tried to conjure up love for that person. I tried to imagine having you in my life for the rest of my life because my child was half yours. Then I tried to imagine *not* having you in my life, even though my child was half yours. And I concluded that if I carried your bloodsucking DNA inside me much longer, I would claw it out with my own bare hands.

I had your abortion because I simply couldn't have your baby.

I had your abortion because I wasn't sober. I wasn't stable. I hadn't stopped spinning my wheels. I hadn't accomplished any of my dreams. I was so lonely I'd developed an irrational, unfounded, call-my-parents-in-the-middle-of-the-night fear of multiple sclerosis (?!)—fixated on something that wasn't a problem because there was so much that was. I was overwhelmed. I was a mess. I wasn't ready to be a mom. It's cliché, but I could barely take care of myself.

I had your abortion because not saving me would've been a greater regret.

So I told our embryo sorry. I told it that I had been lonely and I had been lost, but I could still fix me. Not me and a baby. Not "us." Not me plus one in any capacity, but I could still save myself. I clutched my stomach and whispered, *Go in peace, child.*

WOOZY BLUES

I got a temp gig at the Minneapolis Convention Center. The Learning Annex was putting on Real Estate & Wealth Expos across the country with topics like how to flip houses, how to take every fucking tax deduction you possibly could, and how to start a multi-level marketing cult.

The keynote speakers were celebrity investors, motivational speakers, and financial gurus, including Donald Trump, Tony Robbins, Robert Kiyosaki, Suze Orman, and George Foreman. The whole thing reeked like a scam. Every chart looked like a pyramid.

This is the kind of morally questionable side work that defined this era of my career.

I hit it off with one of their main producers, Vince, who had the vibe of a tough guy '80s movie star and talked with a delightful lisp. "We sure could use the help in Chicago," he said with a whistle. I loved the idea of traveling for work. My life in Minnesota was stagnant and isolated. I was ready to join a cult.

At the same time, I'd convinced myself that spending $18,000 on grad school would help solve my financial problems, so I enrolled in a year-long Master of Business Communication certificate program at the University of St. Thomas.

Working on a small group project for Business Technology class in the library, I went to the bathroom. When I came back, I complained, "My period is late."

My classmate's back stiffened. "Maybe you're pregnant," she said. Fifteen years older, she was trying to have a baby herself.

"There's no way," I replied confidently.

"Famous last words," she said with her hand on her hip.

"I barely have sex," I shrugged. "I just hooked up once with my ex and took Plan B right after."

She stared at me. Her gaze was hot.

In Chicago, during my first road show with the Real Estate &
Wealth Expo, I felt weird, but I couldn't figure out why. *It's probably
just the traveling*, I thought. That always did a number on my
system. Learning about NLP (neuro-linguistic programming)
definitely made me queasy. Plus, convention center food. *That
explains it.*

A week later, preparing for an expo in Boston, I realized
my classmate was right—I was pregnant—but I had to wait to get
the abortion until after my trip because I couldn't afford to take the
weekend off.

State law in Minnesota required a phone call with a
clinician after a twenty-four-hour waiting period in order to get
approved for an abortion.

On the plane, I tapped my leg anxiously as we swooped
over Boston Harbor, worried that I might miss this call and thus
lose my appointment. Once we landed, I rushed through Logan
International Airport with one eye on my cell phone.

Juggling my suitcase at baggage claim, I got the call. The
doctor explained the medical risks of abortion and of continuing
the pregnancy. "Do you have any questions?" she asked.

Yeah, I thought. *Why does it feel like the only option and also
impossible?*

"No," I said.

My high school bestie Karissa was going to Northeastern
University in Boston, so I met up with her while I was in town.

After Friday's work at the convention center, I took the
T to the bar where she worked, though it was her night off. She
was in a phase of exploration—I could feel her newness—but she
still cracked her knuckles and had the same snort-laugh as she did
back in the day. I met her new boyfriend, and after the first drink,
she nudged me and whispered, "Hey, wanna do some coke in the
bathroom?"

I leaned against the stall and watched Karissa do a big rail
off the toilet paper dispenser, unable to speak my great truth of that
moment—my great sorrow and my great relief: I would be getting
an abortion the day after I got home.

"This is really good shit," she said, sniffling her nose. I smiled and did a line, trying to forget the unforgettable. I closed my eyes as I inhaled. There it was running on ticker tape in my brain. "YOU'RE GETTING AN ABORTION. YOU'RE GETTING AN ABORTION. YOU'RE GOING TO BE THE TYPE OF WOMAN WHO'S HAD AN ABORTION."

I wanted to expel that truth out of my body, just like I would do to the fetus in less than a week. But I could barely believe it was happening to me, much less say it out loud.

I woke up the next morning with a raging headache, three missed calls from Vince, and puke in my hair.

Oh shit, I'm already 90 minutes late.

Picking off the big chunks in front of the bathroom mirror, I heaved and turned to retch into the toilet, barely making it in time.

After a quick rinse in the shower, I sprinted from my hotel room to the convention center, stopping to puke into a trash can along the way.

As I ran into the breakout room, out of breath, I bumped into a sea of attendees leaving the second session. Vince pulled me aside. "I heard some bad reports about last night." He informed me that in my drunken, coked-up stupor, I told some of my colleagues, "I'm really good at doing drugs."

"I like you, but this is going to make it hard for me to get you hired back for the next show," he said.

"Fuck, I need the money," I said, palming my face.

Vince shook his head. "Work your ass off this weekend and I'll see what I can do."

He paused and looked at me sideways, "So what kind of drugs were you doing last night?"

I admitted to being blackout drunk.

Which I was. I just had fragments. I had no idea how I got back to the hotel. Who peeled me off the cobblestone? Who wiped the puke off my face and got me a taxi? I guess I'm really good at doing drugs.

For the rest of the weekend, I worked my ass off—shouting the sales pitch like a carnival barker, funneling attendees into upsell workshops, and processing their credit card transactions before they could realize what they'd done—except for the dozen or so breaks I took to run to the bathroom and vomit. My body definitely knew I was pregnant now; I could barely eat.

Monday morning, I flew back on Sun Country Airlines. I forced myself to eat their free hamburger for lunch and tasted it again in Terminal 2 as soon as we landed, washing my mouth out with a grimace.

That evening, I went to the Mall of America on an empty stomach to buy some full-coverage underwear at Victoria's Secret. The nurse had told me I would need to wear pads until I stopped bleeding. My thongs weren't going to cut it.

Tuesday morning, I went to Planned Parenthood for my first dose of Mifepristone. I had anti-nausea pills for lunch and dinner.

The next morning, I went into the shared bathroom of my St. Paul rental with my follow-up dose of misoprostol wrapped up in a towel. I crouched over the toilet and inserted four pills into my vagina.

I stumbled back to my bed, bracing myself for the cramping. I rummaged through my oversized purse for another anti-nausea pill, which I chased with warm Diet Mountain Dew. I tried to focus on my business technology handouts, staring at the same page until I felt a stabbing sensation in my uterus an hour later.

By 10 p.m. I was writhing around on my bedroom floor, moaning. I was in and out of the bathroom all night. My roommate, a mid-thirties ad agency copywriter, peeked in late at night with his video game headset on. "Are you okay?"

"Yeah, just not feeling well," I lied.

The next two days were a deluge of blood and tears and vomit. Thursday evening, I had to miss the presentation for our group assignment.

My professor seemed to be staunchly religious. The only instructor who reinforced the fact that the University of St. Thomas was a Catholic institution casually in his lectures. In my email, I

told him I was sick. "Really sick," but I couldn't be more specific.
I couldn't say "because I just had an abortion." I couldn't say it to
anyone, but especially not him.

I got a C+ in his class. The lowest grade I'd ever received.

Somehow, Vince pulled some strings, and I went to New York a
week later, mere days after my abortion.

The expo in New York was so wildly successful that each
of us got a $300 bonus check for helping attendees part with their
money. I forgot my check in a breakout room and had to sprint
through the Javits Center to retrieve it, blood seeping out the wings
of my giant pad as I ran.

There was an afterparty at Cat's Bar on 48th Street, and at
that party, I drank my feelings and indiscreetly felt up a much older
real estate guy from San Diego with leathery skin. I knew that it
was not a good look, but I had the woozy blues and couldn't muster
the give-a-fuck to act better.

The woozy blues felt like drunkenly wading through
quicksand, even when I was totally sober. All of my energy had
gone to the planning and execution of my clandestine abortion.
Now I was waterboarding myself to keep the secret. It had been a
sad choice to make, but for me, the real tragedy was feeling like I
had to cover it up like a murder, though I thought of it more as a
compassionate release for all parties involved.

I ran into the booker wearing her sleek, sexy suit in the
bathroom. *She has her shit together*, I thought, looking in the mirror
at her while we both washed our hands. I caught her rolling her
eyes at me as she jacked the paper towel dispenser. *Fuck*. She'd seen
my over-the-pants hand job. Everyone had. That was my final straw
with The Learning Annex. Not even Vince could save me.

Six months later, I was sick of spinning my wheels. I'd started
hatching a plan to get back out to Los Angeles. Probably catching
a psychic whiff of my desire to move on with my life, Derek finally
called me back. He still had no idea about the abortion, but by this
point, part of me was relieved that he never called back, that I never

had to tell him. I knew I didn't want to have a baby with him, and he'd never been helpful in our relationship, not even one time.

Derek called because he was bored with his girlfriend. I was bored too, so I let him come over and fuck me in the ass, my first time, with lotion instead of lube. I was very open to masochistic suggestions at that moment. Had I been a writer, I would have chided myself for being too literal with the self-torture, but I wasn't yet, and that's what I thought I deserved at the time. The next day, at my temp job, I power walked to the bathroom with a subtle limp. *Now you're done with him forever*, I promised myself.

Finally, my $18,000 certificate program was over. I made plans to move to LA at the end of the summer. I wanted to work as much as possible before I left the Twin Cities. I applied to be the emcee and producer on Hallmark's "Daddy of All Dance-offs" Father's Day tour.

I was smoking a lot of weed, so I refused my drug test. They still hired me. Big mistake. Huge.

They flew me down to St. Louis for training, and I had a friend of the craft services guy drop off a whole bottle of Adderall at the warehouse where we were loading up our branded trucks.

The other producer ran his mouth incessantly. He said it was a good thing that his sister had been talked out of getting the abortion that she'd wanted because it "forced her to grow up." He told me that I was "a nine"—not perfectly attractive, I did have some flaws, but attractive enough that it made my life easier. I didn't tell him about the rapes or my own abortion. I didn't say, "Why the fuck are you rating me on a numerical scale?" I entertained his perception of me. So fresh off Girls Gone Wild, less than two years later, I put myself on the scale more than he ever could. So I just quietly hated myself and hated him and hated that we were stuck together until I was driving the truck one morning, and I hit the blind spot mirror off another car in the parking lot as he was yelling at me.

It was a minor accident, but it totaled our relationship.

The tour ended in disaster. The refused drug test, Adderall rumors, and accident meant another company I was blacklisted from.

In Minneapolis, I unpacked my suitcase in my little room in a big
house with six other people near the University of Minnesota. A
few weeks later, we got two new roommates: an Irish lad named
Ronan moved in with another fresh college grad, both of them over
on J-1 visas to work for the summer.

During the day, while I did guerrilla marketing for brands
like Clinique, they both worked construction—literally laying
bricks. Coming home dirty, sweaty, and sunburnt only amplified
my initial attraction. Though Ronan was shy, I could tell he was
interested in me.

I hadn't dated anyone since my abortion. I'd made a deal
with myself: *Nice guys only from now on.* If I didn't trust him to be a
father or pay for my abortion, much less tell him I was pregnant, he
couldn't be my boyfriend or even a sexual partner.

But Ronan was a nice guy. Safe. Reading *Angela's Ashes*
at a malleable time in my sexual development had made me a bit
of a hibernophile (lover o' the Irish). The struggles, the accent, the
humor, the twinkly eyes—all those things were appealing—plus
I've always been a fan of the underdog, an identity they take very
seriously as a culture. Beyond the general Irish attraction, Ronan
traveled with more books than anything else, and I knew whatever
was going on in that head of his, I wanted in.

One night, not long after they'd arrived, Karissa was in town, so
we all went out together. We sat around a large table at a loud,
bustling bar. I whispered to Karissa, "I think the skinny one is cute,"
and proceeded to pursue my attraction with the subtlety of a bugle
boy. I was so excited to be socializing and so out of practice that I
accidentally dropped my wine glass. After two more broken glasses,
they asked us to leave.

Back at the house, everyone trickled off to bed one by one
until it was just Ronan and me. There was a long conversation, and
a point when I thought he was going to kiss me, but instead he did
an awkward bow and went upstairs.

I sat on the couch for five minutes, drunkenly plotting my next move, slowly psyching myself up until I traipsed up to Ronan's room, tripped, and fell on his air mattress. All of a sudden, we were both horizontal, so I hit him with "Why don't the Irish say what they feel?"

He kissed me, or I kissed him—either way, the feeling was mutual—and the rest is sex-on-air-mattress history.

The summer heated up quickly—my twin bed became ours, we said the L-word, he met my family, and we thoroughly enjoyed each other's company. We tested every greasy spoon diner in Minneapolis-St. Paul and he taught me Irish phrases like "What's the craic?" We came up with the pet name "meine baba," which we called each other constantly. There was so much softness between us. He was waking me up after a long depression. Showing me I could be desirable. Showing me what it was like to be treated well. Laughing with me. Loving me more tenderly than I had ever been. Putting me back together again.

I got a job setting up a laptop in a hotel lobby in St. Paul on game days during StubHub's early years. It was perfect because they had a regional office in Southern California, so I would be able to transfer my job and thus have at least some part-time income to rely on after I moved.

I took long walks around Lake Harriet to get in shape for LA. I wanted to move there as my best self. I wanted to be ready to make it this time.

As Labor Day approached, Ronan helped me pack all my shit into my Chevy Malibu and drive halfway across the country. He was able to extend his visa and stay with me in LA through the end of September, until he had to leave for grad school in Belfast.

Neither of us wanted our relationship to be over, so we decided to try long-distance. Ronan got a headset and Skype, and I bought phone cards and a plane ticket to Ireland for Christmas.

Ireland was moody, but I was taken with its charm. I met Ronan's nerdy finance friends in Belfast, hung out with his family in Letterkenny, drank at quirky pubs, and visited ancient ruins and old IRA battlegrounds. At a Christmas fair, we drank hot cocoa, and I bought winter bulbs as a gift for my mom and grandma. The weather was gloomy, but not me, until he took me back to the airport. I cried as I watched him head back down the escalator, during the customs search where they confiscated my contraband bulbs, and the entire eleven-and-a-half-hour flight home.

Ronan got a ticket and came to visit in February.

By the end of March, however, nobody had a ticket, and my latest phone card was running out of minutes. I offered to marry him—to end the separation, to get him his green card, to figure out if we even wanted to be married to each other.

But he did not accept my offer. He had a better offer—a job with an international company. He was sure he'd be able to work his way over to LA in an indeterminable amount of time.

On the phone with Ronan, meter running, I looked out the window at the lush garden outside of my Mar Vista apartment and asked, "How many phone cards until we don't need them anymore?"

"No more than five," he said optimistically.

After we got off the phone, I couldn't stop thinking about my dwindling phone card minutes and all the California left to explore. My woozy blues were breaking, and I was beginning to trust my instincts again. Ronan was great, but five years was an unfathomable length of time to a twenty-four-year-old, and LA was teeming with warm bodies. Maybe I could find a nice guy a little closer to home.

So before the minutes ran out, I rang him one last time.

MR. SKIN

One sunny late spring SoCal morning, I pranced around outside of a Circle K, hollering out to male customers as they entered the door. "Hey there, hun! You gotta try M-150. It's the perfect energy drink to perk you up for the day." I forced a big smile.

A guy slowed his walk as I untwisted the cap and poured him a sample. I'd been twisting so many caps off bottles that I had a raw callous just under my left ring finger.

I hadn't been back in LA for very long, maybe a year and a half. I was living with Danielle in a two-bedroom apartment in Mar Vista near Venice High School (better known as Rydell High from *Grease*). Danielle had a little edge to her now—long hair, more of a rock and roll vibe, and a penchant for Vodka diets—but we still ran a stoner household, with a small bong the centerpiece of our coffee table.

I was still working promotions, shilling for startups and Fortune 500 corporations. The gig du jour was launching a new energy drink called M-150, which tasted like a fruity cleaning agent, outside of convenience stores around metro Los Angeles and Orange County in booty shorts and a spaghetti-strap tank top.

During a tiny lull in the foot traffic, I snuck a glance at the email on my cell phone—a relatively new feature—and *HOLY SHIT!* I held up my phone like it was a winning lottery ticket. I'd gotten a teaching gig at a summer camp for high school students planning to become doctors.

It wasn't just another gig, but a well-paid off-ramp from the hustle. It would deliver me to just the right financial situation that would allow me to pursue my acting dreams fully for a few months instead of day jobbing my time away. This is why trust-fund kids have the upper hand in Hollywood. They're rarely wilier or more talented, but in addition to connections, they have more time and money, and thus are afforded more opportunities, a more professional reel. That's one of the things I needed: a new reel, new headshots, the fees to upload them to the casting sites, a package of casting director workshops, the list went on and on. But soon,

I would be able to buy those things! This job was going to pay me over $6,000 (in 2008 dollars). It was also going to buy me time.

Knowing I was almost out of my M-150 misery, it was a lot easier to smile the rest of my shift. I plastered one on from ear-to-ear and yelled at a man getting out of his Jeep, "Hey there, hun! Stop by and see me on the way out. You're gonna *looove* this new energy drink!"

For the first day of training on the UCLA campus, I sat down at a table in the middle of a large classroom, surveying the room keenly. My new coworkers were also filing in. One of them looked like a younger, tanner, taller version of Darrin from *Bewitched*. His nametag said Felix. He wore a crisp polo shirt. There was something super hot about his preppiness. Felix looked at me, I looked away.

I was there to focus on the job. I paid careful attention as we talked through every page in the manual, practiced the lessons we would do with the students, and did a dozen rounds of roleplaying. It all seemed straightforward enough. I didn't need to be a doctor or have attended med school myself; I just needed to confidently lead the students through the curriculum. I could do that. Other people were there to be the experts. I wanted to be the expert on Felix.

Felix was on summer break from med school in San Diego. Maybe his allure came from the fact that he was going to be a doctor and that his life had an order and stability mine didn't. Whatever the reason, I felt warm whenever Felix was around. I had a boyfriend, but it didn't suck to have a work crush. I wanted to impress him while at the same time ignoring him—it wasn't brain surgery, but close.

The most eventful part of training was a phone call from Zoe. "I'm pregnant!" she said.

"Oh my god, dude. Do you want to be?" I asked.

"Yes!" she shrieked through the phone.

I listened to the rest of her update with a stunned smile, watching birds flit around a tree outside the window. After the

excitement about bringing new life into the world plateaued, Zoe
and I devolved into swapping stories about our work crushes.

"There's a hot trainer I work with at the gym," she said.
"I'm about two squats away from jumping his bones."

I watched Felix do standing stretches out of the corner of
my eye. "There's a cute guy at my new job, too," I whispered.

"These kids are curious," they told us towards the end of training.
"They'll want to know personal stuff about you," they warned. "If
you're worried about your search results, come see us after lunch."

As I walked to the cafeteria, I thought of my own: my
acting résumé, an interview for *The Poisoned Court*, occasional
Facebook posts (sometimes silly, but never alarming, and regardless,
my account was private). If they looked me up, they would see that
I was an actress.

The first day of camp, I put on khakis, a button-up shirt, and ballet
flats, and I walked over from the teachers' dorm. The kids were
already arriving with parents and siblings in tow. Hundreds of
voices clamoring with questions. The energy was electric. My mom
and dad were teachers. I'd always turned my nose up at that as a
job—"those who can't do, teach" and all—but this awakened me to
the possibility.

Standing in front of my class for the first time, I cleared my
throat. "Okay everyone, let's get started." I scanned their hopeful
faces as I waited for the whispering to stop. "We're gonna have
fun," I promised. A few of the rowdy boys pumped their fists. A
few of the girls giggled. We pushed the desks aside, and everyone
scooched into a circle on the floor.

I quickly discovered that I was good at this teaching thing!
I was adept at negotiating with the kids. They wanted to listen to
me, impress me. They liked me. I felt like I was making an impact.
I was nearly a decade older than these kids, and my perspective
seemed relevant and helpful to them. It was more rewarding
than trying to get guys to buy energy drinks outside 7-Eleven or
handing out free stuff at the Santa Monica Pier, that much was

sure. Aside from a vomit-inducing live video presentation of a knee surgery, during which I had to leave the auditorium, I loved my job.

I settled into a stimulating rhythm of lessons with my class, camp-wide assemblies, meals in the UCLA commons, and trying to flirt with Felix's stiff ass.

"Everyone, grab your workbook and open it to page 12," I said one day after lunch. Pages rustled as I continued, "This afternoon we're going all the way back to ancient Greece to learn about the Hippocratic Oath." There was a knock at the door.

"Hey, what's up?" I said, greeting one of my fellow teachers as they stepped inside the classroom.

"I'm here to sub for you. They want to talk to you at the office."

The sun stung my eyes as I exited the building. I sighed and began to jog across UCLA's sprawling campus, impatient to get back to my students. The office was half a mile away. When I finally got there, I was winded and sweating through my button-up.

"What could be more important than medical ethics?" I joked as I entered.

"Hi, Courtney. Go ahead and take a seat," the director said, unamused.

"So how's it going?" she asked.

"I'm *loving* this job. It's even better than I expected."

She nodded and paused. "There have been some complaints…"

"Really?" I said, clutching the arm of the chair. "All the kids are so great."

"It's not the kids. It's their parents." She informed me that some of the kids had googled me and found naked stills of me from *The Poisoned Court* on the celebrity smut site Mr. Skin.

"I didn't put those on the internet!" I exclaimed.

"It doesn't matter," she said, her face tight. "Their parents aren't happy. Why didn't you tell us during training?"

"I didn't think it would be an issue. I mean, it's art—it was for an independent film." I couldn't believe it. Nobody even saw that movie, how could it lead to my firing?!

Next thing I knew, I was back to hawking M-150 outside Circle K. My issue wasn't the glass ceiling; it was the tits and ass ceiling. Even more confining. I went to college, but my acting pursuits meant the only decent-paying jobs I could get and keep required me to wear booty shorts and sweet-talk men. A legit acting job resulted in some rando on the internet making a topless collage from the film that branded me a certain kind of woman, a sex object, not to be trusted with kids or polite society. I wasn't sure how much say I'd had in the branding, but it didn't matter. I couldn't find any way around it. The damage was already done.

"Hey there, hun! Wanna try some M-150?" I called after a guy who blew past me with no eye contact.

I adjusted my tank top and sighed. My new reel would have to wait.

HOW TO SET YOUR OWN TRAP

STEP ONE: BAIT THE GUY

"Okay gang, we're gonna need more energy on this next take!" the greedy assistant director hollered into a megaphone.

It was my first day as a Central Casting extra at a fake high school prom on the set of *CSI: New York*, and I was forced to do the unthinkable: dance.

Adam, a cute guy I'd just met that day and was learning the ropes from, was given a camera prop and, thus, had the luxury of lurking on the perimeter of the dance floor. I was envious he was assigned a role for which no rhythm was required.

"Action!" called the director.

I flailed around as energetically as I could muster on a Thursday morning at 10 a.m.

"I'm gonna need more energy," Adam whispered teasingly as he pretended to take photos of me.

"Cut!" the director yelled into his megaphone.

While the crew reset the shot, I grilled Adam for the inside scoop on how to get my three SAG vouchers—the golden tickets that could get me into the union and out of the group holding pen ASAP. He told me everything he'd gleaned about background acting in his few months of experience.

"Today, I'm hoping for a looong day, or at least a meal penalty. After twelve hours, we get paid double time," he explained.

The director called "Action!" again, and I gyrated.

"Looking good, muffswangs!" Adam hissed in a Jim Carrey voice as he pointed his filmless camera at me. I rolled my eyes and laughed silently, busting out a disco move.

Between takes, Adam was good-natured and eager as a puppy, keeping me entertained with funny voices, philosophical questions, and countless rounds of party games like Fuck/Marry/Kill. I'd been dreading my foray into background acting, yet my cheeks ached from giggling all day.

By the twelfth hour of our workday, it felt like we'd known each other for years. The lights dimmed, and we were instructed to slow dance. We clutched each other tenderly, and Adam told me about the abortion he'd paid for right before he moved to LA. "I was hooking up with a coworker at a Wing Shack back home," he whispered.

"Did you love her?" I asked.

"No, I wasn't that attracted to her. But I would've stayed if she wanted to have the baby. Become a dad. Married her. Done the right thing."

I gazed up at Adam's piercing blue eyes, earnest, sad, and relieved. Harboring my own secret shame of an abortion where the impregnator was MIA, I fell in love with him a little bit in that moment.

"I almost didn't make it to LA," he said, chuckling softly. I felt him grip the small of my back tighter.

"Wow, fourteen hours and forty-five minutes. Not too shabby!" Adam exclaimed as we waited for the extras coordinator to sign our vouchers at the end of the day.

"Can I get your number in case I have any more questions about background?" I asked.

Adam raised his eyebrow at me, maybe because I'd mentioned my Irish boyfriend.

"Sure," he said, scribbling on my notepad. "I should get yours too." He looked up at me, and his eyes twinkled. A pleased-with-himself smile spread across his face like butter on toast.

Adam and I worked together a couple more times that balmy early April week. When I wasn't booked with him, I was booked with his best friend. I was technically taken, but Ronan lived on another continent, and our romance was gasping its last breaths. The time I spent with Adam was refreshingly warm and easy. I liked him, and after six months of playing phone tag in a long-distance relationship, I wanted a boyfriend I could actually touch.

Unfortunately, the flirtation process was dragging out far too long for my liking. Adam had coordinated a group hang with our roommates and always stayed close to me on set, but a week of mixed signals and missed opportunities became two. Became three. He wasn't making a move even though his gazes, arms touches, and gentle teases told me that he wanted to. But I was ready for him and too horny to wait for him to figure it out on his own, so I set up a trap.

In my defense, the ruse came about sincerely. I was sitting on the floor in the background holding pen, texting Danielle about my crush.

Dude I think I like him wish he was on set

Back in 2008, the process of texting was not unlike using a rotary phone. I pressed each button multiple times to eke out the message.

I had plenty of time to realize that this text was unintentionally addressed to Adam, who was also its subject. I tapped hastily to delete it. But before I could finish, I had a flash of inspiration. Perhaps he just needed a little nudge? An assurance that any effort on his part would not be in vain.

I scrambled to my feet and swayed enthusiastically as I retyped the end. In under a minute, I restored the message, pressed SEND, and began contriving my "omg embarrassing!" shocked response, like a remorseless serial killer.

Then the game was afoot. Our conversations become more blatantly flirtatious.

I used my calling card for the last time to officially break up with Ronan. I'd been mourning for months after a bittersweet visit to Belfast for Christmas. Saying goodbye felt inevitable. Breaking up wasn't ripping a Band-Aid off a fresh wound, but letting an overripe bandage fall off to reveal healthy skin underneath.

A couple weeks later, I was planning to roll ecstasy with Danielle, her cousin, and his roommate, so I invited Adam to join us. The rendezvous began at our lush Secret Garden apartment, where we took the tablets, chasing them with Diet Coke. Waiting for them to kick in, we drove several blocks down to the Venice Boardwalk and ran shoeless along the beach until the sand felt unbearably tickly on my feet. Back at our apartment, Adam and I sank to the couch and melted into each other. I loved how fresh he smelled, like Irish Spring and Old Spice. We were soon glued together horizontally like a quesadilla that could make out with itself. A double dose of the hug drug finally lubed us up enough to consummate the fledgling romance. Adam wasn't as mature or successful or even as smart as my bucket list boyfriend, but he was a good person and (very critically) physically present, and, having not seen one in a while, I thought he had the perfect dick.

STEP TWO: MAKE HIM YOUR PROJECT

Adam and I hit the ground running, hardly ever spending more than a night apart.

We were both twenty-four. He was scraping by doing non-union background for minimum wage ($64 per eight hours), living on a couch in a one-bedroom apartment with two other guys in Monrovia, California, which was bumfuck-adjacent by 2008 standards. It was so far away from my apartment in Mar Vista that he might as well have lived in San Bernardino. I was on my promo model/auto show hustle. My dreams were still out of reach, but I was making a much more comfortable living than working non-union background afforded—at least I could live within the LA city limits.

Adam saved his precious dollars to make the diagonal trek across the metro to see me while gas was exceeding a crippling four bucks a gallon. I hated to see him sweat the check whenever we went out, so I'd usually cover both of us.

We got in our first fight about a questionable hang with one of his female friends who very clearly wanted more. "If you want to date other people, that's fine, but I don't want to be part of it," I said firmly and hung up the phone. Ninety minutes later, Adam called from down the block. "Look out your window," he told me. I pulled back the blinds and saw a heart-shaped balloon animal on the hood of my car, along with a note. I went outside and opened a three-page list of reasons why it was worth it to drive all the way to Venice to see me, which included points like:

- *Because of how she makes her bed so perfect.*
- *Because she makes me brush my teeth.*
- *She cries during movies.*
- *She has a great personality, in fact, that is one of the strongest parts of her personality!*
- *She is a ravenous independent.*
- *Her mind is always at work, figuring out the world and where she fits.*
- *My mind is always at work, figuring out her world and where I fit.*
- *When I get up to go to the bathroom, she will drape herself on my side of the bed.*
- *Because she makes me like her so much I hate it!*
- *Because her lotion has sun protection!*
- *Because she reminds me of the ocean.*
- *Because she will make fun of me for this.*
- *Because she makes me feel like doing crazy shit like this!*
- *Because I'm crazy about her.*

A few weeks later, Adam moved in at my behest.

Those first six months were magical. We did everything together, and he could make me laugh so hard. Danielle's mom came to visit and told me I was beaming.

Our first Christmas was at the onset of the Great Recession. We'd both lost some gigs, and money was tight, so we decided we wouldn't do gifts. Unbeknownst to me, that wasn't really the plan. Adam began a clandestine gift-making project. Whenever I stepped out of the apartment, he was painstakingly crafting a scrapbook of magazine clippings, favorite inside jokes, cute emails we'd sent each other, paper mementos he'd collected, and photos of our favorite restaurants and other haunts in LA. Inside the front cover was a sleeve containing a mix CD entitled *Muah*. The first page of the scrapbook said: "Time defines us and leaves us knowing who we are. This is about the time that's gone by. Oh, the time…"

Seventeen years later, as I write this, I will run my hands over this scrapbook, examining every page. I will see on the subsequent pages such an accurate rendering of myself at that time, it takes my breath away. There is, of course, the stuff that will make me cringe, like how exacting I was with our financial splits—"Adam, you owe me $87.54 check only please" and my Subway order "plus change"—the money pressure will come rushing back to me. But beyond being cheap, more tenderly, I was a person discovering myself. Him too, but in this scrapbook, he was showing me who I was at twenty-four, a glimmer of who I would become, and who we were together. We were so sweet. It was my first love that felt both encompassing and safe—so safe that in his arms, I could whisper for the first time, "I had an abortion too."

For the humble means he was working with, Adam wooed me with everything he had. Beyond the poems and Post-it love notes, he treated me like a queen on a daily basis. In return, I showed my love and appreciation by molding him with all of my extra clay. Teaching him basic adulting and how to hustle, two things that came naturally to me.

He didn't know how to break out of background acting and wasn't super savvy about how to pursue anything else, so I sat with him sifting through Craigslist ads, rewriting résumés, and composing cover letters. He finally got a day job as a receptionist at a lemon law firm; he had to be there by 7 a.m. He began going to bed early, he hardly ever drank. He turned into a serious person. We hiked Runyon Canyon every day, motivated to get in better shape together. We became involved in the same theater groups, took the same acting classes and workshops—even did a play together.

He was a fixer-upper, but I was a budding architect. I wanted him to reach his potential. For him. For us. For me.

STEP THREE: SHIT WHERE YOU EAT

Sloane Greer was my fairy godmother. I was her "biggest mistake," frequently needing time off for auditions and rehearsals, which made things awkward with her other employees. Sloane owned Sterling Legal Services, a legal support staff company specializing in employee-side employment law, which in California meant big class action lawsuits.

One of her first hires, I came off as a highly capable potential protégé. I have a solid résumé and typically give a great interview.

I not only worked at SLS myself, but, within three months, I'd gotten Adam a job there too. His résumé was thin aside from his few months working at the lemon law firm, but mine was impressive enough for the both of us. So we sat in little cubicles across from each other and called class members and got them to tattle on the meal and rest break violations they'd endured on their employers' watch—and what did we care if they exaggerated?

Adam and I were always together. We drove to work together from the house on top of Mount Washington, where we were living with another couple—Tatum and her boyfriend of a few years, a tennis pro named Richie—collectively house- and dog-sitting for Richie's uncle, a documentary filmmaker, while he and his family were abroad. We tentatively drove Adam's Hyundai or my Chevy Malibu up and down the narrow, winding Mount Washington roads. The compound we were keeping watch over had a yard, a pool, and a view—amenities far above our current LA caste—it was our own private oasis atop the madness down below.

It was a short-term rental, but Adam loved living in Eagle Rock. Its gentrification was in its infancy, and it still felt like a fairly remote portion of the city.

I hated it. It wasn't walkable. It was too quiet. It was so far from everything. My non-Tatum and Richie friends were on the other side of the city. As were most of my gigs, favorite restaurants, rehearsals, and auditions. Frustrated with our lifestyle and feeling like I was treading water acting-wise, I started taking Adderall again for the first time in LA. Adam knew about Adderall from college and didn't like that I was doing it, but I wanted to buy myself some extra time so I could work full-time to support myself, and still have the energy to stoke my acting career at night.

My acting problem was hard to fix, but we could at least change our location when our sublet was up. I could hardly wait.

STEP FOUR: FIND A CAGE

A few months before it was time to leave Eagle Rock, I had my antennas up for apartments with cheap rent. Cheap rent is a crucial tenet of being an actor without a trust fund. As such, Adam and I were both worried about our post-house-sitting options.

On a warm fall afternoon, I was sitting outside in extras holding, working on *NCIS*. Background acting is the kind of excruciatingly boring work, mostly waiting around with the added element of being held captive in a literal holding area, that leads you to divulge personal facts about yourself to complete strangers in casual conversation, just to pass the time.

"My rent is only $400, so sometimes I just take off and travel," Jay mentioned as an offhand detail in another story.

"Seriously?" I said, my eyes wide. That was the best deal in town—I knew because I scouted Craigslist every day.

Jay looked like an overgrown Dennis the Menace and lived in a studio at the Brevoort Hotel on Lexington and Vine in Hollywood. I was determined to get us a unit in his building. I became a rabid dog, biting at his leg for more information.

"The building manager is a fickle old bastard," Jay warned me. "He's the ultimate New Yorker—if he doesn't like you, you're not in."

"What's not to like?" I said, undeterred.

Jay smirked at my confidence, "You're gonna need my vouch."

The following week, I stopped over at the Brevoort to smoke a bowl, and Jay gave me the Cliff's Notes of the building's lore. As we smoked, I was already unpacking in my mind.

The Brevoort Hotel was an old white four-story Spanish-style building that was currently something of a tenement, but used to be an actual hotel—and a swanky one at that. At the dawn of Hollywood in the 1920s, actor Gary Cooper was rumored to have "taken lady friends to several of the tiny bungalows out back, and swum in the Brevoort's walled plunge," according to an *LA Times* article (itself several decades old). Apparently, it was also Regis Philbin's first Hollywood home when he was hired to host KABC-7's *AM Los Angeles* in the '70s. But its real claim to fame is that the Black Dahlia, otherwise known as Elizabeth Short, lived there shortly before she was murdered.

But much like the building itself, the current residents weren't as chic as they once were. In 2009, it was mostly populated by burnouts, out-of-work actors, and costumed characters from Hollywood Boulevard.

After Jay and I were both sufficiently high, we set out to find the building manager, Joe, so Jay could make the introduction. I'd been informed that Joe was actually former actor and Warhol disciple Joe Dallesandro, so I couldn't wait to catch a glimpse.

"Hey, Joe," Jay called out in the hallway.

Joe looked down from screwing in a lightbulb and blinked at us, confused. He was attractively grizzled, like a middle-aged Johnny Cash. He struck me as simultaneously exhausted and still running off the intoxicating fumes of an indulgent, well-spent youth.

"This is my friend, Courtney," Jay said. "She loves the building and wants to live here."

"It's gonna be a while," Joe grumbled, warning that he rarely had openings.

His voice sounded like gravel and, as promised, he was gruff. But I actually found Joe to be quite charming. Once an actor, always an actor, and his curmudgeon persona seemed an apt choice for his current role as the super.

"I can wait patiently until December," I said with a pleasant smile. Joe grumbled something unintelligible and squinted at the lightbulb, getting back to work.

After our introduction, I rode Joe hard, calling him regularly for a month. I left him sweet, persistent messages.

"Hi Joe, it's Jay's friend Courtney. Remember me? I'm calling because I still want to reserve your next available studio."

"Hi there, it's me again… Courtney. Just checking in on your next studio avail."

"Hi Joe, it's your old friend Courtney…"

Surely realizing there was no way I would ever leave him alone, he finally called me back with an opening.

STEP FIVE: LOCK YOURSELF IN

We gawked over the fence at the "Joyously Enter Here" sign above the main entrance when Adam and I arrived to see the unit. I called Joe's cell phone to let him know we were outside. It went to voicemail. I called again… and then again. While we waited, a costumed Charlie Chaplin and Marilyn Monroe exited the building, probably on their way to Hollywood Boulevard, just a few blocks away. Eventually Joe peered out from the reception window like a pirate.

"Oh hi, Joe!" I waved.

Joe led us through the lobby. There was a real McCoy vintage quality to the place. The carpet was varnished with a sticky, slightly damp topcoat, like it had gotten wet sixty years ago and never quite dried. There was also a cigarette-infused musty smell that seemed as foundational to the building as the wooden beams themselves (and probably the same age). He opened the door to the first-floor unit I had pleaded for, and it was… well, tiny.

"It's 200 square feet," Joe informed us as Adam and I bumped into each other trying to check out the bathroom and closet.

But then he gave us the price: "Since there's two of you, I gotta charge $420 a month." Adam and I tried to suppress our smiles. $210 each. Same for the security deposit. Plus, it was month to month. It was cheaper even than our house-sitting sublet had been. Just one block over on the corner of Lexington and El Centro, our friends were paying what seemed like an astronomical

$1,600 for their one-bedroom.

Joe looked on bemused as we tried to determine how we could Tetris our shared shit into the dollhouse of a studio apartment.

"I give it three months," he grunted, as if he were betting at the racetrack.

"Us? Oh, we're good," I laughed confidently.

He shrugged, and a knowing smile cracked through his craggy veneer. "I've been doing this a long time."

The act of moving seemed full of possibility. The alienation I felt at the top of Mount Washington was about to dissipate as I came back down to sea level, or at least 354 feet, the more manageable elevation of Hollywood. I was thrilled that I'd be back in the city, walking to run my errands, mingling with strangers on the street.

Back in Eagle Rock, we seemed to be floating through time and space, going through the motions, not really thinking or communicating too much. There were some tears around my birthday in September. We recovered quickly, but what stuck around was the tension of two people unable to grasp their dreams. That lack lived alongside us. Lay in the bed next to us. Slithered in between us as we fucked our daily fuck.

We'd always had matching sex drives. He was always ready, and I was always down. But as September became October became November became December, and we were gearing up for the move, the sex became more mechanical—two actors hitting our marks, saying our lines, moaning our moans. There was something missing between us. Something I couldn't yet identify. *The move will fix everything*, I thought.

After all, it had been a hard fall. It had become clear that Danielle's boyfriend had a drinking problem. He was charming and she was patient, but his lies were growing more preposterous by the day. I couldn't even keep up with the fact-checking anymore, and the dissonance was driving me wild.

"You can't trust anything that comes out of his mouth. How are you supposed to have a healthy relationship with him?" I said during one of our increasingly rare phone calls, after she told me he'd just totaled his car. I was exasperated, but I missed her and felt guilty because I'd introduced them—he'd been one of my roommates in St. Louis.

On Mount Washington, Tatum finalized her plans to leave LA for good. She and Richie were breaking up—she would move back to Tuscaloosa, Alabama, and he would continue to be a tennis pro in Southern California—but they were doing it gently, together through the end of our lease. It was a pre-Gwyneth conscious uncoupling.

As Tatum's moving boxes started to pile up in the living room, Richie discovered that his parents had been swingers throughout his childhood—and not careful ones because his brother was actually his half-brother, and he'd just learned he had another sibling that he'd grown up thinking was a family friend. Over eight-dollar bottles of wine, we pondered the alternate reality of his younger years and how things aren't always what they seem.

The saddest part of leaving Mount Washington was leaving the dog. I liked him, and Adam loved him. We didn't go home to our families for Christmas and instead spent the last two weeks at the top of the hill, just us and the dog.

"We should do ecstasy again," I said as we were packing up, hoping for a recreation of our first night together—dancing and petting each other, two magnets recharging to their original strength, drawn together on the couch, unable to be separated, attracted and entangled all night.

Adam was enthusiastic about the idea, so I tracked down some molly and we took it on one of our last nights on Mount Washington. We looked at each other expectantly, waiting for it to kick in.

A couple hours later, we should have been melted and magnetized into each other, but instead, we repelled. Touching each other felt forced; not touching each other felt sad. We didn't fuck all night. We didn't fuck at all. I went to bed while Adam did some leftover coke and played video games till dawn.

All around us, the energy was shifting. We were in transition—of course we couldn't be perfectly aligned. We just needed a reset. I was sure of it. We would be happier in Hollywood.

STEP SIX: TRIP THE TRIGGER

The next week, we rented a U-Haul and moved everything ourselves. We were at the age where we were expected to hire movers instead of being cheap mooches and asking our friends for help. But we were broke, so we were our own labor.

It was a tight squeeze in the new apartment. There was no kitchen, just a bathroom. One tiny sink to wash everything, our faces and our dishes, an impossible feat to keep clean. Plates, bowls, cups, and kitchen utensils in a tote under the bed. One tiny closet to cram all our clothes. My desk was stacked with administrative supplies: folders, mail, paperwork, pens, and pencils; we each cordoned off a rectangle for our laptops. A wall of IKEA Connect 4-style shelves stored literally everything else we owned. Looking out our only window, all we could see was the neighboring wall. Everything about it was cramped.

I felt newly invigorated though. Our friends were just a block away, and they invited us over for dinner shortly after our move. Another night, I walked up to iO West, watched Adam's improv graduation show, and hung out at the bar for a while after. I was rehearsing for a play—a Shakespearean take on *Pulp Fiction*—at a theater around the corner on Santa Monica Boulevard. Getting out and about in Hollywood, I felt an ease that I hadn't felt in quite some time. It felt like we were finally home.

But there were a few hiccups at our new home. Soon after we moved in, I got sick like I'd never been in our relationship—not since I was a child. Adam had to drive me home from work at the law firm. I got out of the car and immediately puked on the curb. Adam grimaced, but stepped in to pull my hair back as I heaved again. Trapped inside our little cage, there was more vomit and other bodily smells as I recovered over the next few days. It was gross, but we laughed about it. Weirdly, it made me feel closer to him.

Adam had a birthday in late January. Turned twenty-six.
I threw a party for him at the Libertine, across from the Chateau
Marmont on the Sunset Strip. We invited our mutual friends, his
college friends, and some actors from a new play he was doing.
I was there at the beginning—greeting everyone. I had fun, but
went home early. I wasn't in rager mode. I needed to run my lines
for *Pulp Shakespeare* and prep for an upcoming audition. While I
wanted him to have a great party, there was no way I could last until
bar close. He got a ride after shutting the place down with a couple
of friends. So drunk he came home and peed in our bed. A stain
that would stay on the mattress for the rest of its life.

At work—Sterling Legal Services—Sloane assigned me a special
project: to make a database. That meant I was no longer on the
phones, calling class members about their rest and meal break
penalties. Instead, I was freestyling in InDesign. Eventually, she
realized that I was just moving shapes around, and if she really
wanted a database, she would need to bring in someone above my
pay grade.

That meant special training sessions with Ezra. He was a
handsome fortysomething man with one eye. He was enthralled
by me and would spend most of the training sessions subtly and
not-so-subtly hitting on me. As Adam became more distant, the
attention was flattering.

On Saturday, I went to get a haircut in Venice. I asked Adam to
drive over to go on a Westside date with me afterward. I thought it
would be like old times. But as I was paying, I got a text from him.
He wasn't coming. I called him when I got back to my car.

"Hey," he answered flatly.

"Why don't you want to come? We used to have so much
fun over here," I replied, cajoling him into changing his mind.

He let out an exasperated sigh.

"What's wrong?" I asked, confused.

"I'm not sure I'm in love with you anymore," he said, his
voice high and wavering. My body didn't respond—I didn't believe

him. I was sure it was misplaced stress. He'd always been *so* in love with me. Wasn't this the same guy who made me a scrapbook just two Christmases ago?

STEP SEVEN: GET CAUGHT IN THE TRAP

Three months into our lease, the walls were closing in on us. A week or two after the weird phone call, Adam stayed behind when I went to work—he said he was sick.

I called to check on him on my lunch break. "Hey baby, how you doing?"

"I don't know," Adam said. His voice sounded strained.

"What's wrong?" I prodded gently.

"I found your Adderall stash…"

"So? Why are you going through my stuff?"

"I just— I'm not sure I'm in love with you anymore," he said, sounding like a stranger.

My stomach dropped, no longer hungry. Who was this cold, different person? I jiggled my leg all afternoon and left work thirty minutes early, anxious to find out who would greet me when I got home.

When I got home, our apartment was half empty. All of Adam's books and knick-knacks were missing from his side of the shelves. My jaw dropped, shocked. I swung open the closet doors to discover his clothes were also gone. I tore down the hallway and ran into Joe. "Have you seen Adam?" I said, my voice jumping an octave.

"Earlier today he rented the open unit upstairs," Joe said. "Maybe he's in there?"

I sprinted up the stairs, noticed a unit with the door ajar, and ran inside. "What are you doing?" I shrieked.

"I'm moving out—er, in," Adam said, hammering a poster to the wall. "This is my new apartment."

"But why?!" I cried.

Adam hit the hammer and smacked his finger. "Ow!" he

yelped.

"Here, let me help you," I said, stepping toward him.

"No!" he said, his face pained. "I can't even hang a poster. I have to learn how to do things without your help."

I begged and pleaded, unable to understand. At that point, I could barely feel the waves of discontent that are clear to me now. My mind was reeling. I put my fingertips to my temples like a detective with a head injury. Why was this happening?

A few weeks prior, a dude I had met through MySpace one of the first times I was in California, when I was twenty-one, came to our studio to sell me a bottle of Adderall. I thought it was a totally normal interaction. The guy didn't try to hang out or flirt with me or anything. It was a straightforward drug deal, no funny business. I don't even think we exchanged a quick hug or anything, but Adam was *triggered*, like a guard dog ready to tear the MySpace guy's fucking face off.

I didn't think my Adderall use was out of control; I could justify it because I had a lot on my plate. I needed to work, I needed to audition, I needed a banging body. It all made sense to me. I certainly didn't think my Adderall use was serious enough to be a dealbreaker, but Adam obviously did.

This sounds wildly dumb and immature, but I think subconsciously I was under the assumption that he would never leave me, could never leave me. How could I be abandoned by someone with abandonment issues after I'd been so useful? He needed me—emotionally, logistically, everything. I thought I made myself essential, but I'd inadvertently turned myself into his mother, a thankless, unsexy job.

I cried everywhere for weeks. Target. Trader Joe's. At home. At work. To friends. To strangers. I couldn't be in that haunted room by myself. I went on long walks all the way down Melrose or Sunset—sometimes all the way to Doheny, almost five miles to Beverly Hills—just to wear myself out. After the breakup, I had to be with someone or in motion. That was the only way to not die.

Because it frequently felt like I would die. My heart was broken. Literally broken. I read about broken heart syndrome on the internet—a broken heart really can kill you. And that's what it felt like when I thought about Adam and how much I loved him, and what if I couldn't control the future and get him back, and what if I never found anyone I loved as much, and what the hell was so wrong with me that he wanted to leave in the first place?

I'd made his life so easy. I helped him so much. I must truly be heinous to negate all that goodwill. It wasn't just my heart that was broken. It was me.

STEP EIGHT: FLAIL LIKE A MOTHERFUCKER

Needless to say, I did not take the breakup well, but I never had a chance to properly get over it. I could hear his toilet flush. It was torture. I don't know what possessed him to commit such existential fuckery as moving upstairs. I understood the broke factor, but I'd found this apartment and he was the one who broke up with me. Sticking around was demonic. Every night as I parked my car after driving home from the job that we still worked at together, I saw his window and easily surmised whether he was home or not. Saw glimpses of other people. Wondered who that red hair or tank top belonged to. Was he by himself? Did he look kind of sad? I couldn't look away. It was impossible for me to play the cool girl when he was still in my apartment building and at my job, so I didn't even try.

I stayed in the unit we'd lived in together. It had been cramped with our combined stuff, but now it felt intolerably empty. Everywhere I looked, things were missing. A few cups and bowls. A couple pots and pans. It didn't matter; there was nowhere to cook. I wasn't going to cook anyway. I was too devastated to eat. Mostly what I missed was being enmeshed with another person. I felt like all the patches had been ripped off of me, and I was totally exposed. If I could just get my person back, I could sew the patches back on and be whole again.

When I couldn't go into work anymore, I started working from home. I couldn't focus at the office, but it wasn't any easier in my haunted apartment.

On the one-month anniversary of Adam moving upstairs and across the hall, I skipped out on my afternoon calls and walked all over Hollywood trying to ditch the ghost. I cried as I walked up Vine and across Hollywood and down La Cienega—so far that it wasn't Hollywood anymore, it was West Hollywood. I walked and walked and walked until eventually I heaved my way up to Sunset and tried to distract myself with the sights of the Strip, until I got to Cahuenga and took a left on Lexington, and I was back at the Brevoort. When I got to my unit and looked in the mirror, my skin was burned red.

Alas, the walks weren't accomplishing much beyond raising my risk of skin cancer—and arming me with an enviable breakup body with which to exact my own form of torture, but I wasn't aware of that yet.

So I lost my everloving shit.

It was an ugly scene.

I couldn't work, I couldn't be by myself, and I couldn't even sleep unless I took two extra-strength Tylenol PMs. I was annoying my friends with incessant wondering about what I could have done differently, whether we would get back together, and how I could fix myself. The only person who could tolerate me was Jay, my background actor friend who lived downstairs.

Jay was like forty, which seemed ancient at the time, and was as unconventional as everyone else in that building. When he wasn't a movie extra, he was a screenwriter and a hedonist and an off-the-grid type of guy. He philosophized as I cried on his futon.

Eventually, even Jay grew tired of my shit. He'd still hang out, but he would challenge me to get better.

I truly thought my life was over if I couldn't be with my ex-boyfriend. No one wanted to see that.

One day, Sloane Greer asked me to come to the office for a meeting. When I got there, glancing around shifty-eyed, looking for signs of Adam, Sloane grabbed her purse and put on her Audrey

Hepburn-style sunglasses. "We're going on a field trip," she said, dragging me out to her sexy two-door convertible coupe.

She screeched out of the Century City parking garage and onto Santa Monica Boulevard. Windows down, wind tousling our hair, music blaring. We were en route to a newly opened Billabong store because Sloane had a "man friend" who was teaching her how to surf, and she needed some chic flippers. It was a bright breezy spring day, perfect for fucking off.

"So how are you doing?" she asked, coming out of the dressing room in a wetsuit. "I'm good!" I chirped, and then every other line was about fixing myself and being patient and wanting to get back together. She furrowed her brow and shook her head vehemently. "Stop right there," Sloane said. "You're doing this wrong. The last time I got dumped, I got my hair done, my tits done, and started making a loooot of money. Of course, that loser eventually wanted me back, but by that time, I'd already moved the fuck on and I was over it. That's how you get even!"

Sloane was preaching what we all know is true: looking like a bombshell and being successful is the best revenge.

But I wasn't in revenge mode. I was in sad sack mode.

Sad sack mode looked like making puppy dog eyes at Adam whenever I passed by him at work—or worse, serving him a tear-stained face. Red blotchiness. Mascara streaks running down my face. Pathetic.

A few weeks later, Ezra was finishing up his consulting gig on the database.

He stretched out his last day of training way longer than it needed to go. He kept asking, "Do you have any questions?"

Finally, I teased him back, "Do *you* have any questions?"

"Yeah, actually." He glanced over at Sloane's desk, then leaned towards me. "Can I take you out for dinner?"

A short laugh escaped my lips before realizing that he was serious. "Sure," I said, after a beat.

I'd heard Adam was already on OkCupid, so I figured why

not? I don't think I was consciously trying to make Adam jealous—
it was more an attempt to make myself move on.

Ezra got us reservations for a hip sushi spot called Katsuya on
Hollywood and Vine. It was four blocks up from the Brevoort.
Getting ready beforehand, I decided to wear a black V-neck shirt,
long duster sweater, jeans, and my gold and black zebra-striped
ballet flats. I wanted to look cute, but not too cute. More on the
casual side. I didn't want to be Ezra's girlfriend, so I didn't want to
be too alluring. I could tell he was already sprung.

I straightened my hair and doused myself in Clinique
Happy perfume for the first time in a long time. Tonight wasn't
even about Ezra; it was about showing myself I could be attractive
again.

On my way out of the apartment building, I ran into
Adam. "You look good," he remarked. "Where are you going?" he
asked casually, moving closer to breathe me in.

"Just grabbing dinner with a friend," I replied, smiling
tightly. Heading toward the door, I said, "Have a good night," and
waved goodbye.

He could tell that wasn't quite the whole truth.

At Katsuya, Ezra was waiting outside in a suit. He greeted me with
a kiss on the cheek. I was flattered, but flustered.

Inside, he ordered an extravagant spread. I told stories,
asked insightful questions, and we laughed easily together, same as
back at the office. I snuck a peek at my phone as we were finishing
the edamame and saw that I had five missed calls and a string of
increasingly frantic text messages from Adam:

Good to see u

U looked hot

R u on a date?

I was distracted by the time our food arrived. I nibbled on a
California roll and pretended to listen to Ezra's story. My phone lit
up again:

I miss u

I couldn't take it anymore. "I'm so sorry, but I have to go," I
said, rising up from my chair unceremoniously. Ezra was mid-bite.

By the time he swallowed I was already out the door. I ran home in the rain, tears streaming down my face.

When I got there, Adam's body was weak. He steadied himself by grabbing on to me. "I don't want anyone else to have you," he panted, pulling my V-neck over my head. I lay back, beaming as he inhaled my face, neck, and cleavage like a hungry dog.

We fucked for hours on my pee-stained IKEA bed in our old apartment. The one Joe cursed before we moved in.

But that rendezvous didn't change Adam's mind. We were still broken up. I would go on another sort-of date with Ezra. Adam was dating too. I found out that he'd hooked up with a girl from his play and another from his improv class. I had a hunch and demanded confirmation. I was keeping track of his roster by pure energetic connection, his window curtains, and Instagram stalking like a forensic detective. The Brevoort became insufferable, a toxic torture machine.

STEP NINE: HATCH YOUR ESCAPE PLAN

One day, about six weeks after the breakup, I had an epiphany. I knew the Brevoort was the best deal in Hollywood, and I also knew I had to leave. I couldn't give it up for anything more expensive, but there is one thing better than cheap: free.

I came into work and proclaimed to Sloane Greer and her assistant that, "I would be a great apartment manager."

Little did I know that stating that intention aloud allowed it to manifest almost immediately.

Sloane Greer leaned back in her office chair and cocked her head. "I know a guy," she said. "My mentor owns a dozen buildings in Hollywood and K-Town." Kreative Habitat was the name of the operation. "Look it up," she advised me as I made my way to my cubicle. "Kreative with a k."

Back at my desk, I perused the Kreative Habitat website. Less than a minute later, I called over my shoulder, "This looks amazing, Sloane. Can you put me in touch?"

A few days later, I went to the Kreative Habitat office on my lunch break to interview with the manager of the apartment managers. I wore a little blue and white sundress that showed the triangle at the top of my thighs when I bent over—either a really smart or really dumb outfit choice.

"When are you looking to start?" he asked.

"Yesterday," I replied.

"How about next week?" he said. "I'm going to have to fire someone first."

"I can wait," I said, grinning widely.

Nine days later, the manager of the apartment managers met with me again, this time at the building on Hobart Boulevard, where Thai Town meets Little Armenia. The building itself was an aging four-story with exposed brick walls and genuinely distressed hardwood floors. It was worn and weathered, but I liked the aesthetic and, most importantly, Adam was a mile and a half away.

"What do you think?" the manager of the apartment managers asked me.

"This'll do," I said, nodding. "This'll definitely do."

He dangled the keys in front of me. I grabbed them with a satisfied smirk.

I started moving in that night. Just me and my laptop to start. I slept on the floor. That's how bad I needed out of the Brevoort.

To get the big stuff—the Connect 4-style IKEA shelves, the bed frame and mattress with Adam's big pee stain in the middle, and my desk—I rented a U-Haul and guilted Adam into helping me. Aside from a few brief breaks to help move boxes, I spent the bulk of the day letting Adam know he had wronged me and hurt me and he was making the biggest mistake of our lives. I had just played Hecuba in a workshop of her eponymous Greek tragedy, and I brought the same energy to this moving day.

Just because I moved, didn't mean we made a clean break. It was my turn to haunt him.

A few times, I showed up unannounced in the middle of the night, knocking on his door mid-panic attack. It's really hard to break up when you're codependent and the person you were dependent on is gone.

Jay came over one day as I was continuing to unpack. We walked over to Food 4 Less and bought a garbage can, broom, and a bottle of budget vino. I dumped generous pours into my new 99 Cent Store wine glasses.

"To your new place," Jay said, holding up his glass. "To new possibilities." We clinked in agreement.

Jay reached into his pocket, pulled out a compass, and presented it to me as a symbolic gift. He'd been helping me cope when he lived downstairs, but he wanted me to know I was capable of finding my way on my own.

"You don't have to believe that's possible right now," he reassured me, "You'll believe it when you get there."

Another friend gifted me Pink's *Funhouse* album, which became my breakup anthem. It was her breakup album too, made while she was separated from her husband, Carey Hart. Now they were back together—they'd actually broken up and gotten back together *multiple times* during their courtship and then marriage, and now they were reunited and seemed happier than ever—so it only fueled my hope for a second chance.

I was still obsessed with the idea of getting back together with Adam. I continued asking everyone whether they thought it could happen, would happen, even if they had never met Adam and barely knew me. I would milk them for stories. "Do you know anyone who broke up and got back together?" Had their parents? My parents had broken up in high school, but got back together in college, and they were still together. I was greedy for other examples. I would ask the internet: "how to get back together with my ex-boyfriend," "how do I make my ex come back," "break up get back together." I even paid some breakup guru $27 for a PDF guide.

Adam himself told me it was pathetic. That I was above my handling of the breakup. I knew he was right.

STEP TEN: FUCK YOUR WAY FREE

It felt like I was going to be stuck on Adam's hamster wheel forever, so I made a manic list to get a new dick inside me posthaste. At the top of my list was Theo. He was tall, dark, and handsome. 6'2" or 6'3". I knew him from acting class at the Antaeus Theatre Company (where Adam was also a young company member). We had recently done a scene together, from Tennessee Williams's *The Night of the Iguana*. I sent Theo a flirty email, and he responded enthusiastically.

Beyond the physical, I was attracted to him because he was the opposite of me. He baked bread. He rode a bike. He lived in a loft-style apartment that you accessed through a storefront in Boyle Heights. He was principled. He didn't want to play "the game." He didn't want anything that smacked of networking or superficial bullshit. He tried to be a purist, even when that philosophy seemed to fuck him over.

On our first date, Theo and I ate Thai food and were serenaded by heavily-accented renditions of American pop classics like Blink-182's "All the Small Things" and Nancy Sinatra's "These Boots Are Made for Walkin'."

Then we migrated a couple short blocks east to Jumbo's Clown Room. Jumbo's is an iconic bikini bar, basically a strip club where the thongs stay on. Courtney Love used to strip there. In 2010, it was staffed by the type of hipster chicks who would pole dance to The Beatles.

Theo and I, by this point quite drunk, were soaking up the sexual vibes.

When the next girl onstage smacked her lucite heels to Ginuwine's "Pony," my hand drifted down to grab Theo's dick over his jeans. She didn't even have a chance to finish her number before we were stumbling out the door, right on Hollywood, left on Hobart, down the block, and up the stairs to my fourth-floor apartment, huffing and puffing and laughing and reaching for each other until we reached my door.

He leaned down and kissed my neck as I fumbled to unlock my new manager's gate and then the unit door. Finally open, we lunged across the room toward my shitty IKEA bed like slow-mo cheetahs attacking their prey, ripping each other's clothes off with our hands instead of our eyes, as we'd been doing the whole night up to that point.

My top-floor apartment, no curtains yet, was lit by the pink, blue, and white sign from the 99 Cent Store across the street. We tore into each other in full view of the homeless people and passersby outside on the corner—not that they gave a shit.

Theo had a long, thick, uncircumcised cock, and we fucked in countless positions, an earnest attempt to break that shitty-ass bed. It would have been worth it. I still get wet when I think about that night.

The next morning, we went to Food 4 Less and he bought supplies to make chilaquiles. He told me when he got my email, he "had to find out what this was all about." After that night, I wanted to find out too.

STEP ELEVEN: TRAP YOURSELF AGAIN

Right after I fucked Theo, I got an email from Adam. I read it with my heart in the back of my throat. *I am sorry for treating you with such cold disregard. You deserve a lot and I hope it is not too late to try and have some kind of warm relationship with you, where I am able to show you that you do actually mean something to me.* I misconstrued it as a reason to hope. I was nothing if not confused. Theo had just popped my cherry to possibility, the glimmer that there were still other guys who could turn me on. I'd been so loyally in love for two years, since the scrapbook, since right away, really. Now Adam was willing to get back together.

I don't think that was his intention with his email, I think he just felt the psychic pull of me finally starting to move on and was scared to let that happen. But either way, I couldn't say no. I wanted Adam, and I wanted Theo. I wanted them both. Did I want

an open relationship? Adam and I tossed the idea around. Maybe
we could employ a "don't ask, don't tell" policy. We decided to give
it a try.

It was technically aboveboard, but when I went out with
Theo again a couple nights later, it felt like cheating.

So it was back to being miserably monogamous with
Adam. Unable to find our footing with each other. The innocence
was gone. The illusion of trust was broken. We could see its failing
structure underneath. We could feel ourselves trying and not
finding the other.

We went to a Tool concert for one of our last-ditch dates. It was
Adam's favorite band, and even though I didn't like their music, I
was determined to recreate our manic early-relationship energy, so I
made it my mission to blow him in the stairwell. I felt an obligation
for sparks to fly, to be memorable, which sounds so stupid—I mean,
I'd been his girlfriend of two years, after all.

We went in and out of the stairwell several times, trying
to lose the security guard. We eventually got a sliver of privacy
when the other concert-goers headed to their seats. I rushed to
unbutton Adam's pants and suck on his soft cock. Somehow,
despite the pressure, he got hard and then I really went to town,
giving overenthusiastic head. The security guard came in again and
peered around suspiciously. We scurried further up the stairs. I was
determined to finish, urgently trying to make Adam cum. After
another minute or two that felt like an hour, he stopped me and
said, "I'm worried we're going to miss the concert."

Amid plans to move back in together, we broke up again. The
second breakup came on my twenty-seventh birthday. I went to
meet Adam in our new apartment—Hobart #401, I'd convinced the
apartment management company to let us have a one-bedroom—
and he was sitting in the dark.

"I'm sorry, it's your birthday, but I don't think we should do
this," he said.

He wasn't sure what he wanted and he was scared to leave,

but when he left the second time, self-preservation kept him from looking back.

I was blindsided by both breakups, though the second one any idiot could see coming from a mile away. Our divergence seems inevitable when I think about it now, but at the time, I was incredulous. I was so content and comfortable in the warm bath of a reliable relationship. I couldn't stand the thought of shivering in the cold air.

It felt like I was in purgatory. I still wanted to be with him so bad, and he was constantly in my periphery. I kept running into him at Antaeus. In our Stylized Comedy class, he had everyone in stitches. My scene partner suggested we make a last-minute change to a gender-bending rendition of *Rosencrantz and Guildenstern Are Dead*. Underprepared and out of my element, having to perform in front of him was humiliating. I wanted to crawl under the stage and hide until class was over.

Ultimately, I set my own trap. I'd allowed our lives to become so intertwined that even in a city as sprawling as Los Angeles, I could not escape him. My investment of time, effort, contacts, and support in growing him into a man made me painfully aware that I was picking up the pieces all by myself.

STEP TWELVE: BREAK FREE
(FOR REAL THIS TIME, YOU STUPID BITCH)

The pieces came together slowly. First, Danielle moved into my apartment building after going through her own breakup and then having a stalker in Van Nuys.

On a warm November day, we went to the animal shelter. The male dogs barked relentlessly as we walked through the caged aisles. On the female side, Danielle took her time, crouching down in front of a tan American Staffordshire named Polly. They locked eyes, and next thing I knew, Danielle was filling out adoption paperwork.

On the sidewalk outside, I snapped a photo as Danielle tied

a kerchief around Polly's neck and Polly licked her cheek. Watching this moment of bliss, I knew instantly I wanted a dog of my own. Getting over Ellie was hard, but I was more mature and ready this time. I was sick of fixing up guys; I needed to find a more suitable being to put all that caretaker energy into. I wanted a four-legged best friend, baby, and constant source of accountability rolled into one. That was what I needed, and I knew it.

I went back to the pound where Danielle had found Polly, but I didn't find a spark with any of the dogs on the girls' side, and the boy dogs were pure chaos—all the barking and peeing on stuff seemed like a bad idea. I didn't need another dick in my life.

I launched an epic search to find the perfect fit: a girl dog, at least a year old, ideally potty trained. I slacked off at work, combing through online listings. I didn't know exactly what I was looking for breed-wise, size-wise, or looks-wise, but I knew I would recognize it when I saw it. I inquired about a couple of promising prospects, but one was already taken, and the other was at a rescue that wouldn't place their dogs in apartments. After weeks of searching, I clicked on a Craigslist post, and there was a photo of a gawky-looking white spotted puppy in the grass. It was love at first sight. The listing said Georgia was a pit bull/Dalmatian/boxer, recently rescued from doggie death row. Her foster mom already had two dogs and her landlord had discovered Georgia, so she needed to rehome her, like, yesterday.

I went to meet Georgia at her foster mom's in West Hollywood. I was wearing a gray V-neck shirt. Georgia couldn't stop licking my cleavage. I think she liked my Clinique Happy perfume. Her foster mom tried to get her to stop, but I just threw my head back and laughed. Pure joy.

I loaded Georgia in my car and we went to the Silver Lake dog park with Danielle and Polly for a trial run. Instant besties, Georgia and Polly chased each other in circles, between our legs, and around the park, kicking up dust. I didn't want to give her back, but I'd promised.

Georgia's foster mom called me the next day. "She sat by the door for an hour after you dropped her off," she told me.

"Really?" I said.

"Really," she replied. "She's yours if you want her."

Yes, I wanted her. Finally, a little reciprocity!

Soon Georgia and I were walking all over Hollywood, West Hollywood, back through Hollywood, Los Feliz, Silver Lake, and even over to Echo Park sometimes. We couldn't get enough steps. Her with her pent-up puppy energy, and me attempting to walk off my breakup anxiety. She made it feel safe to walk at night and live alone. She followed me around wherever I went and always had kisses for me. She was the perfect companion.

I had my best friend one minute away and my dog by my side. Now I just needed to write this new chapter.

At work, I came across a pitch call for TheGloss.com's "I Regret Everything" series. I peered over the top of my cubicle at Adam, knowing exactly what I would write about.

That night, I stayed up late working on my submission, feeling like I just had to make the deadline. At 4 a.m., I closed my laptop, bleary-eyed, after finishing a rough draft.

The purge of writing the essay was incredible. It gave me a place to process my feelings. And I was good at it! The next day at work, I polished it up and pressed send. When it got accepted and published—the first byline of my adulthood—I wanted more.

The experiences I'd had since leaving Minnesota had begun piling on top of each other, weaving together into the stories of a complicated young woman who was finding herself, demanding to be seen, demanding to be told. And this young woman was discovering she had a lot to say.

INTERMISSION 2

It was all starting to make sense.

For as long as I could remember, I'd kept Post-its and scraps of paper with smart words I wanted to remember, bits of dialogue, and funny or interesting premises. There was never any indication as to why I was doing it. Just a habit that felt natural.

When bad things would happen to me—feeling lonely in my darkest days with Derek or existential angst on the Girls Gone Wild bus—I would have a nagging whisper in my ear that this wasn't all for naught. *I will use this*, I thought. How was unclear. Presumably character motivation for acting?

But the way *I will use this* nagged at me was deeper and more primal than pretending to be another person.

Besides, the more bad things that happened to me, the less I wanted the stage and the more I wanted to unpack the nuanced reality of it. The more I wanted to write the script. The more I wanted to tell *my* story. The more I wanted to put myself back together with words.

"I think I'm done with acting, I want to be a writer instead," I said, spitting it all out before taking a breath.

I paced around the Laurel Canyon Dog Park, kicking grass and keeping an eye on Georgia. I thought my parents would be happy at the new development, and I was right, they were relieved. It wasn't med school or becoming a lawyer as they'd hoped, but at least it seemed more stable.

I was relieved too. Part of me just needed to say it out loud, state my intention, which had been harder than anticipated to do. For months—years, even—I'd been stuck in a prolonged denial that I would ever, could ever, give up on my original dream. Acting had been my center of gravity for so long, it felt like I was cheating on myself by changing which art form I wanted to pursue.

Georgia was busy engaging in her signature dog park move: chase. She was a gawky puppy, a little over a year old and the fastest dog in almost every pack. She got the other dogs all hyped up and sprinting after her around the perimeter, then swerved between the humans who stood looking down at their phones. The other dogs dropped out one by one, panting, until she was back to where she began: running in circles by herself.

I'd had some close calls that, had they gone another way, may have kept me in the acting game longer: A *Californication* audition where the casting director mulled over my potential out loud in the room, but ultimately decided I looked too young, too innocent (ha!). A *Criminal Minds* audition that was maybe a little too method. I was supposed to play an addict, so I took Adderall and stayed up all night working on my line. I looked so tweaked out and authentic that the casting director was probably concerned I would steal something from the set to buy meth if he cast me. An audition to play a mobster in a Honda commercial—I did my best Joe Pesci impression after a night of crying over Adam.

Unfortunately, nothing substantial was happening for me on

screen, but I had found a more reliable outlet to get my fix—on the stage, performing Shakespeare and other classical theater for free, or nearly free, at non-union or 99-seat Equity waiver houses around town. LA is an impossible city if you're trying to make a living from theater, but there are still plenty of plays to perform in because there are so many actors desperate for stage time.

Acting was starting to feel like a gambling addiction—hard to tell if I was chasing my dreams or ruining my life.

My last big hurrah as an actor was an internship at a classical theater company called A Noise Within. At that time, they were housed in the old Masonic temple on Brand in Burbank, across the street from the future site of the Americana. Their fall season consisted of *Measure for Measure*, *Great Expectations*, and *Blithe Spirit*. I was cast as pregnant Julietta—a key character, but a small role—in *Measure for Measure*. I was on the crew for *Blithe Spirit*. I also understudied Estella in *Great Expectations*—my favorite thing I did during the internship. I had great love for the company and fleeting moments of performance euphoria, but my heart wasn't in it anymore.

Although I was hitting all my marks, I wasn't my most alive on stage anymore. My head was offstage, calculating how I was going to pay my bills, or noodling on scenes for a script. Late nights after rehearsals and shows, my castmate and new friend, Ariana, and I were writing a screenplay. It was a terrible screenplay, a thinly veiled fictional telling of our experience in the internship—very much a first screenplay—but it was a start and, more importantly, writing it lit me on fire.

That excitement was in sharp contrast to how I felt about acting, which had become a hardship and was accompanied by a looming sense of dread. Its pursuit was like tending to the most fickle flower, needing the perfect amount of sun and the perfect amount of water. I sucked at keeping plants alive.

During *Measure for Measure* performances, I loved to talk shit with Stephen Rockwell, who played our bawdy, gossipy Lucio, in the wings.

Towards the end of the run, we were waiting outside the

stage door, whispering, when he gave me a note: "The script says, 'What shall be done, sir, with the groaning Juliet? She's very near her hour.' You're great in the scene, but I've never heard you groan."

"I don't want to steal focus," I responded defensively.

I did get accused of scene-stealing in my early days of acting and had since made it my mission not to chew the scenery in my performances—I wanted to work on camera after all. But the more I thought about it, Rockwell was right. In my previous years as a passionate thespian, I would have tried every interesting choice on the menu. Sometimes it was too much, but I was an actor genuinely excited by the process of becoming someone else, and that made me fun to watch.

Now I was over it. Plus, I noticed that even the company's "stars"—the people I most looked up to—were barely scraping by from play to play, even if they were lucky enough to book a TV spot. I tried to imagine a future where I was satisfied with regional theater as the pinnacle of my success, and the ongoing hell of auditioning for creative opportunities, and what kind of life that would be. Forget not being able to afford health insurance or plane tickets and always needing a day job. Even creatively, it made me wince. I was becoming disenchanted with the art form in part because it was so ephemeral. There was nothing lasting about stage work. I didn't want to toil away as a firefly, I wanted my work to have some staying power—at least that of an LED light bulb. I also wanted my art to be less dependent on getting other people's stamp of approval. I wanted more control, to be closer to a project's origin—I was tired of being a muse, I wanted to be an auteur.

I had to get back to a writing session with Ariana, so I called out to Georgia (not yet knowing that she was deaf), and chased her until I had a leash on her collar and could corral her into my Pontiac Bonneville.

We drove down Laurel Canyon's long, winding boulevard— paved with the longing and lyrics of Joni Mitchell—and turned on to Hollywood with a new vision for the future. One that wasn't just bumbling around in my head. I could finally say it out loud.

Now I just needed to learn how to make my words sing.

TRAGEDY + TIME

We met at a comedy show called Gonzo. Well, we didn't meet exactly, but we saw each other. Made an impression. He was performing—doing stand-up in a silver jacket—and so was I, my best coquette. We didn't talk at all that night. Yet somehow, without exchanging any words, we lit each other's fuse for the love-at-first-sight fireworks show that goes off in your gut when you meet somebody special.

I went to the show with Ariana, Sam, and a coworker from the Kreative Habitat office. Sam had recently moved to LA, now an investment banker. We were still not dating, and perhaps not exactly friends after everything that had transpired between us. Ariana was my writing partner, and we were taking a TV writing class together at iO West. That's why we were at the show in the first place: our classmate Sofiya was hosting. Within the next few months, Sofiya and I would become writing partners, a relationship that would span the next decade.

But that hadn't happened yet.

It was May 19, 2011, and we walked down Sunset Boulevard from my apartment on Hobart to Club L, a funky brick warehouse-style venue with no sign and no number at the corner of Wilcox, a block from the old Amoeba Records location.

After getting a drink—a shot of vodka with a Diet Coke back, my then drink of choice—we settled down on a comfy couch in the front near the stage.

About half of the way through, Wes took the mic for his set. Opening jokes are where comedians often call out the obvious thing about themselves to get the audience on their side. Wes started, "I'm sorry about my face…"

He was really funny. Endearingly self-deprecating. I got up halfway through to get another drink, and I felt him clock me, his eyes warm on my body.

When we left later that night, he was smoking by the door, and I felt his eyes exploring me again.

When I got home, I curled up with Georgia and my laptop on my IKEA bed, first popping on Twitter to tweet about the stand-up show—perhaps hoping I might feel those eyes again someday—and then opening Celtx to work on my script for the TV writing class. The next thing I knew, Wes was in my DMs. *Who are you?* he messaged me. I could almost hear his incredulity.

Our first hang was a long walk with Georgia all the way down to Larchmont and over to West Hollywood and back to my place in Hollywood, while covering a lot of ground in our backstories.

"My mom's a physician's assistant, and once I had to call her because I put a toothbrush in my ass and it got stuck there."

I burst out laughing. "What?!"

"Yeah, I'd just learned about milking the prostate, and I wanted to see for myself," he said with a sly smile. I was enamored with his honesty.

He was smitten in his own way. "Walking down the street with you is like being with a famous person," he marveled. It was an apt observation. I was twenty-seven, and the guile of youth meant everyone was looking at me, whether I liked it or not.

A few weeks later, Wes came to my showcase at iO West. Michael McCarthy was our instructor—he'd worked on *Saturday Night Live* and *The Drew Carey Show* and was now on the downturn of his career, but was a great teacher and gave good advice, doling out practical wisdom like "If you want to get anywhere in this business, you have to focus like a white-hot light."

Ariana wrote the first draft of our *How I Met Your Mother* spec, which I punched up with extra jokes. I was a little more gung-ho, so I wrote our spec for *Bored to Death* by myself. Even though it wasn't glamorous—for a few frenzied weeks, I was propped up in bed with my laptop, rocking dirty hair and the same yoga pants as the day before—I'd absolutely loved the process; how I was able to take some of my favorite characters on TV and create a very "me" episode that existed within the world of this beloved show.

I'd asked an ensemble of my favorite actors to perform our pilots in a staged reading, which we taped for the industry interest we were sure to garner. The casting was perfect. The audience laughed at the right times. I knew Wes was in the audience, and I was happy to have his attention, but I had bigger fish to fry: introducing the project, directing our actors, and making sure we got a good video.

After the showcase, Sofiya, her boyfriend, and Wes were standing around near their folding chairs. They showered me with compliments, clearly more impressed by the reading than they had anticipated. Sofiya's boyfriend, a then-budding screenwriter who went on to become a successful showrunner, raised his eyebrows. "That was actually really good."

I beamed, not offended, but proud. I had no idea how to get this TV writing thing off the ground, but I was hooked.

After everyone filed out, Wes and I sat in his PT Cruiser extending our time together. He played me a cover he'd done of Daft Punk's "Something About Us."

"This is actually really good," I said, raising my eyebrows.

"You hungry?" he asked.

"I could eat."

We drove a few blocks to Kitchen 24, and everything came with a large side of tingles. Wes said he would send my script to his agent. I think he felt like what he had to offer me were industry connections, which of course I was receptive to, but that wasn't why I liked him. I already thought he was superlative in all the best ways—funniest, smartest, weirdest, most curious and creative. He was prickly on the outside, but soft and sensitive underneath. Figuring him out was like solving a Rubik's Cube, and I loved puzzles.

Several days later, we had dinner again, after I'd followed up with him on his offer to send my script to his agent. As he sipped his coffee, he accused me of using him. My jaw hung open at the ludicrous suggestion—he was the one who'd brought it up and said he wanted to help, after we were already out on a date. I shot back, "If I was focused on using people, don't you think I'd aim a little higher?"

We had some awkward hiccups like that early on, which led to an on-and-off dynamic. He was a few years younger and hadn't had much relationship experience yet, and along with all of his good qualities came frequent bouts of anxiety and depression. I had my own issues too. I was still chafed from the aftermath of my relationship with Adam. This was after I'd picked up all the pieces, but before I'd put them back together again.

But we loved hanging out, so soon we were dating despite our hesitations. We were obsessed with watching British comedies, like the UK version of *The Office*, *Peep Show*, *That Mitchell and Webb Look* ("That's Numberwang!"), and Sharon Horgan's *Pulling*. He wasn't big into working out, but I cajoled him into taking long walks and hikes with Georgia. Sometimes we would reward ourselves with giant burritos from Tony's Mexican Grill at a strip mall near his place. I was happiest when we were riffing and cracking each other up. We sat outside and talked and laughed as Georgia dug up the backyard of his Valley Village rental.

There was a palpable attraction, but Wes was psyched out about sex, despite his desire. We made out incessantly, almost devouring each other, but when we moved to take our pants off, the vibe fizzled. Skin-to-skin was a boner killer. "I'm so sorry. I really want to, but when it's go-time I get in my head and my dick jams out," he said. It was a mental block he just couldn't get over. "It's because I think you're so hot," he confessed. I took his ED as a compliment.

But three months later, I was getting impatient. We were now officially boyfriend-girlfriend, and I wanted to fuck my boyfriend. His mom had to get involved, and he wound up getting prescribed boner pills so we could finally get it on.

When the relationship was on, it was really good. He could be so sweet. I went out of town, and he surprised me with a typewriter when I came back. He made me mix CDs: *The Kiss &*

Make Up Mix, *Songs for Courtney*, *Mix for Courtney - Part Deux*, *Autumn to Winter Mix for Courtney*, and *Lovey Dovey Winter Mix for Courtney*. The Flaming Lips, The Pixies, Fruit Bats, The Beatles, Joni Mitchell, Neutral Milk Hotel—always with lovey-dovey liner notes, handwritten or typed on a typewriter, art of its own. We took a festive road trip to Seattle for Christmas, so he could visit his best friend and headline for the weekend.

I had continued to pursue my own comedy writing ambitions by enrolling in UCLA's Professional Program for Screenwriting, a year-long program that I put on my credit card and crossed my fingers would give me the foundation I needed to launch my TV writing career.

During a weekend workshop that fall, we had a guest speaker, a showrunner and the co-creator of a popular show. At the end of his lecture, he gave us his email.

I jotted it down eagerly and emailed him a follow-up expressing my interest in gaining experience in a TV writers' room.

Weeks later, I wound up interviewing and getting a job as the Writers' PA on a USA Network TV show called *Necessary Roughness*. I had my foot in the door and was determined to make the most of this industry gig. One of my first days in the room, I pitched a long story arc that made it into the show. I took this as a green light to keep sharing my pitches and interjecting my opinions, likely to the chagrin of the main creator/showrunner who never really took a shine to me. I didn't understand hierarchical writers' room politics, and I've never been one to hold my tongue. Instead of being satisfied with my win and sitting back to keep the fridge stocked, take notes, clean the dry-erase board, and learn, I was trying to climb the ladder as fast as possible.

As the season progressed, I eventually took over the writers' assistant duties (without a raise, natch). It was a great opportunity, and I was grateful for the title bump, but the show was not quite the right fit for my interest in comedy, and I was too impatient or stupid to fake it. I felt like I'd already paid so many dues as an actor that they should roll over into my new creative venture. In fact, I was effectively starting over.

My biggest problem was that I was being ambitious, not strategic. TV writing is about networking as much as it is talent.

It's essential that your superiors like you so they'll help you get your next job. Instead of trying to get my words on the page, I would tell my younger self to shut up and politely beg and flatter the older writers into mentoring me.

Wes was floundering through his own career struggles. He hated LA in general, the cliquiness he felt within the comedy scene, and his own failure to launch. After appearing on *Last Comic Standing* and being selected for Just for Laughs, he'd gotten some buzz but was frustrated that his career wasn't further along. I could relate, but sometimes he would get jealous of my little wins and was an asshole about it. "You got your Writers' PA job because of your tits," he once said in a huff. I knew it was because he felt bad about his situation, but I didn't need that sort of bullshit misogyny from my own boyfriend.

By this point, we were working together on a YouTube series, a sketch show based on our relationship called *NORMAL*. This was around the same time *Broad City* went from a quirky web series to a breakout Comedy Central hit. That was our end goal. The experience of making the weekly episodes vacillated from sublime—cracking each other up, barely making it through our funniest takes—to exasperating late-night fights over self-imposed deadlines. Wanting it to be good and successful and on time added extra pressure to our dynamic. Wes was resentful of having to do all the editing, but we didn't know how to work through our issues productively. He would be critical of me. I would ask for space. It would send him into a tailspin. They didn't feel like "real" breakups to me, but we were stuck in a destructive cycle that was eating away at our foundation.

Keen to enhance my résumé, gain more writing experience and bylines, and because I was poor, I pitched xoJane a Morgan Spurlock-style series called "99 Days at the 99 Cent Store" as *Necessary Roughness* was gearing up to go on hiatus, and it was accepted. I committed to shopping at the 99 Cent Store—there was one across the street from my apartment building—exclusively, for

99 very long days. Every week I would write about it. I think I had a hunch that *Necessary Roughness* wasn't going to hire me back if the show was renewed. As the experiment took over my life, I inflicted scarcity on Wes by proxy.

As of that Christmas, Wes and I had been dating for a year and a half. Back in LA after two weeks apart on respective holiday trips, we were thrilled to interlock our fingers and share the same air supply. Wes had sold a joke to a famous comedian, so he went nuts buying presents for me, even though he knew I wouldn't be able to reciprocate. He revealed them to me like he was Oprah. "Look under your chair!" He gave me a leather jacket, an eighth of weed, a soundbar for better movie audio on my tiny TV, a calendar, and a bunch of other little gifts. Absolutely spoiled me.

I gave him some vintage books, including *The First Time*, a collection of essays from famous people like Maya Angelou, Mae West, and Liberace about how they lost their virginity. I added some candy from the 99 Cent Store to zhuzh up the gift bag. "Seriously, I loved that book as a child," I raved as he opened it. "You're gonna think it's hilarious."

He tried to force a smile as he read the back cover. But the dichotomy in the quality of our gift-giving was obviously bugging him. He seemed disappointed that I hadn't cheated on my experiment for him.

A couple months later—on March 1, the last day of my "99 Days at the 99 Cent Store" experiment—Wes came over to pick me up for a date, but we didn't wind up going anywhere. He seemed subdued when he walked in the door. He sat on the couch as I finished getting ready. Something was off. Mid-mascara, I put the tube down and crawled onto Wes's lap. "I can't do this anymore," he said.

I was so surprised, I didn't even cry. Wes did, though. Georgia licked the tears off his face. "I'm really going to miss her," he said. I laughed. The whole situation was absurd. Just two months prior, he'd been showering me with gifts. Now he was breaking things off. I was just getting comfortable.

How did I not see it coming? I wondered. Same as with Adam. I thought my relationship with Wes was healing me, but when it was over, I felt more shattered than ever before.

During the back half of my 99 Cent Store series, there were publishing delays on xoJane's end and writing delays on mine, so I was still wrapping up my articles while nursing a broken heart. I should have written about the breakup for my final installment; it would have been a poignant end to the series, but I couldn't. I was too distraught to tell that story. Instead, I focused on the dollars and cents. But even writing about money made me cry.

On Twitter, I saw that Wes went on some podcasts after the breakup. I couldn't resist listening. I leashed up Georgia, put in my headphones, and listened like an absolute sicko to every last minute of him talking shit about me as I walked Sunset Boulevard down to Echo Park and back.

I went home and marked off another day on my old-timey romance calendar. *I will get through this*, I thought, though it felt untenable at the moment.

My heart leapt when I rediscovered the 2013 calendar Wes had gifted me, in its then-dusty plastic, soon after the breakup. It had been one of my Christmas presents, initially unappreciated amid the deluge of other gifts. The cover said LOVE and featured a sultry "Lady in a Reckless Mood." Across the top read: *Vintage Pulp Romance*.

I restored the old-timey romance calendar to its rightful place above my kitchen sink and started counting days, auspicious new moons, and fraught full moons as I took long, hard looks at the cracks in my porcelain. As I marked off the days, I painstakingly clamped, swabbed, and epoxied my broken pieces back together. I could see time pass, myself growing stronger, and I felt Wes's presence there with me, helping me find my way.

Ironically, much of my post-breakup growth involved becoming more independent and decentering my desire for partnership, but the calendar allowed me a lingering connection to a man I'd loved so deeply.

My other compass during this period was writing in my

diary every day. Early in our relationship, I became obsessed with the journaling practices of famous writers and began keeping my own, which allowed me to organize my thoughts, catalog events, and let my voice stretch out on the page. It also made it nearly impossible to lie to myself. During this period of self-reflection, I realized I didn't just want to date a comedian—I wanted to be one myself. I wanted to take my art as seriously as Wes did.

I started reading my work at storytelling shows around town and writing stand-up bits for myself to eventually perform onstage. I wrote lifestyle roundups for *Bustle*, packed with as many jokes as possible. Sofiya and I produced and performed in a semi-scripted podcast with a cast of up-and-coming comedians. We also started submitting writing packets for gigs on late-night TV and almost booked a Comedy Central show on our first try.

On unemployment and recently dumped, I spent a lot of time at the dog park with Georgia. I discovered Cheryl Strayed through Maria Popova's Brain Pickings newsletter. The issue was about the heart-remodeling Dear Sugar column in which Cheryl's mom gives her a coat that she initially doesn't love—the last gift she would get from her mother—and she doesn't think to say thank you until her mom's dead and it's too late. I was gutted. It gave me perspective beyond my own pain, which I'd been drowning in. I was instantly in love with Cheryl and her plainspoken prose. I ordered *Tiny Beautiful Things* and read it at the dog park with day-old mascara running down my face. Her hard-won wisdom helped me find my footing in the throes of breakup hell. I then read *Wild*. Cheryl became my lodestar. She felt kindred to me. She also grew up in a tiny place in Minnesota.

I set an intention in that dog park that I wanted to be Cheryl. Not her exactly, but my own version. It comforted me that she was forty-three when she finally broke through. Maybe I didn't need to be in such a rush. I would still feel the thrum of wanting to make it vibrate in my core. I would still identify as a hare. But I would act like a tortoise in developing myself as an essayist and memoirist.

I discovered Chloé Caldwell's *Legs Get Led Astray* on Cheryl's recommendation in an online interview and was delighted to find an accessible peer who showed me another vision of who I wanted to become.

The calendar wasn't the only way I found to feel connected to Wes post-relationship—I finally read the Tom Robbins novel *Still Life with Woodpecker*, a demented love story he'd given me as a birthday gift that I took as a sign we were fated to get back together again. I kept a "Wes" doc in Evernote, and whenever I heard about some amazing-sounding day trip or thought, *I should get another pillow*, or *I bet Wes would have liked it if I had a coffee maker at my place*, I added it to the list. I made him a mix CD with carefully chosen songs, including Liza Minnelli's "Maybe This Time," The Velvet Underground's "I'll Be Your Mirror," Cat Power's "Sea of Love," and The Concrete's "Miss You." I tried to go no contact as long as possible, but I kept thinking I saw his black Ford Focus everywhere I went.

Summer rolled around, Danielle packed up to do a show at Boji and move back to Missouri to be closer to her family, and she and Sofiya both told me it was time to move on. I knew they were right, so I unenthusiastically downloaded Tinder. I winced my way through hundreds of profiles, but made myself swipe right occasionally.

I was getting ready to meet up with a bestselling author's brother for a drink at the Drawing Room when my phone lit up with a text from Wes.

We need to talk soon.

I felt a flurry in the center of my chest, but I rolled my eyes at the timing. I called Sofiya to rant. "So predictable," she said, laughing.

"Why are dudes always like this?" I lamented. "They can sniff it from a thousand miles away when you're finally ready to move on."

I decided to wait to respond until after my date. After months of practice, I could play it cool for a few hours.

After a wary welcome, the date quickly escalated to confrontational. The bestselling author's brother said he didn't like being written about.

"Oh," I said with a laugh. By this point, I already knew I

couldn't have a boyfriend who didn't like or at least tolerate being written about. It would never work out. I fidgeted through an hour of hostile small talk, but couldn't wait to get out of there.

I texted Wes back later that night. He said he was leaving LA soon; he had shitty medical news. Immediately done playing games, I drove over to his house at midnight.

We leaned against my car under the cloak of darkness. His forehead crinkled, and he said, "I have cancer."

Fuck, that wasn't the sort of reconciliation I was hoping for. But I would take it.

Wes moved back to Nashville for treatment, and we stayed in touch via text, sext, and occasional phone calls.

In September, I went to Nashville to visit him. It was fun, but not romantic. Given our spicy pre-trip communications, I didn't know what to make of it. He'd been sending me dick pics, but seeing each other in the flesh, it felt like he wanted to keep me at a distance. We had a blast watching live music, checking out his dad's new bar, and dipping in and out of intimate conversation. But when I went in for a kiss, I could feel his body stiffen. I was trying to be empathetic, but it was a mindfuck. I don't think that was his intention—juggling treatments and wrestling with his own mortality, he had a lot on his plate. However, it was also clear that there wasn't any extra room for me.

When I returned to LA in October, I expressed my concerns, and it took him days to respond about whether or not he wanted me in his life. I had to take a step back.

At the end of November, when it was time to flip the page on the old-timey romance calendar, I sighed. It was officially the last month of my beloved calendar. I was proud of what I'd accomplished in the nine months and nine glimmering new moons since our breakup. I had done a lot of necessary work on myself and decided I would take myself seriously, even when no one else was. After Adam had broken up with me, I was not excited to live alone, but I had begun to cherish myself as a companion, preferring the solitude even. I was single, but I finally felt whole.

Soon it was Christmas again, and the old-timey romance

calendar was out of commission. I was sad to put it away. But I got news that Wes's cancer went into remission. It was a relief knowing he was healthy again as we went our separate ways.

I nudged myself into dating again by reassuring myself that when I woke up in the morning on the day that Wes and I met, I didn't know he was coming—it wasn't on any calendar. Likewise, I didn't know what magic pixie dust the universe had up its sleeve for the next year or next month or even that night.

For a long time, I wished it would have worked out between Wes and me, but when one of us was hot, the other was cool; we never met each other at the same temperature. Still, I'm grateful for what he showed me. How to be an artist in the solitary, obsessive, writerly way, how to be a comedian, and how to give something—and someone—I deeply desire my best shot, and then let go and let time march on without trying to bend it to my will.

It's funny how fickle fate can be about having its independence.

DAY OF THE DEAD

We met up at a friend's house to put the finishing touches on our costumes. Wes was dressed up as a cop, featuring a creepy fake mustache, and I was a before-and-after from "The Faces of Meth." I braided one side of my wig and teased the other into a ratty mess. Wes checked himself out in the mirror, adjusting his aviators.

Once the group had gathered, we walked up the street to join the WeHo Carnaval, the biggest, queerest Halloween street party on the planet. We began the parade route with a comedian friend and his producer girlfriend, dressed up as Wall-E and Eve. People kept stopping them to take pictures, so we lost them at some point among the costumed revelers bumping and grinding their way down Santa Monica Boulevard.

For weeks, I'd had a weird premonition. That something bad was going to happen at the parade—maybe a shooting? It kept popping into my head like a jump scare while I was working out, washing my face, walking Georgia, but I shrugged it off as superstition, thinking I had invented it as an excuse to be antisocial, a manifestation of convenience, not intuition. Leading up to the holiday, the building next to mine had an open casket with bride and groom skeletons displayed out front. Maybe I was just unnerved by the decorations.

Trepidation turned to relief by the time we trudged along Melrose, returning to Wes's car. We'd bopped through the parade route and watched some drag queen witches rock out on the stage, but it was otherwise uneventful. One of my Goodwill heels was falling apart, my fingertips were numb from the cold, and conversation with Wes felt a bit forced, but none of that would kill me.

We stopped at Starbucks so he could get a coffee and I could warm up. An eerie wind hit me as I opened the door and we resumed our trek.

"Did you feel that?" I asked with a shiver. Wes took a sip from his steamy cup and shrugged.

It wasn't Halloween that felt particularly scary. The parade was campy, silly, and fun. But there was something else, something ominous in the air.

"Love is a drug," say Stanford scientists, hack poets, English pop group Bananarama, 1,040,000 Google search results, and me.

Wes was my boyfriend, but by this point, our relationship was running on fumes—more of a bad habit than anything. My longest relationship and most passionate love affair was with Adderall, nearing a decade of on-and-off use.

With Adderall, it wasn't an addiction per se. I refused to claim that mantle. Any thought of rehab or a twelve-step program was quickly dismissed—I could quit whenever I wanted, I told myself, knowing that wasn't exactly true. But it didn't matter because I didn't want to quit anyway. I didn't think of myself as a drug addict or even an abuser; I would abuse Adderall, and it would abuse me, but that word didn't fit either. Obsession maybe? I was obsessed with the warmth, the focus, the drive, the creativity, the corporeal current, the escape. My early days with Adderall felt like puppy love—giddy, consuming, impossible to resist. When my chest burned pink and my tummy tingled warm in the backseat of Danielle's white Ford Escort as we drove the backroads of Columbia, Missouri, and I unclenched my jaw to exclaim, "I would love to do Adderall every day."

But I wasn't satisfied with just my love of speed. I also craved partnership. I felt like I *should* have it. I wanted to live with my boyfriends immediately. Crawl into their skin, burrow them in mine. Enmeshment, I think they call it?

Obsession was driving my life in this era. I took a million showers. I wrote a dozen journals of desperate, incomprehensible musings. I had Post-its all over my room, trying to map the plot of my interconnected obsessions with lovers and speed.

I met Geoff through my friend Jeff, a TV writer, who also bought drugs from him. I had a medical marijuana card, but needed my Adderall dealer more often and more urgently than I would like to admit.

Geoff wasn't what you'd expect of a drug dealer. Nondescript, save for a nerdy, quietly pervy Woody Allen-like energy—showing me pics of him and his girlfriend in a hot tub in Vegas and casually hitting on me when I looked good—and neurotic as fuck, which seemed like a great cover. I always wondered how he found the time. His life was packed with activities, including defending alien theories, financial advising, being the CEO of an online roleplay sex gear company, and proudly fathering a son. You might assume some weird shit about Geoff, but you definitely wouldn't suspect him of being a drug dealer. And maybe he wasn't. Maybe he just sold his prescription to me, my friend, and the revolving door of Angelenos who stopped by his house.

Geoff was a self-taught alien scholar, mentored by one of the big gurus. He was a talking head on a show about alien encounters. His son lived with his baby mama in Pasadena, and occasionally, driving home from hanging with his son, he would stop by to service me, instead of making me come to him. I would run downstairs and find him waiting in the Hobart median in his BMW. "We had a fun day at the park," he'd say, smiling, showing me a photo on his phone. "That's super sweet," I'd say, tucking a tiny bag of pills in my pocket. We'd drive around the block exchanging money, pleasantries, and pills.

Whenever I went to Geoff's place, he greeted me at the door with his Shake Weight. He always wanted to show me something— photos, videos, clothes, a new scab on his body—anything. When I first met him, he was simply a means to an end. Though our relationship was purely transactional, he was a loveable weirdo with a genuine desire to connect, and I quickly developed an odd affinity for him.

Geoff's associates were Camila, a balayaged and budget-luxurious Brazilian babe, and a skinny goth rocker dude named Riley. They were an interesting trio, working together in an ambiguous capacity. Through my interactions with each of them individually— stopping by Geoff's house, meeting up with Camila outside of nail salons, chatting in Riley's car with Evanescence bumping—I learned more about their strange amalgamation of a business.

It wasn't just drugs they sold, though clearly that was a huge part of it. The only reason I was a customer, after all. But they also sold clothing. Racks and racks of bodycon dresses, bikinis, colorful scarves, and accessories for furries—people who like to dress up like animals and fuck.

Literally every time I went to that house, into the weird office/living/receiving room, I thought, *god, this is something I should be writing about!* Every time Geoff answered the door with his Shake Weight, I thought, *Seriously, why are you wasting any time? Do you think he'd let you trail him and the crew? Like formally agree to be your subject—under the table, of course, like everything else.*

The day after Halloween, the Day of the Dead, I put away my mangled meth wig and spent the day in and out of my apartment—catching up on errands, walking my dog, and periodically calling and texting Geoff, Camila, and Riley. I kept getting Geoff's voicemail. Irritated I couldn't reach him on a whim the way I'd grown to expect, I finally left a message. "Hey Geoff, I know I called earlier, but I would love to come see you, like tonight if at all possible… so call me." I tried to sound cool, but I was jonesing.

At 9:53 p.m., I fumbled with my keys, wallet, purse, and phone as I opened my apartment door.

My friend Jeff had just called—just, as in that very same minute. I fantasized that he was calling to recommend me for a job. Maybe they needed a new writers' assistant on the TV show he wrote for, and he thought of me. My mind wandered to what it would be like to work together as the transcript of his voicemail popped up on the screen:

> *Hey Courtney, it's Jeff. I know it's been a long time. I wish I were calling for a social reason, but, unfortunately…uh, I just have to tell you something really fucked up. Um, it's gonna be weird…but…I just need you to call me back when you get this. Um…also, in case we don't talk, don't text Camila or Geoff or Riley anymore. It's important that you don't text them anymore. I'll explain when you call me. Bye.*

I tried to call Jeff back immediately, but couldn't reach him. I paced around my studio apartment, making wild guesses about what was going on with Geoff and his crew. *They must be under investigation*, I thought. *No fucking way!*

After I got over the bombshell of my prophesized FBI investigation, it wasn't that surprising. The previous year, there had been a period when Geoff wanted to be more careful on the phone and meet up a couple blocks from his place. It was kind of annoying, but it wasn't like I was going to call the Better Business Bureau on my drug dealer.

I took a bong rip and assumed it would blow over like last time.

Hours later, after midnight, Jeff called me back with the news. Geoff was shot. Dead. On his porch in Mid-Wilshire. On Halloween. Catching the same shiver I caught coming out of Starbucks, I gasped.

"Crazy, right?"

"Yeah, super crazy."

"Sad, right?"

"Yeah, super sad."

I had a million questions: Did the cops know about the drugs? Was there going to be an investigation? Do you know anything about the funeral? It would probably be weird if we went, right?

Jeff didn't know any of the answers.

We said goodnight and hung up. I paced around my apartment in shock. I stayed up for hours sans Adderall, trying to process how Geoff could be gone.

The next morning, as I was leaving my apartment, I noticed that the coffin was still alongside the sidewalk, but now it was closed.

It stayed on the curb like that for weeks, confronting me every time I came home, transforming from garish Halloween decoration to genuinely spine-tingling. The coffin was an embodiment of my mental state: When my mind wasn't specifically trained on another task, it kept wandering back to Geoff's tragic, untimely death. I needed to know the circumstances of the shooting. I was constantly googling, searching new sites and social media for clues.

My head was thumping with the simple facts: *My drug dealer died. My shooting premonition was real.*

I wasn't sure what to do with that information. It felt like I should probably quit drugs. It was a very heady era, but I wasn't self-absorbed enough to think that some higher power would smite down Geoff for the sole purpose of teaching me a lesson. Still, I had to admit, it felt like a sign. If I didn't need a drug dealer in the first place, then I would not have developed this oddly intimate relationship with someone whose funeral it would be inappropriate for me to attend. I would not have subjected myself to this bizarre new form of grief without closure.

How do you mourn the loss of your drug dealer? The question echoed in my mind.

My other mental loop was stuck on my relationship, which was also on its last breath.

I got mad at Wes for sucking on my ear. A little while later, I got mad again when he licked my cheek. Except: "It wasn't a lick," he said. "It was a kiss." But it felt slobbery and gross to me. Disgusted by a kiss from my boyfriend—did I not want to be with him anymore? Was I hanging on because I hoped he was going to become a totally different person any day now? Was I just scared to be alone?

I would much rather stay in a relationship far past the expiration date than break a heart. But I knew it was unwise to stick around waiting for my partner to change. Or maybe it wasn't about him—maybe I was just looking to be more of myself. Either way, it was a lead-weighted feeling in the pit of my stomach, and I couldn't shake it. I couldn't continue indefinitely when our stars brightly burned, yet they were not aligned. They were going to eat each other. *That's how black holes are made,* I thought.

As terrifying as the shooting was, I preferred to think about Geoff. Perhaps I'd become obsessed with his death so I didn't have to deal with the issues in my own life.

Meanwhile, I tried to quit Adderall. I really did try. But it was hard to stay sober. I bought some extra pills from the other Jeff and played hide and seek with myself. Putting away my stash in the back of my closet and deciding unequivocally that I was done. Then digging it out and taking a pill two hours later. Putting the pill bottle away, getting it out, putting it away again for real this time, and bam, I got it out one more time! Quitting for sure, and then not quitting a little while later because… well, because there was still some left in the stash. I could go back to quitting tomorrow. It was a dangerous cycle, especially for a grieving addict-adjacent mess.

I waited like a month, and then I couldn't wait any longer. I needed my drugs from a reliable source. Somehow, I got a hold of Camila (with a new number, obviously) and drove up to North Hollywood to buy Adderall. I had so much I wanted to ask her. I wanted to give her a big hug and tell her I was sorry, and if she needed to talk, I was there for her. But she didn't look like she wanted a hug. When we were finally face-to-face, neither of us had any words. Mine were right on the tip of my tongue, almost jumping off, but there was a hesitation.

I broached the conversation with the obvious, "Crazy, right?"

"Yeah, it's crazy," she responded.

"Sad, right?"

"Yeah, it's very sad." …and for a while, nothing else.

Towards the end of our transaction, both of us standing in the dark parking lot, she revealed that one of his other coworkers had found him. So the cops didn't find anything suspicious.

Back in the car, I broke off a chunk of a 30 milligram Adderall and washed it down with Diet Mountain Dew. When I got home around midnight, I walked around East Hollywood with Georgia. Fluorescent lights jumped off the buildings and zapped my overstimulated pupils like a taser. I wondered if I would do Adderall until my retinas popped out.

After the initial shock subsided, we were both back to our old tricks—Camila selling whatever the fuck she sold, and me driving to different neighborhoods to get my fix.

But there was a new world order. Camila wasn't the grunt anymore; she was the boss, and she handed me off to a new dealer in the heart of Hollywood. I'd drive over near the Walk of Fame (shame?) and wait on the street for fifteen to twenty minutes, sometimes longer, for my new dealer—a twentysomething dudebro who didn't give a fuck about customer service—to eventually mosey down and sell me ridiculously overpriced pills.

One time, I was down there so long that I listened to a whole episode of the *Dear Sugar* podcast.

Summer turned into fall turned into winter turned into Wes and me breaking up for good.

Summer turned into fall turned into winter turned into a Tinder situationship with a new guy who had such sexy tattoos on his chest that he made me rethink my whole life. He didn't know about my pills or where I got the energy to fuck him all night, but I knew if he did, it would probably be trigger-y for him because his mom had an issue with drugs when he was growing up.

I'd been happily single for a while, but I'd begun yearning for a boyfriend again. I felt like Adderall had been fucking up my relationships—a third wheel that only one of us liked. I didn't want it to be the reason for another breakup, not with this new guy or anyone else.

Before I could convince myself to quit for good, our casual relationship came and went. As it petered out, I flushed my last pill down the toilet as an internal show of strength.

Going cold turkey was hard at first. I leaned on my intense walking routine for all the natural dopamine I could get. I continued guzzling diet soda and energy drinks, trying to get my fix through caffeine.

A couple times, I felt weak and texted my new dealer for addies, but I came to my senses before scheduling the pickups. I just left him on read. Until I stopped craving it anymore.

Ironically, when I quit Adderall and stopped living my life like a neverending finals week sprint, I got more done. But I had to face some uncomfortable truths: I'd been acting anxious for *years* because I'd been jazzed up on speed. It had made me overly intense about work. It had made me bad at eye contact. It had brought out the worst parts of my personality. The upside of quitting was that I liked myself more.

I'm sober as I write this—or at least California sober—and I've been Adderall-free for nine years. But I can't get Geoff out of my mind. He's been stuck there for almost a decade. Periodically, I google him to see if there are any new developments, and eventually, I find the case file online and read it all in one sitting.

A guy robbed Geoff and was arrested. Geoff was set to testify against him. The guy went to jail, but talked to a homie on the outside. The court transcript has him saying, "Somebody else has got to fight this case for me on the streets… this shit gotta disappear."

On Halloween, Geoff's security camera showed his killer wearing a costume. There were actually two people present. Geoff went out and looked at them because of their costumes. The killer was drunk. He shot Geoff twice in the back of the head with a 12-gauge shotgun. Afterward, they went to the beach to throw the weapon in the ocean.

The killer, the accomplice—who'd supplied the weapon, costume, and location—and the co-conspirator were all convicted of murder. The killer claimed incompetence and the accomplice claimed battered women's syndrome, but two special circumstances—lying in wait and killing a witness to a crime—were found true. The killer and accomplice were each sentenced to life in prison without parole, while the co-conspirator received a lesser sentence after pleading guilty to second-degree murder. In the case file, they read so young and dumb, and like they realized the horror of what they'd done too late. "We shouldn't have did that shit," one of them said. But that doesn't bring someone back from the dead.

The mastermind, the person who'd ordered the hit from behind bars, perhaps in a last-minute act of contrition, asked his attorneys not to defend him against the death penalty, and he was sentenced to death.

I'm no longer religious, if I ever was, but these days I'm more agnostic than atheist, and if anything puts me in conversation with God, it's the razor-thin line between life and death.

As I process the details, I pull up a video of Geoff speaking at a conference months before he passed. There he is in his element in a white button-up adorned with a big nametag and black slacks. He speaks of his friend and mentor, and his beloved alien theories. He shows a photo of himself as part of his PowerPoint presentation. Pointing to it, he's beaming in double. "This is me on top of the Pyramid of the Moon in the city called Teotihuacan, right near Mexico City…"

I think of Geoff with his Shake Weight, swinging by my place in his BMW, showing me pictures of his son. He was a gentle soul; it's unfair that he's gone. Then I hear him say, "Teotihuacan means the city where men become gods."

After he finishes his presentation, I close my laptop and say a prayer for Geoff in his last gasping moments. I say goodbye, I say thank you, and I say a prayer for life itself, even in its soberest moments.

I CUM ALL OVER MY CLOSET FLOOR

The car clock read 1:47 a.m. Feverishly driving to Hustler, the adult toy store on Sunset Boulevard in West Hollywood, I had to make it before closing in 13 minutes. Past the ArcLight. Past Amoeba Records. Past the Viper Room, Whisky a Go Go, the Roxy, and the Rainbow. Only the drunkest, most degenerate Angelenos were still out howling at the moon. I was not drunk, but I was something of a degenerate—out of my mind horny. So fucking sick of swashbuckling Tinder dudes with their tiger profile pics and other such false advertising who went shy when I dared to initiate a hookup intended to take place on that very same night. I didn't want to go on a fucking date, I didn't want to text incessantly, I wanted to get laid. I thought it was supposed to be a fucking hookup app? I was so horny, every sentence was trying to fuck.

I don't know what makes masturbation taboo. It's solitary. There is no predator, no victim: it's pleasure without power dynamics. So pure. You discover when you're young that it's fun. And then almost immediately you learn that it's wrong. Or maybe you skip the "fun" part and go straight to wrong.

I will never forget being scolded by Mrs. Driscoll for rubbing my vagina against my desk. And fair enough, I shouldn't have been doing that in class, but the shame of being found out as a pervert stayed with me for decades after. I masturbated a bit in my teens and twenties, but guiltily and infrequently. Because of that moment, because of religion, because of the ingrained idea that pleasure belonged to men. Nearly twenty years later, that was all about to change.

I skidded into Hustler's parking garage and slammed on the brakes, locking the car with my fob as I ran to the elevator. When I got inside, I made a beeline for the phallic section, stocked with so much polyurethane the scent led me there. Silly stuff like the plastic pickles beckoned me, but the veiny, hyperrealistic cocks also caught my eye. There was too much selection. Did I want something realistic or ridiculous? How many settings? What color? It was overwhelming. With a real partner, you don't get to choose.

"The store will be closing in five minutes," a sales associate announced over the PA system.

Shit, I had to pick a dick fast. I scanned the vibrator aisle mentally fucking all the inventory like I was the Bachelorette. I grabbed something manageable. Six inches. Battery-powered. Purple. A couple of silicone veins. It looked like it could get the job done. Compared to the other options, it honestly looked discreet.

My thong was wet as I ran to the checkout.

One night in high school, I was watching TV in the basement, and I felt this same fever come over me. I can't remember if anyone from my family was home. If they were upstairs, I didn't care. I rummaged for something, anything, I could put inside of me to break that fever. I found my travel toothbrush holder. It was orange, like the fire I was trying to extinguish by wedging it between my legs until they shook. It was so feral and innocent at the same time. I lost my virginity to a toothbrush holder.

Then there were boyfriends with fleshy human penises. At this stage, my toothbrush holder was merely a functional sheath, not a pleasure device. *I just need a boyfriend*, I thought. That's what society told me. No need for any assistance or solo play. I would get all my pleasure from men.

Now I was single, holding a disembodied cock at the cash register. I loved being footloose and fancy free, prioritizing myself and my friendships with women. For the first time, I was too empowered to wait around for a real dick worth fucking. I wanted a fake one that would be happy waiting in my nightstand, ready for me 24/7. From now on, I would cum on my own terms, whether that involved another human or not.

At the register, I grabbed a little novelty dick sucker— another impulse buy—and handed over my credit card. I couldn't wait to jerk off. The ultimate debt relief.

I jabbed the elevator button again and again as if it were my clit. I sprinted through the parking lot, out of breath, my body vibrating in anticipation. I felt an urgency to put the car into drive, but also tear into the millimeter-thick hermetically sealed plastic packaging as I swerved between eastbound lanes on Sunset Boulevard, past the Rainbow, the Roxy, Whisky a Go Go, and the Viper Room, already twisting at the nob and putting the dildo a half-inch inside of me, desperate to scratch my itch.

Nothing! Not even one buzz! I cut over to the right lane and made a quick right on Fairfax. "Fuck you!" screamed a man with his window open, honking behind me. The thing is, I *was* trying to fuck myself—it just wasn't happening fast enough. I pulled the dildo out of me and tossed it in the passenger seat, hoisting up my yoga pants as fast as I could. I sprinted into CVS, hurdling over someone sleeping outside the door and making a mad dash from aisle to aisle, until I jogged up to the cashier and asked breathlessly, "Do you have any batteries?"

Back in the car, I jammed those batteries into my Barney-colored dildo just as roughly as I wanted to jam that vibrating rod in my hungry cunt. I never called it a cunt, but pussy seemed too demure for this expedition. I drove back to my apartment with my legs chattering and a death grip on the steering wheel. I somehow parked and made it up to my fourth-floor apartment in a horny stupor. The rest of the night was a blur.

After I bought my grape dildo, I didn't get as much work done. I "worked" from home, but I was frequently distracted by something more powerful than my fingers, which didn't vibrate and tended to tire easily.

In a feeble bid for privacy, either Georgia or I had to be in the closet, and it was quieter me than her. Still, I would hear her panting, pressed up against the closet door. Surely my neighbor heard the endless vibration on the other side of his wall. The cyclical moans. As the apartment manager, technically my neighbor was my tenant.

Luckily, there were no sounds of porn involved. I didn't need it. I thought only of myself when I masturbated. Did this make me bisexual, a narcissist, or both?

I had never squirted before. When I worked at the Martini Bar in college, my coworker buddy told me explicitly how he made his girlfriend squirt, though it always sounded so extreme. But now I was masturbating so much I found a new ridge in my vagina. A rough, squishy button. And when I pushed on it really hard with my firm plastic dildo, I made myself gush with pleasure. Good thing I'd put a towel down for comfort.

Over the next month, I did this gushing a couple more times, cumming all over my closet floor again and again.

My ex-boyfriend Adam came to visit me. While he was in town, we had sex a few more times for old times' sake. We came together, like we did back in the day. He didn't make me squirt— only I can do that—but he could tell something was different.

After Adam left, I shut myself into the closet. I put a towel down, kneeled on top, and stuffed my Barney cock inside me. I turned to my favorite setting—the jackhammer: fast, hard, and constant. I thought of myself and came over and over and over again. I heard my tenant flush his toilet as my toes curled, a tiny squeal escaped my mouth, and I relaxed into a gush. My jaw went slack, and I leaned back on my knees, into the pleasure.

When it was over, I collapsed onto the damp towel and caught a vision of Mrs. Driscoll. Was she smiling at me? I couldn't help but laugh.

THE SELF-ESTEEM POLICE

After sixteen months of Netflix and chilling, mostly by myself, and not a single IRL prospect, I was back on Tinder. It wasn't my first time on the app, but it was the first serious attempt. This time, I was fully over all exes and ready for a relationship.

After a week of nonstop sorting potential boyfriends—in line at Walgreens, in stop-and-go traffic, on the toilet, basically anywhere with cell service—I fell in love at first swipe.

Him: a forty-year-old dirty blond tatted up former architect with a vintage furniture store in East Hollywood (my hood) named Luke. One of his profile pics was casually shirtless, surrounded by tools. The next was one with his mom. I wanted to write him off as a douchebag, but I was too turned on. Plus, he went so far as to describe himself as happy—an adjective that always makes me swoon.

Me: a thirty-two-year-old basic, yet effectively beautiful artist/apartment manager. But he wouldn't know that last part because there was nothing in my bio. Why bother? I was the one screening here. My M.O. was to reel 'em in with pics themed like Tinder's Seven Dwarfs: Friendly, Funny, Sexy, Goofy, Dog Lover, Beach Goer, and Stone-Cold Heartbreaker.

I had already spent a long night swiping and squeezing subtext out of random faces and bios before my bleary eyes came upon him in all his glory. What more was there to look for? I swiped right on him and fell asleep, cuddled up to my phone, the heart eyes emoji plastered on my face as I melted into dreamland.

The next morning, I awoke to a new match. (There were several, but his was the only one that mattered.) It was mutual! I wanted to wait to text him, but not even breakfast was a worthy distraction. I'd barely finished chewing before I broke down and messaged him my classic, "Drink soon?"

Six agonizing hours later, he replied favorably. A highlight reel of our entire relationship projected in my head until: there we were in old age, and I was stricken by the fact that one of us was going to have to die first. I thought solemnly, *I love him so much, I'd rather it be me.*

A few days later, we were avoiding eye contact for the first time at hip Thai Town bar Harvard and Stone. There was a sexy spark between us, but we were both nervous, so we fidgeted and stole glances until our first drink allowed us to lean in and lock eyes.

Then it was on. We casually touched each other's arms and thighs for emphasis when making a joke or ardent point or finishing a sentence. We lightly inquired about each other's relationship histories.

His thumb grazed my forearm as he revealed, "I haven't been in a long-term relationship in over five years."

I nodded, silently accepting his challenge.

After three hours of standard first date fare supercharged by palpable attraction, he walked me home and kissed me goodnight at the front gate.

I was worried that I'd forgotten how to kiss during my drought, but Luke's lips made it easy to remember.

I got a text as I took off my shoes: *I had fun tonight. Thanks ;)*

Later that week, he made himself available to reconvene on Valentine's Day (!!!), and after getting buzzed at a bar in the Arts District, we consummated our sexual chemistry until 6 a.m.

Until this point, my online dating experience was limited to mostly messaging. So, after several more dates, I wasn't sure how to proceed.

My best friend had regaled me with wild tales of New York City dating and flitting among men, many of whom she met on Nerve.com. Her stories led me to believe that playing hard to get was the gold standard. They became my strategic inspiration: Be the cool girl. Online dating was like poker; to be forthright about your feelings was to lose.

The trouble was I'm bad at bluffing. I was obsessed with Luke immediately.

It was like his number was constantly being called in Hot Guy Bingo. His chest tattoos were a sexy mishmash of aesthetically pleasing drunken mistakes. He was building a loft in his furniture warehouse with his own hands. He texted me a selfie covered in visible wood chips. There were mirrors strewn around the perimeter of his bed and nailed to his ceiling so I could watch the livestream of this gorgeous man ravenously eating my pussy and fucking the shit out of me whenever we had sex.

I tried to play it cool, but I would win a Razzie for this performance.

Every time I saw Luke felt like a jolt of lightning—with a persistent tingle the rest of the time (UTI notwithstanding). It didn't take long before I was plotting to get him to commit to me. I could be the one! His last monogamous relationship ended because she cheated on him, and they were basically married, raising her three kids together. She broke his heart. The only reason he had been single ever since was that he's too sensitive. This bachelor could be tamed!

Six weeks after our first date, we traced each other's bodies after a particularly breathless tangle in the sheets. I looked up at us intertwined in the mirror and officially lost my chill. What more evidence did he need that we were an awesome match? I was incredibly dense, but I'd still managed to pick up on the fact that he was bringing other dates—*a lot* of other dates—to Tony's Saloon, a pool hall near his place in downtown LA. One of the bartenders seemed annoyed that I was mooning over a dude who was basically fucking a revolving door. I tried to feel out the vibe when Luke went to the bathroom. The bartender forced a smile and said, "Yeah, he comes here a lot."

I stewed and stewed over how to make him want only me. I wanted a boyfriend, not a time-share. Looking up at his perfect body entwined with mine, I wanted to know that other women didn't share this same view.

He nibbled on my neck. I closed my eyes and relished in

the sensation until I couldn't take it anymore.

"What are we?" I demanded, dropping the ultimate post-coital bomb.

I felt his body tense up immediately. "We barely know each other," he protested, as we lay next to each other completely naked.

Just fifteen minutes prior, he'd eaten my ass. Needless to say, we weren't on the same page.

Then it was fits and starts for our budding relationship. I would come on strong; we'd take turns running away. We would alternate between passionate and passive-aggressive date nights, always ending in explosive sex. I would text, he would ghost, then turn up a week or two later to start the cycle over again. It was all pain, frequent urges, and trouble voiding. Nothing could bloom in this environment.

Come early June, I found something questionable on Luke's Instagram and folded. I had a hunch he wasn't being honest about why we couldn't hang out. Late one night in my bed, dark except for my phone screen, I went down a rabbit hole until I found a full photo set of him as the wedding date of one of his other fuck buddies. I also discovered they'd been on a camping trip to Joshua Tree, another time he'd been MIA.

On our next date, I asked him about it by candlelight, across from each other at a swanky Arts District restaurant. His eyes flickered with recognition, but he laughed it off and said she was "an old friend." Judging by her captions, she thought he was her boyfriend too.

And she wasn't the only one. My social media sleuthing uncovered evidence of several other love interests. He had a small harem of beautiful women at his beck and call. I came to know their personalities and patterns with Luke like an omniscient narrator. It was too much. I didn't want to moonlight as a detective anymore.

So I walked over to his furniture store on Vine, sat on a red mid-century modern chair, and said, "I can't see you anymore."

He was disappointed. He told me how much he liked me, that he was going to miss me. I savored his eyes on me, his hangdog face, and his penitent musings. However, I had already workshopped this scene with my therapist.

"Maybe you'll be ready someday—I hope you are—but clearly it's not today," I said, firm but breezy. I wanted him to remember me at my best.

I gave him Cheryl Strayed's *Tiny Beautiful Things* with a Frida Kahlo bookmark—as much a gift for me as it was to him. I thought of Cheryl's book as a panacea. Maybe he would read it and decide to fix the part of him that wasn't ready to commit.

A month later, on Independence Day, I texted him. He responded enthusiastically, but he seemed to be holding back. He said he missed me but wasn't ready to meet up in person.

We flirted on a text-only basis until August sweltered and I cracked. A Saturday evening stroll around my neighborhood turned into an obstacle course of couples holding hands. When I got home, I threw down Georgia's leash and texted point-blank: *Can we talk soon?*

He was in the desert until Monday, at which point it came out: he'd started seeing someone exclusively for the first time in six years. He was confused by it, but he was trying. "I was really sad when you ended things. It made me realize I should try to get serious," he said.

"With the next girl?!" I wailed in disbelief. "If you missed me so much, why didn't you call me?"

He didn't know. It happened kind of fast. He said he still thought about me.

I was livid. I couldn't believe it. I wanted some sort of closure.

"You could come over tonight," he offered.

We arranged to meet that night at his Arts District loft; sit across from each other like grown-ups and suss out what went wrong. At first, we succeeded in this mission. My therapist later identified this brief period of composure as my "higher self."

The conversation was going well. Too well. Leon Bridges was crooning about "Coming Home," as we traced each other with furtive glances. We were at least four feet apart, but I still felt the warmth of our chemistry. I didn't want it to end. As I gathered my things, I tried to leave my hair tie behind—easy bait for any hawkeyed girlfriend—but he quickly scooped up the band and handed it back to me with a gentlemanly grin.

After he waved goodbye, I took a right at the end of his street. I felt the "what ifs" and "why not mes" bubbling in my chest as I cruised past several cop cars. The next block, I called my best friend with an unsatisfied Yelp review of this latest encounter and a brief manifesto about why Luke was the love of my life.

"Uh, sounds like you guys had a good talk," she said. "Just go home and digest it."

But I didn't want to go home.

My "inner child" made an illegal U-turn and drove defiantly back to his pad. Whatever just happened was not gonna cut it. I was seeking an appeal. He met me at the door with matching anguish on his face. We talked, grazed lips, and nuzzled until sunrise. I didn't feel right about sleeping with him, but the option seemed to be on the table. At 4 a.m., he walked me out to my car and kissed me before I left.

This did not lead to closure. (Duh.)

The following morning, I zipped down Melrose trying to make it to my brow appointment, windows down, phone in one hand, yelling at him over speakerphone—raising a few brows along the way, I'm sure. I needed an explanation. "Do you randomly kiss her in the street? Do you have better sex with her?!" I demanded to know.

"You're the best sex of my life," he responded quietly, which enraged me even more.

At the height of my soliloquy on why he should pick me, why I should be his girlfriend instead, I blurted out, "I... love you?!" I didn't even know if it was true. It didn't sound right.

He didn't say it back.

Instead, I heard sirens.

I was being pulled over.

The voice I'd been screaming at suggested we finish the conversation later.

"No!" I growled.

The officer approached my window and asked me why I was driving while on my phone. "I'm having relationship issues," I cried.

The voice on the other end of the phone was silent.

The officer gave me a $165 ticket and a last look of pity before hopping back on his motorcycle.

His face said it all: It didn't matter what was printed on the citation—whether it was issued by the LAPD or the self-esteem police—it was a stern warning that I was acting pathetic. I couldn't beg someone to be my boyfriend. I needed to read the cards better, and, more importantly, not pretend to "be cool" until I exploded. If online dating was indeed poker, I needed to find someone I felt comfortable showing my hand to from the beginning. Someone who didn't want to play games.

There was barely a delay between getting pulled over and realizing that I was a dunce. Inexplicably, I had made Luke stay on the phone to witness my humiliation with his ears.

I didn't want to let him go, but by the end of the call, I knew it was over. Any glimmer of "us" had been a mirage, and I didn't want to spend more time walking through the desert, thirsty and sun-blind, making up false relationships in my mind that don't materialize in the flesh.

My coulda-shoulda-woulda-been boyfriend was still on the line, but I was finally ready to hang up.

"Goodbye," I said, meaning it this time.

After I got off the phone, I made a pact with myself that this breakup would be different. I would not botch my dismount as I had done before. I wouldn't spend any more time wallowing over Luke or any other guy who didn't really want to be with me. No more obsession with second chances—I was determined to start fresh. Standing between me and my future happiness was the ability to let go.

Before driving away, I checked Tinder and saw that I had a new match. A guy named Wade had superliked me. I recognized him—we'd matched before. In fact, we'd matched three times. I sent an urgent message, there in the car, still smarting from my ticket.

"Drink soon?"

We arranged a date for that very night. We met at the 4100 Club in Silver Lake and hit it off right away.

Two spicy skinny margaritas in, he asked, "Are you hungry?"

"I'm starving," I said with a grin on my face. You don't expect much from a Tinder date. I was just trying to get back out there, not looking for my future mate, but this guy was fun—I was definitely down for dinner.

We migrated down Sunset to El Condor. Standing at the crosswalk—me an inch taller in Converse—he glanced over, trying to gauge if that was a problem. I met his gaze. It wasn't. At the restaurant, we had tacos, more drinks, and more laughs. We talked for hours about everything from hypnotherapy to grief. It was easy. It felt like we could've had fun running errands at Target. It was the best first date of my life.

"He's going to be really great for somebody else," I reported back to my best friend the next day. I was skeptical of the timing. *Literally the day I let go, I meet my husband? Unlikely*, I thought. "I'm just going to keep dating around until I meet the right guy."

A week later, Wade came over to help me hang up my bulletin boards—a good omen for how supportive he would be of my career.

A few weeks after that, I watched him shine at his restaurant opening.

Six weeks in, he made a thinly veiled joke that he wanted to be my boyfriend. "We'll see," I joked back.

We recently celebrated our ninth anniversary, and I haven't gotten a ticket since.

THINGS DON'T ALWAYS STAY
WHERE YOU LEAVE THEM

For as long as I can remember, I've been obsessed with ephemera. I collect things. I'm a packrat, my dad says, my boyfriend says.

When I lived in Jackson, probably at sixteen when I could drive, I took a workshop in a nearby town about paper ephemera. It was led by two middle-aged women, one in a festive sweater and the other a cardigan, holding up retro-looking branded calendars from the '50s, newspaper clippings, and elegant early 1900s stationery. I sat on a folding chair in the front row, looking on rapt when out of a special, perfectly pH-balanced box, they pulled out a handwritten note from the turn of the century, tinged yellow by time.

"Paper Americana holds a rich cultural history," the lady in the sweater informed us.

"These items were only intended to be used for a short time, but the way they illuminate the period they are from so precisely is what gives them their enduring value," her partner in the cardigan chimed in.

"They're irreplaceable. Once they're gone, they're gone forever…"

I remember very clearly sitting in that class and imagining myself in the future. The ladies passed around a few of their more durable paper treasures, and as I rubbed my thumb over the rough texture of decades-old cardstock, I wondered, *Where will I be in three decades? Even two?* It seemed unfathomably far away.

I couldn't quite envision what my future would look like, only a glowing blank space in my mind where I started to sketch out a fantasy. Maybe one day I would come back in a limo and leather jacket and treat the whole town to a party. To celebrate me making it, of course—moving to the coast and accomplishing all my dreams—ironically, success I had to leave to find.

Thinking back, it surprises me that the fantasy I had that day was local. I guess it makes sense that my fantasy sought the

approval of the only people I knew thus far in my life. But most of
my fantasies at that time took place elsewhere.

Growing up in slowpokey ol' Jackson, Minnesota, I couldn't
wait to leave. My hometown made me claustrophobic with all
the wide-open space. I felt like a big city girl in a metropolis of
cows. I mostly daydreamed about my impending life as an actress:
auditioning, on set, rubbing elbows on red carpets, bicoastal living
in New York and LA. My Grandma Betty would say I was born
with stars in my eyes.

Long before my senior year, I had uncovered every shred of
mystery that still existed in Jackson. I knew what was inside every
building. Where everyone lived. Their struggles. Who they loved,
cheated on, or otherwise disappointed. How often they went to
church. How often they went to BuckSnorts for a beer. There was
nothing left to discover. There hadn't been much to begin with,
but now every rock was overturned. Nothing felt ephemeral about
Jackson. It seemed like it had been stuck in a time warp since the
'70s and would never change again.

I left town the day I graduated from high school. Moved to St.
Cloud to be with Derek. My parents and I had been through a
rough couple years, that spring in particular.

We were already in a fight as I packed up my getaway
car. The same fight we'd been having for the past two years: I
was leaving home for a destination completely incomprehensible
to both of my parents, the only map I had was based on all the
daydreams of my life, and nothing they said seemed applicable
to that journey. Thus, they no longer had the appetite to give me
advice because I was so devastatingly uninterested in taking it—and
yet they couldn't resist—and yet I still did not care.

So we hugged each other with the energy of a shove and
said goodbye through pursed lips. I threw up my middle finger as I
pulled out of the driveway, turned right, and drove the quarter mile
to my Grandma Betty's.

She was my last stop before skipping town.

We sat across from each other in her living room, perfectly
lit by the afternoon glow that poured through her big picture

window. She told me she loved me and how proud she was of me and that she was going to miss me and that I should try to be good. She laughed wryly about the turmoil with my parents. As a mother of nine, her sense of humor was finely attuned to appreciate inevitable family drama.

"Oh, they just love you, Courtney," she said and gave me a parting squeeze.

She watched from underneath her open garage door as I walked back to my car and got in. She hollered, "Don't do anything I wouldn't do!"

I rolled down the window, rolled my eyes, and shouted back, "I'll try not to, Grandma. I love you!"

We waved goodbye until we couldn't see each other anymore.

When I was a child, my Grandma Betty purred, "Gee, you got a round, fat face," as she outlined my face lightly with her smooth finger. She traced my features as she softly announced them: eyes, nose, lips. Then again. "Gee, you got a round, fat face." Her finger drew a calming sensation on me that radiated to other parts of my body. I did, I had a round, fat face, and she was literally the only person in the world who could say that to me and remain unscathed. In fact, I would beg her to say it to me. This was my original ASMR, and nothing else will ever come close.

I only had three grandparents for most of my childhood, but the ones who were still alive lived in Jackson, and I would see them on a weekly, almost daily basis.

My mom's parents were Marge and Joe, and my dad's mom was Betty. Betty's husband, John, died of a heart attack when I was a baby. I knew him from a photo of the two of them together, looking very happy in their jackets next to the misty Pacific Ocean on a vacation in California. The photo was always perched on the same shelf in her living room next to a large conch shell she got on the trip. When I was little, I held it to my ear, and Grandma Betty would say, "You can hear the ocean in that shell."

Having grandparents nearby and actively involved in your life is an underrated luxury. It's like having extra parents who are often nicer than your real parents.

We kids—my brothers, me, and my cousins—were always hanging out at Grandma Betty's. She had a big property at the edge of town with a rambling yard, an extra garage, a parcel of farmland, and a large wooded area that went all the way down to the river.

During the winters, we went sledding down her back hills. One time, Ashley and I went down her biggest hill in a sled at top speed. We hit a bump and veered off the course, landing in an enormous cocklebur bush.

I was dragged back up to my grandma's house by my Uncle Buck, bawling my eyes out, my face red and splotchy. I had some scratches and soon-to-be bruises from my high-speed tumble, but the worst part was my big mop of curly hair hadn't been brushed yet that day, and now there were dozens of cockleburs burrowed in it, decorating my head like ornaments on a Christmas tree.

"Oh, sweetheart…" My grandma couldn't help but let out a low chuckle when she saw me. She gave me a big hug and then set to work painstakingly picking cockleburs out of my tender scalp.

A couple of hours later, she draped me over the sink and patiently coaxed out the last few holdouts.

My busy, working mom of four said, "You're lucky it was her and not me."

I *was* lucky to have a Grandma Betty—for a lot of reasons, but one being that she set the perfect feminist example while being far from the perfect feminist. I honestly don't think she would have identified with that term. Catholic, yes. Democrat, yes. Pro-life, yes. Feminist… I don't know. But it doesn't matter. When she went down to the grocery store to get milk with her hair in curlers, no makeup, looking kind of a mess but not giving two hoots what anybody else thought about her, she was teaching me about feminism. She would look cute later, however, for brunch with her birthday club ladies. That's when *she* wanted to look good. It was always her choice.

Grandma Betty managed her household and finances since my Grandpa John wasn't around. He didn't leave her much except the property, so she had to work as an aide at the school to get by. She worked with the kids who needed a little extra help. She was so sweet to them. Her smile would span her entire face, recounting funny stories about the "little stinkers." She never failed to have a soft spot for even the biggest rascal.

She decided she didn't want to date anyone after my Grandpa John, despite having an awful lot of suitors for a woman who already had nine kids. She didn't need to find another man; she had a lot of other fulfilling things in her life. Even if she was a feminist by accident, she taught me about it nonetheless.

It's impossible to keep track of time in Southern California. Seasons glide by nearly indistinguishable. Days bleed into weeks, months, years until a decade has gone by in a hazy flash. It takes so much hustle to live there; I wasn't that good at keeping in touch. I rarely went home. I missed a lot of Christmases. My mom would warn me that I should come home more often. "Things don't always stay where you leave them," she would say.

On a random, meandering SoCal spring day, soon after my grandma's eighty-eighth birthday, I was puttering around my desk, organizing rent checks, when I got a call. Grandma Betty had had a heart attack.

At first, it seemed like she was going to be okay. She was stable in the hospital. I missed a call from her as I was getting out of the shower, primping for a guest spot on a comedy show. I toweled off while listening to the voicemail my Aunt Mary left: "We're just calling to chat. There are no doctors in the room at the moment, so Grandma wanted to say hi." But I was hustling around, trying to finish getting ready for the taping, already running late. *I'll call her back when I get there*, I thought.

But I got caught up in the filming and didn't have a free moment until I was walking back out to my car, giddy from the riffing, guilty that I hadn't yet returned Grandma's call, and relieved that there hadn't been any emergency updates in the meantime.

On the side of the road, I dug through my purse for the key and felt a shiver as the sun crept down toward the horizon. Still fishing around when I heard my phone ring, I pulled it out, lit up with Aunt Marcia on the caller ID, and put it up to my ear.

"Courtney, you need to come home."

I knew she meant now.

I bought the earliest ticket I could, but there were hours to kill in the meantime. I wielded them against myself, viciously, chastising myself for all the times I didn't go home and all the times I could've called but I didn't. Why didn't I answer earlier? Who cares if I was late to that dumb comedy thing!

I bargained with a man in the sky, whom I thought I didn't believe in, to let me see my grandma again. *Please keep her exactly where I left her. I promise I won't leave her there for so long this time.*

When I anxiously arrived at the hospital, my grandma was alive and awake.

She greeted me with, "So when are you going to move back to Jackson?"

I laughed. This was her favorite question, despite the fact that we both knew the answer was never. I didn't know exactly what to say except "I love you" and the pure demonstration that I was there, that I had come from my faraway land, and I was happy to see her still alive in front of me. I would wait to say more until later, a quieter moment when everyone else wasn't gathered around her bed.

The minutes I sat by her bedside felt longer, time suddenly sated with relief.

Then those slow sands morphed again into dominos, each toppling the next irrevocably in its wake.

The doctor came in, and Grandma Betty stared straight ahead with a look of dread as he explained some possibilities for what her life would be like if she recovered—and that was a big *if.* They weren't sure when she'd be able to walk again. She'd need a hospital sling bed and near-constant monitoring. She probably shouldn't eat any of her favorite foods anymore.

She shook her head.

Within an hour, she was sharply declining.

One of the nurses put a dragonfly outside her room to signal the start of hospice.

After that, no one wanted to leave her side. My quiet

moment alone never came.

In the middle of happy family gatherings, Grandma Betty had a knack for reminding us, "You know, when I die, please make sure you wet my lips." Her sister Marie had such dry lips on her deathbed, and my grandma never got over it. We'd laugh it off. It was too morbid. We didn't want her to die.

Because she'd been saying it for as long as anyone could remember, when she started going downhill, we all knew exactly what to do. We got little mouth sponges from the nurses, and my aunts took turns dabbing her mouth.

It seems odd to call death beautiful, perfect even, but that's what it was. This amazing night where we held her as she murmured and writhed her way out of her body. We cheered her on as she crossed over the threshold of life like she was finishing a marathon.

"We love you, Mom!" "You did everything you were supposed to do!" "We're going to be okay!" "Go see Grandpa John!"

Frightening, yet magical. A messy miracle. Like childbirth.

Soon after 1 a.m., Grandma Betty died in the room with the dragonfly, surrounded by many of her nine kids, a few of their spouses, and me.

She died with lips so wet it would make her hoot with laughter.

Everything was just how she would have wanted it.

For a while, she was still warm, and I felt myself yearning to nestle at the hearth of that moment indefinitely. And then she wasn't—and it bowed me that she wouldn't be again. In an instant, it was over forever. No more Grandma Betty on this Earth.

I missed her immediately and in a way that I knew would seep into my marrow, a permanent perversion to my DNA. There was life before Grandma Betty died and life after, but I was not the same.

I thought I would go crazy waiting a week in Jackson for her funeral, so I assigned myself a project. I would make a book in memory of Grandma Betty to preserve her—capture the firefly of my grandma in a jar before it went out.

Plus, it made me edgy to watch her stuff get divvied up. My aunts negotiated the porcelain, my cousins negotiated the furniture. All I wanted was for everything to stay the same. After that, I wanted the conch shell. Oh, but I wanted it!

I needed a distraction, so I asked my family to email me their stories, and I compiled our memories. Her signature moves came up like when she would ask for a "million-dollar favor," which usually meant "piddly stuff like getting her something from the kitchen," my cousin Nick remembered.

Another one of her greatest hits was for birthdays and special occasions, she gave banknotes—typically in low denominations, but the bills were always exceptionally crisp. It would just be a ten-dollar bill, but she would turn it into a big pageant, making meaning from the letters in the serial number, saying, "This 'M' is for Matthew, and the 'B' is because you have such a big heart."

On the last night before the booklet printing, it came time to write my own memories. By that point, my cousins' memories felt like they belonged to me, too.

I think it's natural when people die to remember every single time you were shitty to them, even if it was just in your mind. Those bad memories came to me in flashes as I tried to write my ode to Grandma Betty. I remembered rolling my eyes when she asked for help on the stairs when I was a teenager and Karissa was over. I remembered telling someone I thought my other grandma was prettier. I remembered being embarrassed when she arrived to pick me up with her hair curlers in. But as I chastised myself for these cringeworthy indiscretions, my mind also summoned sweeter Grandma-related memories. Her smooth pointer finger tracing the perimeter of my face in a hypnotizing circle, cooing, "Gee, you got a round, fat face."

For the booklet, I wrote about Grandma Betty enabling

Ashley and me to ruin countless boxes of Jell-O as we "learned how to cook," the infamous cocklebur incident, and how she hated when she couldn't see the Jackson water tower.

By the time the funeral visitation rolled around, superstitions were running high. My dad—who I'd heretofore appraised as irksomely rational—found a delicate blood-red flower on the passenger seat of his car. "Did you see the flower?" he asked me enthusiastically. "Clearly it was on the seat, and then it was gone. Your grandma left it. She wants us to know she's okay."

He told that story at the visitation and the levee broke.

My Aunt Cathy was next. "I saw circus peanuts at 7-Eleven and I knew they were from Mom," she told us.

More signs followed.

Everyone was starting to sound so crazy, I had to interject, "You know they sell circus peanuts at 7-Eleven, right?"

But the truth is, I was envious. I didn't get a sign. I mean, I get it. I hadn't been around for a while. Maybe she was mad at me. Or maybe, perhaps worse, she forgot.

During the funeral service, I read a poem about a dragonfly whose "life had been fulfilled rather than ended." I admitted to the congregation that the past week had made me wonder anew about the existence of God, or at least an afterlife.

Pretty soon after that, too fast, they lowered my grandma into the ground, and it was time to go back to LA. I packed up my shell and got on a plane. Before we landed, the pilot announced the temperature—a balmy May day in Los Angeles.

But when I walked outside at LAX, it felt chilly. Days went by, and still I couldn't warm up. All I could see was the rat race. Nobody gave a shit about my dead grandma. Or the book I'd made for her.

Sometimes I held the shell up to my ear, but I couldn't hear the ocean over the din of my grief.

I was barely trudging through the June gloom—dating a guy who didn't want to be my boyfriend, working a job I didn't like, and not even making good art. I didn't know why I was out there anymore and felt sorry for what I'd left behind.

I shut the car door behind me in a strip mall parking lot before I
went inside. Looking around, I saw steel, rubber, concrete, nothing
unusual. When I came back out, there was a crisp hundred-dollar
bill right next to my car door.

What luck! I put it in my wallet and carried it around. My
bank account was nearly empty at the time, and it made me feel
safe. Like I had a hundred-dollar backup plan.

At the bank a few weeks later, I thought, *This is dumb—
why am I carrying around a bill this big? I'm either going to lose it or
someone is going to steal it. I should deposit it.*

While I was filling out the deposit slip, I glanced at the bill
and, for the first time, noticed the letters. There was a "B" for Betty.
I scanned to the other side and found a "C" for Courtney. And
in between, there was an "L," which she would say stood for love.
Betty loves Courtney.

I knew I didn't find that Ben Franklin. He found me. A
special delivery from my Grandma Betty to remind me that she'll
always be with me. Even if neither of us goes back to Jackson again.

I took a storytelling workshop the fall after Grandma Betty died.
When I was still chapped with grief. I workshopped an early
version of this story, but I couldn't get through it without crying.
At the end of the eight-week session, we went to KCRW's old
studio in the basement at Santa Monica College and our instructor
recorded our voice-over.

Listening back, my devastation was piercing. I started
bawling during a line about how I would think about her every day
for the rest of my life. And at that point, I did. I couldn't imagine
not being consumed by the lack of her. But time strolled on, and
my Grandma Betty memories sank from top of mind to a more
manageable, moderate presence to where they are today—sporadic.

Now, when something triggers a memory about her, there's
a tinge of sadness that I don't think of her as much anymore. Life
goes on without her until the next time I remember she's missing.

But I always remember. She comes back to me in many
forms and various degrees of longing: sometimes with a flash of
memory and a smile, sometimes a pained realization of absence,

and sometimes a sharp rebuke of myself.

Since she's been gone, I've realized I look just like her. I see myself walk out of the grocery store mid-morning with no makeup, a hoodie, a sweatpant leg pushed up above my ankle showing one full sock, my hair held up with a clip, unfussy, squinting my eyes at the sun—the whole look is cozy, but tired, and a bit sloppy, certainly not trying to impress a man or anyone else. It's not cute, but that's its charm. For a second, I see myself as someone else would see me and it's clear I don't give a fuck. I am struck by how I look just like Grandma Betty. Which is funny considering my comment comparing her beauty to my other grandma's. Well, joke's on me. We have the same face, the same David Letterman-style teeth. We even have a similar body type. The only difference is the wear and tear. Hers I knew in the flesh only after nine kids, myself childfree, but still, you can tell that it's the same frame. Both tallish and slender, but womanly. Sturdy but delicate.

Though I racked my brain for years over what I wished I'd said the last time we spoke, I recently discovered that I did say my piece. Not at the very end, but close.

Three months before Grandma Betty passed, I mailed her a Valentine's Day card with my handwriting filling up all the available space inside. It was a response to her card. After the pleasantries and thank yous, I got to the point:

> *The part about "California might as well be another country" made me sad. I feel like that sometimes too—I wish I wasn't so poor and it were easier to come home. Even though we don't see each other often, I just want you to know that my memories of you are still strong and no amount of time or distance will change that. You were one of my very first examples of how to be good and soft and strong and I carry that around with me in the part of my heart that's unbreakable. I love you!*

The summer of 2020, I took a road trip back to Minnesota to visit my family, namely my other grandma, Marge. I was trying not to stay away as long as I used to, and I was overdue for a visit. I hadn't been able to come for Easter like I'd planned because of the COVID pandemic. In the meantime, my parents had moved into a new house—Grandma Betty's old house.

Driving up her lane was a shock to my system. There was an overflowing garden off to the left by the shed. My parents' picnic table and a bunch of new chairs were gathered in front. Next to the garage door hung my mom's corn shuck decoration.

My Grandma Betty's house had stayed the same longer than any other landmarks in my life. Seeing it changed, my heart cracked with a sadness I hadn't felt in three years. I visited for six days and five nights. Slept in her bedroom. Took a shower in her formerly pink bathroom. Made a mental note of every minor alteration that had been made in my absence (and there were a lot).

Slowly, I began to realize this was precisely what she'd wanted. And inherent to the plan was that she would never get to see it. "That's a lesson you learn from the school of hard knocks," she would say with a chuckle.

It doesn't matter anyway because she doesn't live in that house anymore. She lives in every cell of my body, in the sayings and memories I've stored in my mind, and in a secret pocket of my wallet.

My Grandma Betty has led an adventurous life since she died. The hundred-dollar bill has been all around the world. My grandma has traveled with me to places she never imagined she would go: London, Paris, Helsinki, Mexico City, Tokyo, Belize. In the Parisian cathedrals, I blotted her tears as they ran down my face. She has kept me safe as I've traveled the world. Kind of an ironic afterlife for someone scared to lose sight of the Jackson water tower.

I stopped praying to God a long time ago, but these days I pray to Grandma Betty almost every day. Maybe Grandma Betty *is* god. Maybe that's why her funeral was overflowing with hundreds of people paying their respects. Maybe that's how she could leave me a little piece of heaven on Earth—a hundred-dollar bill marked with proof that BLC, Betty loves Courtney.

Some things are devastatingly ephemeral, but not that.

DR. DONNA

A month after Grandma Betty died, I was back in Los Angeles, reorganizing my office.

Cleaning out a drawer, I opened a small box and found a shell. Not just any shell, but a heart cockle—a callback to five years prior, during my stint on *Necessary Roughness*, a TV show inspired by a woman who was the performance psychologist for the New York Jets.

That woman was Dr. Donna. Mononymous, like Madonna with a Ph.D. Her fictionalized self was portrayed by Callie Thorne as Dr. Dani Santino. You could easily confuse her real self for a well-kept mob wife, a Real Housewife, a retired Playmate, or Donatella Versace with bigger hair and a better skincare routine. Dr. Donna is not immune to flattery. She is into being hot. But she will also warn: "Don't let the blonde hair fool you."

I sank into my desk chair and cradled the heart cockle in my palm, remembering how Dr. Donna stood in front of the writer's room at the beginning of season two and said, "I manifested this show when I was a busy mom back on Long Island. You can do anything you can dream of if you just believe it's yours."

Looking back in the box, I noticed a business card for Dr. Donna at the bottom. Curious, I opened my laptop and looked her up. What was that dynamo up to these days?

Scanning her website, I found an overview of her services alongside a slick mention of her recent work as the on-camera therapist to Jeff Lewis and company on Bravo's *Flipping Out*. There was also an agreeably ostentatious portrait of her posed with a quill pen. I sat back and beheld her in all of her splendor. She was the answer to my prayers, had they been bolder.

Floundering in my grief, I was in urgent need of a therapist. Unfortunately, the task of finding a therapist tends to be such a monumental undertaking, it'll easily double whatever trauma you're trying to quell. My game plan was to keep my head in the sand for as long as possible. I could heal myself through exercise and cleaning alone, right?

But I knew I needed help and that pompous feather won me over, so I gave Dr. Donna a call. I left her a voicemail, took Georgia for a walk, and soon after I returned to cleaning my office a few hours later, she returned my call. She was bright and easy to talk to as we exchanged pleasantries and she explained how she ran her practice. When she told me her rate, I swallowed hard, but was undeterred. I'd already decided I needed her, at any cost. I was struggling with existential questions, not just about life and death, but also about my career—I needed a Hollywood therapist, ideally one who had sold a show.

I schlepped north on the 101 to Encino for my first session.

There was something soothing about stepping into her bougie all-ivory apartment, like I was stepping into an episode of *Keeping Up with the Kardashians* and Kris Jenner herself was telling me, "You're doing amazing, sweetie." I immediately spotted the quill pen on her desk and knew I was in good hands.

Dr. Donna doesn't fuck around. And oddly, she had the same teeth, smile, and even laugh as my Grandma Betty—a perk that is not relevant to all her clients, but I found the happenstance reassuring.

As soon as I took a seat on her luxurious white couch, Dr. Donna got right down to business. She gave me a copy of her book, *Game On!*, with a message scrawled in her beautiful handwriting: *Courtney, Believe in your power! Dr. Donna*

She asked why I came to see her. I gripped a decorative pillow and bounced my dusty leopard-print ballet flat on her pristine white carpet as I let it all spill out: My grandma, of course. Dating issues—namely, thinking I was in love with Luke, a fuckboy (sorry, fuckman) who didn't want to commit to me. And the uncertainty and struggle of trying to parlay a few recent successes—writing a commercial and on an animated series for Amazon—into the kind of career that I wanted. I didn't just want any writing job; I wanted to be turned on by the subject matter, and ideally, I wanted to be the creator and running the show. It was a tall order. Since wrapping those jobs, my career had been zigzagging more backward than forward, clearly afraid to run straight toward success.

Dr. Donna nodded knowingly. "You need to reset your subconscious tapes," she said, identifying the faulty programming standing between me and an amazing relationship and me and an amazing career. She gave me language to reframe those dynamics. As far as my romantic problems, she instructed me to be honest about what I really wanted and put a Post-it note on my laptop: *choose love, not fear.*

"Are you ready for hypnosis?" she asked after we'd thoroughly talked through my issues.

I nodded enthusiastically. "Yeah, it's my first time."

"Okay, lie down and get comfortable," she directed, making a note on her yellow legal pad. "Today we're going to focus on worthiness." She played soft Enya-style music. I closed my eyes and tried to static my mind. When she woke me, I floated upright on the couch and then out to my car, driving home on the 101 perfectly synchronized with the flow of traffic.

My sense of calm was a temporary relief. The next session, I sat on the couch and immediately burst into tears. "I'm trying to be perfect, but this industry is so hard and I think Luke has been seeing other girls and I miss my grandma," I blubbered. "Why is my life such a mess?"

Dr. Donna had me get a yellow rose out of her bursting bouquet.

"Okay, now pick off a petal and let it drop to the ground."
I obeyed.
"Is it still beautiful?" she asked.
"Yes," I replied.
"Pick off another," she said. I complied again and again, each time agreeing that the flower was still beautiful as its petals fell to the floor.

"Nothing is perfect," she said, "But it's perfectly imperfect and there's always beauty to be found."

I took what was left of the flower home with me as a reminder at the end of our session.

I kept going, and over the next few months, Dr. Donna helped me put myself back together again.

We did all the hits—visualizations about my inner child and higher self. She had me close my eyes and vacuum out my insides and then pour gold liquid inside. She had me picture my very chill and beachy, yet successful and driven higher self at my dream office overlooking the ocean in Malibu. She sent me home with a best self/best move exercise I could use between sessions. She wrote a mantra for me on the back of her business card, "Every day in every way I get better and better." She repeated over and over, "There's no such thing as a mistake." She talked to me about quantum physics: manifestation as scientific fact. I'd come to her with an interpersonal misunderstanding, and she'd nod and shrug, "You're an alpha female. He felt intimidated." I felt so seen. She was also self-made and suffered no fools, so I could trust her career advice. She just got me. My dreams were batshit insane to regular people, it helped to have a licensed professional in my corner who also drank the Kool-Aid.

It was not a cheap session and I was a struggling artist who didn't even have health insurance, but it was worth it. I never left her office feeling the money was misspent. I collected Post-it notes of her shorthand wisdom: *There are no mistakes.*

If I weren't afraid, what would I do?

Choose love.

Her advice was so simple and practical, it was almost hard to grab onto without her help. I told her that in one session. "Complicated people tend to overcomplicate things," she replied.

Dr. Donna helped me stay away from fuckboy Luke and recognize the wonderful qualities in Wade. Soon I was genuinely falling in love and deleting Tinder from my phone.

Wade started going too. And when he and I had an early relationship hiccup, we enlisted her help in fixing it. She did an incredible job in our joint sessions. On the surface, it seemed like only his issue—he was trying to test me in weird ways to make sure I would stay because of childhood trauma from his parents' gnarly divorce—but deeper down it was mine too: How do I trust something stable to last when I'd felt blindsided in past relationships? "Easy. All you have to do is have fun and pay attention." I took her advice and we moved in together. Blissfully, but with our eyes wide open.

Things were so good, I stopped seeing her for a while. She'd moved her office from Encino to Palmdale, so she could start a school, and her sessions went remote. I was still craving the IRL experience. Wade, at this point my live-in boyfriend, and I sometimes mused about daytripping out to the Mojave Desert so we could take turns visiting our favorite shrink—we wanted to optimize, but she'd given us such a good framework for our relationship that there wasn't anything urgently problematic to deal with.

Then, a couple years after my first visit to Dr. Donna, career frustrations began bubbling to the surface again. I had a day job that was distracting me from writing, and I was not happy about it.

My mounting discontent prompted me to book a FaceTime session with Dr. Donna. I sat cross-legged on the IKEA bed Wade and I had hauled with us to our new apartment on Argyle. I gesticulated passionately as I told her about my monotonous, soul-sucking, demoralizing day job drawing up legal paperwork for evictions. I explained that while it was fairly flexible and self-directed work, kicking people out of their homes made me feel like a class traitor, even if they deserved it. I was resentful of any time and energy I had to dedicate to it. "I don't want a day job, period," I said resolutely, "I want to write full-time."

Dr. Donna told me to go for it, quit my day job, and pursue entertainment full-time. "Before I sold my show, I came to LA and signed a lease on an apartment," she reminded me. "Sometimes you have to tell the universe that you're ready."

I could already hear my mom fretting about money in my mind. But Donna reminded me that in quantum physics another, more successful outcome always exists. She had me repeat, "There is a version of me who knows how to be a successful writer." She told me to write it down. I scribbled *There is a version of me who knows how to be a successful writer* on my notebook and circled it. I was giddy by the time we got off the phone.

Days later, my Dr. Donna buzz eased, but it didn't wear off

completely. Weeks later, I was still ensnared in eviction paperwork with no solid plans for how to quit. I sighed when I saw *There is a version of me who knows how to be a successful writer* scrawled on my notebook as I grabbed a document off the printer in my office nook. I hesitated. Where was that version of me?

I glanced over at a Post-it from our session: *What would I do if I had no fear?* Moments later, I called my boss to turn in my notice.

I was tempted to go back and see what else Dr. Donna could fix for me, but then I got an email stating that she was raising her prices. She was now charging her old ninety-minute rate for an hour. I was proud of her. She knew her worth—I just couldn't afford it anymore. I'd quit my job after all. That was all I needed anyway. I needed her to tell me to quit. I needed her to tell me what I already knew. And she was right. We were right. Because that was my last job not related to the entertainment industry.

Dr. Donna said good things were already on their way. She said all I had to do was, "Just get outta your own way, boo!" So I stepped aside in eager anticipation of their arrival.

HOW I TALK ABOUT MY ABORTION (NOW)

With my mom (part 1)

I walked down the sidewalk on Park Street with my mom. I was little, maybe six or seven. It was fall; the election was approaching. I was starting to understand complex, serious issues, but had a lot of questions. Amid the row of quaint houses, someone had a political sign that said "pro-life."

I started in on my mom immediately: "Pro-life? What does that mean?"

She hesitated, "Well…"

How do you explain abortion to a first-grader? I knew about vaginas and penises and had vague notions about how sex worked, but abortion was on a whole other level.

With my dad (part 1)

Throughout my childhood, my dad would say things like "I don't like that" or the more presumptive "We don't like that" when confronted with the topic of abortion. I have always been a feminist—before I knew what it was or claimed it as my own—and I was forever playing devil's advocate with any wisdom my dad attempted to relay, but I don't remember arguing much about abortion. I didn't spend extra time thinking about it. I never thought it would happen to me.

In college

I said, "I'm pro-choice, but I don't think I could personally do it."

With my mom (part 2)

Mom: *Anyway, your uncle and Lori are going to stay with us for the reunion*—

Me: *Can't wait.*

Mom: *Courtney, I need you to be sensitive this weekend.*

Me: *Why?*

Mom: *Just be nice.*

Me: *I'm always nice. What is the big deal?*

Mom: *It's just a sensitive time.*

Me: *What's so sensitive about a reunion?*

Mom: *It's... Listen, you cannot tell anyone this.*

I stop at the stop sign and look expectantly at my mom.

Me: *Tell me.*

Mom: *Lori had an abortion.*

Me: *What? I thought she wanted a baby.*

Mom: *She did. She does. But your uncle doesn't.*

(beat)

Mom: *You wouldn't do that, would you?*

Me: *What? Date a guy like him?*

Mom: *Have an... abortion.*

Me (quickly): *No.*

(beat)

Me: *I don't know.*

Mom: *Have you ever been pregnant?*

Me: *Mom!*

She looks at me expectantly.

Mom: *I'm asking.*

Me: *No.*

Mom (intensely relieved): *Good. You know you can come to us about anything. We would want you to handle that situation in a more Christian way.*

(beat)

Mom: *Don't tell your dad about Lori.*

When I couldn't

Because of stories about Lori and a couple of my other aunts, I was able to go through with my own abortion at twenty-three. I would have a secret just like them. I didn't tell anyone for two years. Alone in my car, I would cry whenever Mary J. Blige started singing

"Runaway Love." After two minutes and forty-nine seconds of tears, Ludacris came on for a third verse about Little Erica getting pregnant, her baby daddy bailing, not having any support, and not being able to afford an abortion, and that's when I bawled so hard it became dangerous to drive.

I became highly sensitive to abortion references in pop culture. Growing up with the insinuation that abortion didn't make for polite conversation, encountering it in media was my only external relationship with the subject. Otherwise, I kept it bottled up. I aimed to do that for my entire life. Why did anyone else need to know?

With my best friend (part 1)

I moved to LA nine months after my abortion. I finally felt like I was back on the right path. Danielle and I moved in together in Mar Vista and settled into a pleasant evening routine of watching TV, weed smoke wafting out our screen door.

One night, something about abortion came on TV—a storyline on *The L Word*, I think.

I wanted to tell her—I wanted to tell her so bad—but I couldn't. I couldn't even say the whole word out loud to another person.

I made an awkward comment, calling it "aborsh" as if it were a casual thing.

Danielle coughed hard after taking a hit. "What???" she asked, confused.

"Nothing," I said, shaking my head. "Nothing."

When I finally could

Part of the reason I fell in love with Adam was that he had gotten someone pregnant before moving to LA. They were just hooking up, not in a relationship. She decided to have an abortion, but he supported her decision either way. He'd told me that the first day we met, when I was still Ariel before she found her voice, and

I loved that he could say it out loud. I loved that the situation made him sad, and he could acknowledge that. And after feeling abandoned in my own situation, I loved that he would've stayed and helped raise the kid.

After we'd been together a little over a year, I distinctly remember driving home against a soft pink Southern California sunset—whisking through the Santa Monica streets, bursting to tell him. I can't remember why. Because I finally could? I loved him, I trusted him, I was so sick of carrying this heavy secret by myself. "I have to tell you something," I said when I arrived.

We sat on our bed and I whispered my story in his ear. He hugged me tight and when he eventually let go, I remember feeling so light I could float up into the cotton candy sky.

With my mom (part 3)

On my next trip home, I sat on the basement couch with my mom and told her about my abortion. She looked pained but acted understanding, striving to live up to her mantra of "you can tell us anything" with an arrow in her heart. As we wrapped up our conversation, I said, "Okay, I guess I'll go tell Dad." She grabbed my arm as I rose from the couch. "Don't do that," she said, solemnly. "It would kill him."

With my dad (part 2)

We didn't. I listened to my mom for once in my life. But eventually, I told her that it was time to tell my dad. I was excited and emboldened to have a conversation with him about it on my next visit home. My mom replied, "Oh, Courtney, he already knows." My temples buzzed. My skin felt warm. *It would kill him*, echoed in my mind. I felt robbed of something I didn't know I wanted: the opportunity to own and articulate my own choice.

On the page for the first time

In the summer of 2014, I applied for a writing fellowship with a twenty-page sample, including a brand-new essay tentatively titled

"I Guess I'll Tell You Now," which gave a sorrowful accounting of the circumstances around my abortion and why I made that decision. I wrote the first draft of it in one sitting while sobbing and rocking myself back and forth, my fingers and tears hitting the keyboard in a frenzy.

I showed it to Sofiya, and she said, "Fuck, I think this is the best thing you've ever written." I agreed. I felt like I'd unlocked a new level by committing my secret shame to the page.

I showed it to a writing mentor, and she said, "This doesn't sound like you." She told me that sitting in front of her was a confident, capable woman, and she didn't recognize her in the essay I wrote.

I didn't get the fellowship, and although I made a half-hearted attempt to publish the essay, it never went anywhere—but I was thrilled that at least now the experience existed outside of my body. I realized that my mentor was right *and* the essay was good: before the confident, capable woman could come to the surface, the one who couldn't even say the word had to learn how to talk about it.

With my best friend (part 2)

She called me in trouble. She was pregnant and thinking about keeping it, but the impregnator wasn't nice.

A week later, she called me in tears: "He was choking me."

I touched my hand to my throat and my eyes began to sting. I imagined her being visited by police semi-regularly for the rest of her life. I thought of what my own life with Derek might have been like if I'd gone through with it.

"I don't want to tell you what to do, but I think you should get an abortion," I said.

I could say the whole word now.

With my best friend (part 3)

My friend got pregnant in a place that was inhospitable to a women's right to choose. She had to drive to another state and take someone (not her partner, who'd recently punched her in the face) along to make sure she got home safely after the procedure. She had to take off work during peak season and pay out of pocket.

While she was recovering, I went to visit her.

We clung to each other for an extra beat when she dropped me off at the airport a few days later. I realized that being there for her was as healing for me as it was for her.

Publicly for the first time

In September 2015, Lindy West, Amelia Bonow, and Kimberly Morrison started the hashtag #ShoutYourAbortion in response to efforts by the United States House of Representatives to defund Planned Parenthood. Seeing other people's stories made me want to start sharing mine. But I didn't. Not right away.

I had a sex podcast, yet I somehow skirted the subject of abortion for three years' worth of episodes. The subject came up a couple of times, and I empathized, but I didn't say, "me too."

Then things got weird; reproductive rights began to roll back.

In 2019, I finally began talking about it on the podcast and decided to "shout my abortion before it's too late" in an essay published on HelloGiggles.com for the forty-sixth anniversary of *Roe v. Wade*. I wrote:

> *Once I became a clandestine abortress, I found myself in casual conversations that illustrated how dangerous it is to hide the real, more nuanced narrative. It felt disingenuous to engage in fiery debates on the topic yet only talk about my experience in the third person. It felt even worse to say nothing. As Bonow writes in SYA, "If we do not tell our own stories, we give other people the power to define us." I barely endured a coworker with a political view based entirely on his wayward sister—"having a kid cleaned up her life!"—before realizing that if I wanted to change the taboo, I needed to start with myself.*

With my dad (part 3)

One gorgeous summer day in my mid-thirties, my parents were visiting me in LA. After hiking Griffith Park, we were downtown at Central Market, across from Angel's Landing, eating at my boyfriend's BBQ restaurant. The patio hummed with other patrons as a steady stream of cars whizzed by. My dad was halfway through his pulled pork sandwich when he casually said, "I wish you would've had the baby and let us raise it."

I stared at him as he took another bite, horrified by this suggestion.

"Are you kidding me? What a weird thing to say and even weirder to want," I finally said.

He furrowed his brow. "I don't understand why," he said, dabbing his mouth with a napkin.

My mom quietly ate her coleslaw.

I pushed my tray away, no longer hungry. It was like he'd spit on my vision for my life. It wasn't like I'd stayed in my hometown, and I was selling insurance or something. I was trying to compete in the Olympics of the entertainment industry. The same goal I'd been chasing relentlessly my entire adult life. Had there been no abortion, this child would now be twelve. Over the twelve years since, I had been immersed in a lifestyle antithetical to motherhood. I wasn't trying to compete, or even just live, with a brick on my ankle. And I certainly didn't want to have a child if my metaphor for its place in my life was a brick on my ankle.

My dad crunched on a pickle and explained how they could have been the type of grandparents who were more like parents while their adult child, who couldn't get it together for their own kid, was out gallivanting around.

I didn't have the words for why I hated that he was presenting this as a better solution than what actually happened. But the issue was that I was missing from their desired narrative. I was a bystander in their scenario. Can you imagine the nagging guilt? As if I would be able to focus on my art while my fucking kid was back with my parents. As if it would be healthy for any of us to still be in any sort of contact with my abusive ex. As if I were some sort of breeding sow, making a whole person without much say in the matter. I tried to say all that, but none of it got to my mouth.

Instead, I shoveled a forkful of mac and cheese and shook my head, "That's the most ridiculous thing I have ever heard."

On Instagram

In Texas, a pair of laws now bans abortion at all stages of pregnancy, with no exceptions for rape or incest and only narrow exemptions for pregnant people at risk of death. The first was Senate Bill 8, known as the Texas Heartbeat Act, which banned abortions after a fetal heartbeat is detected (usually around six weeks). SB 8 was signed by Governor Greg Abbott and took effect on September 1, 2021.

Three days later, I went in for a hair appointment, and while I was waiting for the color to set, I typed out this message:

> *I have been beside myself livid all week that people without uteruses are legislating what people with uteruses are allowed to do with their bodies. Can you imagine if we legislated compulsory vasectomies on their precious balls? And the vigilante "justice" written into the Texas bill is so far beyond the pale it's obscene. I hope the circle of hell these narcissistic dickwads wind up in is an eternity of Satan himself constantly impregnating them like Octomom breeding cows.*

> *On the anniversary of* Roe v. Wade *a few years ago, I publicly "shouted my abortion" for the first time via this essay for @hellogiggles in hope of preventing this type of siege on reproductive rights in this country. And once again I trot out my personal trauma in hopes of preventing this from metastasizing to other states.*

> *Also: my abortion itself wasn't particularly traumatic. It was a HUGE relief that I wouldn't have to abandon my dreams to raise an unwanted child – with a father who was sure to be a deadbeat – all by myself. What was traumatic is the way we talk about abortion in our society with so much shame. But I'm not ashamed anymore. I'm loud and proud, and now I know it's the stigma that's shameful.*

> *I am pro-abortion, and I will never shut up about it. Your "pro-life" is a joke – you don't care about life, you care about control.*

I will fight like hell with the women of Texas to restore their right to choose. Bodily autonomy is a human right. I don't want to be a second-class citizen to a bunch of hypocritical asshats who wouldn't know empathy or anything outside their narrow existence if it punched them in the dick. I hope they're scared of the tidal wave of feminist rage that they've unfurled because this is just the beginning. /endrant

#proabortion #reproductiverights #reproductivejustice #abortionrights #abortionishealthcare #abortionban

I tapped my phone frantically with foils in my hair, pacing the salon as I finished. My blood pressure rose through the roof, and for a second, I was worried that I might have a stroke. I sat back in the chair, pressed post on Instagram, and tried to relax. I tried to reassure myself. About living in California. About being more financially stable than I used to be. About menopause being closer than it used to be. But my self-assurances sucked. Nothing made it better because millions of women were losing agency over their bodies, being abducted by shitty circumstances, held hostage by controlling men, and assuming alternate lives for (mostly male) legislators who shouldn't be involved in the decision in the first place.

I sighed and checked the comments.

A friend replied: beautiful 🩶

Someone else said: Couldn't have written that better myself! Thank you for sharing this!!

A guy posted: Forced birth is actually considered a crime against humanity via un.org. I encourage everyone to use this information and spread it to everyone they know.

With Dr. Diana Greene Foster

In June 2022, I skimmed through a news roundup in my email and came across the headline: "The Most Important Study in the Abortion Debate." I clicked on it like catnip and read Annie Lowrey's article in *The Atlantic* about The Turnaway Study, Dr.

Diana Greene Foster's landmark research that studied the diverging paths of women who were able to get the abortions they wanted and those who were turned away. They began following women in 2008, which was a couple of years after I got my abortion. According to the study, women who didn't get the abortions they wanted were more likely to be poorer, still in contact with their abusive exes, and less satisfied with their lives. I immediately felt seen.

I emailed Dr. Greene Foster immediately, and she graciously accepted an invitation to come on my podcast. By then, *Roe v. Wade* had been overturned. I've interviewed celebrities and people at the top of their field, and I'm typically very chill about it. But with Dr. Greene Foster, I felt like a fangirl. I told her I couldn't believe the findings when I first read her study. Or rather, I could very much believe them, but I didn't expect to see the data illustrate so clearly what I couldn't articulate to my dad.

Now

I talk about abortion like I talk about knee surgery or bankruptcy. It's certainly not exciting. Sometimes it's sad. But it's not scandalous or demonic. (What I see as demonic is a cascade of new laws and bans and amendments designed to hold people with uteruses captive in their own bodies and lives.) Abortion is not shameful. It's healthcare. It's routine. And it shouldn't be endured silently or its pursuit turned into an obstacle course.

With my dad (part 4)

I visited my parents in Jackson recently. One night before bed, I showed my dad a draft of this essay. He nodded subconsciously as he read. When he finished, we talked—him, me, and my mom, who'd read it first and wanted him to read it too. I asked if he understood where I was coming from.

"Selfishly, I wish you hadn't done it," he said.

I underlined the word "selfishly" in my head.

"But I'm not saying you were wrong. Maybe you made the best decision." He continued, half-joking, "Maybe I'd be in jail because I would've killed Derek, who knows?"

Though he didn't say the words I would say or would want him to say, to me it sounded like he understood. And I also realized I didn't care if he did.

It was *my* choice, not his.

EXPOSURE THERAPY

"Ugh, I'm so glad we're not together anymore," Adam said, shaking his head. "It's so you to do something like this."

I was sitting on my ex-boyfriend's couch in suburban Denver. He was on the other side of the room, in the adjoining kitchen, crunching on a big cup of ice. He had the same boyish face, but his typically tight crop was overgrown. It was August 2020, the first summer of the pandemic, and I was on a road trip back to Minnesota to visit my family.

What was I doing that he found objectionable and was so like me? Starting an OnlyFans.

"I'm also glad we're not together anymore," I shot back. "Wade is totally cool with it."

Wade *was* totally cool with it, but the truth is, I hadn't told him yet. I wanted to wait and see if I got any actual fans first. How embarrassing to have a big talk about it and then not get any subscribers. Plus, I already knew he'd think it was okay. I say/write/ do pretty much whatever I want, and it doesn't seem to bother him one bit. Exhibit A: I got a happy ending massage during a Tokyo trip for my podcast seven months prior, and he wasn't the slightest bit fazed.

In the earlier stages of our relationship, I was suspicious that this chillness couldn't honestly be how he felt. I would search for a trace of resentment in his eyes, but I never found it. I think he likes that I'm a little out there. That said, he doesn't usually consume my media unless I say, "Hey, check this out," or more often, "Can you proofread this?" I don't think I could have a boyfriend who was super invested in my work or took it as a personal reflection of himself.

This was about me.

For as long as I can remember, I've been obsessed with sex work.

As a kid, one of my favorite movies was *Pretty Woman*. In 2012, I read an exposé about former Olympian-turned-high-priced prostitute Suzy Favor Hamilton and wanted her job. Not really for the money, though I did need the money, but more than that, I liked the idea of being bought like a luxury item. Yes, I was a woman with agency, but choosing this objectification of myself as part of the transaction, putting a high price tag on myself, turned me on. I lusted over the same thrill that Suzy herself chased in her mania. The eroticism of doing something taboo, and in her case, something illegal. And getting away with it.

But even more so, I liked the exhibitionism of it. Being exposed. Physically, morally, spiritually. For being a bad girl who sells her pussy (and likes it), as well as a good girl who wins gold medals. For being a Madonna *and* a whore.

"It's false advertising. People are gonna think you're Latina and be disappointed," Adam warned me when I pitched a version of Coco Gone Loco that wasn't already taken. "Trust me, I work in online marketing... Or at least I did."

"You're right," I said, deep in thought. A minute or two later, I cocked my head, "How about Coco's Peep Show?"

Adam nodded. That was the one.

Welcome to Coco's Peep Show, I typed into the headline, happily joining the steady stream of sex workers and cash-strapped civilians flocking to online content subscription platform OnlyFans, whose business boomed when we were cooped up at home during the lockdowns. We were living in a bizarro COVID alternative reality, and regular decision-making was out the window.

The idea came about spontaneously in early June 2020, when the George Floyd protests were in full swing. I saw another LA comedian post about offering topless pics in exchange for Black Lives Matter donations, so I launched a campaign of my own: Thirsting for Justice. I tweeted that interested parties were to send me their BLM donation receipt for fifty dollars or more with that day's date—I was a stickler—and I would reply with a three-pack of my best topless and ass pics.

I took off for a protest in downtown LA. When I opened my Twitter DMs hours later, in the middle of a chanting crowd, I had hundreds of messages. I wound up raising $32,685. I know the exact number because I kept a spreadsheet. The lesson was *Damn, sex really does sell*. It woke me up to the fact that there's a market for my tits and ass. The eternal exhibitionist, I absolutely loved doing it and wanted to continue, but the administrative aspect was turning into a full-time job.

Meanwhile, a bunch of comedians I knew were promoting their new pandemic-inspired OnlyFans pages. Sofiya and I interviewed them for a podcast series. OnlyFans seemed like a horny release valve and an easy, fun way to make some extra money. I loved doing photo shoots, posting thirst traps on Instagram, and the response to my BLM fundraiser. Talking with them, I knew it was only a matter of time before I followed their lead.

The night after my stop at Adam's, by myself at a Best Western in Grand Island, Nebraska, I snapped a topless pic in the bathroom mirror and posted an open for business tweet.

My content would be relatively tame—Playboy-style topless, lingerie, and bikini photos, nothing overtly pornographic—and I was upfront about that from the beginning. But still, I got 149 subscribers and made about $1,200 in my first few days. In a quiet rest stop parking lot, I took a topless car selfie to thank my subscribers for their support.

Acting out my sex work fantasy started with a seductive dance in front of the bay window at age four. Since then, it's been an intermittent lure.

Back in college, kicking that guy in the balls for money felt right. In 2019, a podcast interview with a successful dominatrix in New York City really got my wheels turning. The idea of becoming a professional domme became a personal fetish. It seemed like a fascinating job, the money could be life-changing, and the work of it was more psychological than sexual—an empowering and perhaps alleviating experience. I daydreamed about my BDSM business plan for months afterward.

I knew I didn't want to give any more Craigslist massages, but the more strippers I met through my journalism, podcast, and life in general, the more I wanted to join their club. I bought a five-pack of S-Factor strip aerobics classes, created by Sheila Kelley, one of the actresses from *Dancing at the Blue Iguana*. In my fantasy, I was instantly fantastic. I took to the pole like a bike I'd been riding for decades. I waltzed into the legendary Jumbo's Clown Room or Cheetah's in Hollywood and dazzled them with an audition so good that they put me on the best shifts, and I made a ridiculous amount of money every night. The door guy had to escort me out to my car to protect my bangin' hot body and huge bag of cash.

Unfortunately, I was not good. Maybe I could have been with a lot of hard work or a stronger need, but, under the present circumstances, I was not decent enough to moonlight as a stripper without some intensive training—a disappointing revelation.

A few months after I interviewed the domme in NYC, her episode dropped. When I went to tag her on Instagram to promote it, I couldn't find her handle. Her profile had disappeared completely, and her website said she was no longer in business.

As I've discovered through my dabbling, sometimes the fantasy is better than the reality.

"So this is sort of crazy, but I started an OnlyFans," I told Wade over Sugarfish delivery when I got home from my trip a week and a half later. "I've already made almost two thousand dollars," I said with a laugh, popping a piece of ginger in my mouth.

"Really?" he said, impressed.

"It's actually kind of fun. Do you mind if I keep doing it?"

"As long as you really want to do it. If you're just doing it for money, I can help you out." Exactly the sort of good-natured response I'd expected. No wonder we've lasted so long.

Ten days after I joined OnlyFans, Bella Thorne got in on the fun. She made a million dollars in her first twenty-four hours. Long-time sex workers were up in arms. I understood the criticism, but I was also an interloper. When friends asked me what I thought of it, I shrugged and said, "I'm not sure what I'm doing is that much different."

The difference was that I didn't make a million dollars, and I genuinely needed the money. I had a couple contract gigs in the podcast space that were sort of sustaining me at the time, but I *was* buying food and paying bills with my OnlyFans money. I definitely wasn't independently wealthy like Bella Thorne—though maybe she felt financially insecure too. Most Angelenos would tell you that unless you're rich, we're all just varying degrees of poor. Maybe Bella Thorne felt like she'd been selling herself the entire time she'd been in Hollywood. What's the difference between signing your body, voice, and likeness over to a production company to make a movie? I've done nudity in two non-adult films and had no control over their editing and distribution. Even when you're not naked, acting requires you to relinquish all control beyond your performance. At least with OnlyFans, you can do it on your own terms.

OnlyFans is the opposite of my Model Mayhem days. Now I only work with photographers I vibe with. The power dynamic is totally different. There's no predator and prey. I'm always in control.

The key to OnlyFans is sticking to your boundaries. It's harder than it sounds. I've bumped up against mine for sure. What I've seen from the creators that I know and the interviews that I've done is that there's more internal conflict for creators who don't stay within their comfort zone. I get the temptation because it can be a ready source of income—occasionally I have a big bill that comes out of nowhere, and OnlyFans seems like a great solution. I've been super tempted to stick a dildo up my ass and have an outrageous payday. And God bless the creators that do. There's nothing regressive about fuck you money. But that's outside of my boundaries, and I know if I avoid crossing those, the better I'm going to feel about the whole experience in the long run. And I know that's where my privilege comes in.

Unlike most sex work, OnlyFans can be engaged with from

a distance. No clients trying to touch inside my panties. No gritting my teeth while rubbing oil on a hairy back, or worse, a hairy dick. I can do my exhibition on the other side of the metaphorical glass.

When I started my OnlyFans at thirty-six, I was self-conscious about my age. At one point, I thought that I would definitely need to retire before I turned forty, but I don't feel the need to retire anymore. None of my fans has ever made a negative comment about my age. In fact, I interviewed a fifty-seven-year-old OnlyFans sensation, raking in loads of fans and their money. Another refreshing reminder that all the propaganda about beauty and desirability falling off a cliff after forty is false. Some old man Peter Pan must've started that rumor as an excuse to date much younger women.

The truth is, I get better every year. Age really is just a number (and a blessing). Attitude, energy, and even superficial aesthetics don't have a hard expiration date. Quite the opposite. Women are wine, not bananas.

Another interesting thing I have learned from doing OnlyFans is that I don't have to feel great about my body for other people to appreciate it. I'm forever fucked from '90s diet culture, though I've mostly made peace with my body in my adulthood. I have my preferred weight, and I'm fairly regimented in my food and exercise routines to maintain it. Yet even when I'm on the heavier end of my range, my fans don't seem to care or even notice. That's taught me to step off the scale—it may not be the best way to measure my attractiveness.

Maybe the male gaze isn't all bad.

It's hard to pick apart my sexuality from the male gaze. It's so ingrained, like an invisible hand always cupping my ass. The amount of time I've spent looking at before-and-after galleries of breast augmentations. The way I want the tightest pussy possible. How I feel hotter when I'm a little skinnier.

But it's too late for me to fix all my fucked up subliminal desires. At this point, I'm just trying to have a good life without hurting anyone else.

It is not lost on me that OnlyFans is the new Girls Gone Wild—in the absence of Girls Gone Wild, OnlyFans not only became possible, but proliferated. However, they are two very different companies. OnlyFans isn't perfect, but it has improved on the business model exponentially, cutting out the need for porn companies as middlemen and putting power in the hands of adult creators who fully consent to use the service and typically self-determine their own boundaries and marketing—and receive the bulk of the profits.

As of my third anniversary on OnlyFans, I had grossed just shy of $30K. My biggest month was $2,331. It hasn't just given me money, but power and control over the process.

I can't help but wonder what would have happened if I'd had this outlet when I was younger. Instead of selling T-shirts on the Girls Gone Wild tour, would I have started an OnlyFans account instead? Would I have been able to find safe photographers at that age? Would I have been as successful in setting boundaries? Would I have come up faster in my career, or would it have pigeon-holed and screwed me? Would the money have made me feel better about my decision, either way?

In a way, I'm grateful for the Girls Gone Wild experience I did have. The epiphany that came from betraying myself and my gender allowed me to evolve in opposition to that. Not a prudish opposition, but a full-throated sex positive opposition. With my podcast *Private Parts Unknown*, I actively seek to destigmatize conversations about sex, interrogate the patriarchy, and empower people—especially women—to own their desires and take charge of their pleasure.

Recently, I interviewed a clinical psychologist and sexual trauma specialist, and she posed a dichotomy that made my jaw drop: "Is the choice to expose yourself in that way an act of claiming—you know, this is mine, and I either enjoy this, or this feels okay to me, and I'm using a part of myself to engage with the world or advance myself in a certain way—or am I doing this because I'm repeating something that happened to me earlier that

I haven't metabolized yet, or I don't feel like I'm worth anything other than this, or I don't really know how to say no?"

For me, OnlyFans has been a reclamation. It's allowed me to reprocess photo shoots that went off the rails and things I saw on the Girls Gone Wild bus, as well as sexist experiences in the entertainment industry and society at large. Revisiting those scenarios as a fully formed adult with agency, in control of the situation, reaping the benefits, has been strangely healing.

"Yeah, that's really interesting. Yeah, I accept that totally," the psychologist replied. "And also that it can be reparative. I mean, one of the things that one thinks about in terms of healing is, can you go back to some part of the original event and transform it? You know, so can you go back to some place where you felt really unsafe and this time feel safe? Can you go back to a place where you felt painfully exposed and, at this point, feel joyfully exposed? And that changes things."

It does change things.

But not everything. I've had nude photos stolen. I had to hire a DMCA takedown service to monitor my online presence. There are still bad actors, misogyny still reigns. But overall, OnlyFans has been a net positive in my life.

After my latest photo shoot, I pulled away from the drive-thru window, savoring the salty satisfaction as my mouth closed in around a golden, delicious fry.

WHAT HAPPENS IN VEGAS

I always say I don't have any regrets. Everything has made me who I am today, I say. I'm grateful, I say.

I'm full of shit, though, is the truth.

Few of my regrets are the things an onlooker might identify: my $18,000 Master's certificate, my semester in St. Cloud, my eighth-grade haircut. I certainly don't regret my abortion. Still, I have more regrets than there are plastic bags in the ocean. I regret things like not staying in better touch with people, doing Adderall for a decade, and being so determined and optimistic that sometimes I lack or downright ignore the foresight to see when I'm being delusional. I regret even little things: Did I look at her weird? Was I nice enough to the cashier during checkout? Did I say goodbye too many times—or not enough? I almost always regret losing things. Even if it's something small. One of my biggest regrets is the size of my ring finger.

My Grandma Marge gave me her wedding band for my high school graduation. She made a special visit just to give it to me. I delicately ripped the embossed paper and opened the thin white box to discover a beautiful silver ring encircling a lacy white handkerchief. The interior of the ring was engraved. Though my soul had not yet been stretched and deepened by time, I knew how special this gift was.

Weeks later, after a fight with my mom about sneaking off to visit Derek on the weekend, my grandma came over again and took it back, saying, "You're not in the right place to have this now."

She was right. My relationship with Derek was damning evidence. I suspect she was worried I'd do something rash, like marry his dumb ass.

After I broke up with him, she came over and gave the ring back to me. With Derek out of the picture, she was under the assumption that I was back to good, but she was premature.

In a rest stop bathroom on my way back to St. Louis, hopped up on Adderall to stay awake for the drive after a long day working a promo gig at the University of Kansas, I took my rings off to wash my hands. I set them on the ledge in front of the mirror. I leaned forward to peer at my dinner plate pupils. I leaned back to check myself out. In a Tasmanian Devil-style whirlwind, I sudsed my hands, rinsed, and rubbed them together under the air dryer. I gave myself a satisfied glimpse in the mirror and left the rings behind in a manic sprint.

Turning onto Shenandoah Avenue in St. Louis, almost home at 2 a.m., I looked at my hands on the steering wheel and realized they were naked. I'd forgotten my grandma's wedding ring! My stomach dropped to my feet. My body buzzed from Adderall, exhaustion, and self-loathing. My problem, my whole lifestyle, had gotten out of hand.

Inside, I immediately looked up the rest stop maintenance department on the internet and, lit only by the light of my laptop, left a frantic middle-of-the-night voicemail, urging them to help remedy my error, then crashed out in my sleeping bag on the floor. I called back again as soon as I got up in the morning, still bleary-eyed. "Can you confirm what it looks like?" the employee said. Miraculously, someone had found Grandma Marge's ring and turned it in. I couldn't believe it—I had been redeemed! They offered to mail it, so I gave them the address of my room rental.

The woman I was renting from asked me to move out the following week. She seemed to be a drug addict too—and her downer spirals didn't vibe with my upper benders. She would sleep whenever she wasn't at work; I was up all night. I moved my stuff out and returned my key immediately, without any drama.

When I came back for the ring, she wouldn't give it to me. I tried everything I could think of to get it back—"It's a family heirloom!" I pleaded via phone, email, showed up in person a few times, and even tracked down her work email to beg. Eventually I offered her money, so I think by that point she must've already pawned it. It guts me even now, twenty years later. Each keystroke of this story is laced with painful lashes of self-flagellation. It was the most beautiful ring. Delicate etching. I loved how it looked on my finger. I wore it all the time. My grandma's ring.

Grandma Marge and I lived in the same town and were really close while I was growing up. She was my young grandma, my hip grandma, and I tagged along with her on trips to Walmart, Shopko, or the nursery to buy stuff for her garden and landscaping projects. She attended my dance recitals, trekked along to basketball games, came over for dinner every Sunday (lots of other nights too), and watched me when I was sick. She was involved in the daily—at worst weekly—fabric of my life.

I have her journal from my first year of life, back when I was twenty-six inches long and fourteen pounds, as noted by one entry. Alongside her other scrawled musings are frequent, adoring mentions of me: *sweet Courtney, she's changed again… Courtney is really observant and smiles a lot… could hardly leave Courtney.*

I have a guilty feeling about being so close with my family and then moving across the country and leaving them behind. For much of my twenties and early thirties, I wasn't very good about staying in touch. I was so busy working and up my own ass that I would sometimes go months without calling and years between trips. I occasionally sent cards, but only sporadically. On some birthdays, I forgot to call or just left a message. Yes, the phone lines work both ways, but I also know it would have meant so much to my grandma, and I should have taken more initiative to maintain that relationship. The guiltier I felt, the more I avoided it.

For some of those years, I didn't think it was possible to have the relationship I wished I could have maintained with her. It couldn't exist. I wasn't the same person. There was a gap between the girl she loved and the woman I became. Part of me wanted to be seen through my grandmother's eyes as a perfect little girl again, or at least as a rascally innocent. I was stuck in the girlish tension between the twirly skirt fantasy and what's real. The fact that I have given a Craigslist massage and taken someone else's Adderall prescription and gotten an abortion and a laundry list of other stupid shit—and smart shit that polite society doesn't approve of.

Sure, my grandma still loved me, but I wasn't sure she knew me anymore.

Once upon a time, my grandmother went from being a girl to a woman, too. She grew up Mennonite, a conservative sect of Christianity that grew out of the same Radical Reformation movement as the Amish, so she endured a dozen extra layers of shame and restriction that took her almost ninety years to shed. There was a genuine dissonance between who my grandma wanted me to be and who I was, but perhaps I made it bigger by projecting disappointment that wasn't there. And maybe I hadn't noticed a pinch of curious pride—or even envy—in the freedoms I enjoyed that hadn't been accessible to her.

In every relationship that goes on for large swathes of a lifetime, there are phases—people change, and you have to redefine the relationship along the way. In my thirties, I made it a priority to see her at least a couple times a year, ideally more, and send books, flowers, word finds, and other treats between visits to let her know I was thinking of her. That was the silver lining of Grandma Betty's death: an active awareness that people don't last forever.

Losing my Grandma Marge's ring was devastating. She'd entrusted me with the safekeeping of an heirloom. She thought I was mature enough to handle carrying a legacy, but I wasn't. I was offended when she took it back, but now I wish she had held onto it longer.

When my mom called to tell me that my younger brother Matt had gotten engaged, I was excited. There are four of us kids, all grown now, and for the first time, one of us made a move resembling traditional adulthood. Prior to this, there had been no babies. No weddings. Not even an engagement.

"Do they know when they're getting married?" I asked. "Did you know beforehand?" And then, of course, "Where'd he get the ring?"

"From Grandma Marge," my mom said.

I almost dropped the phone. It was my grandma's remaining ring. Ironically, this ring was one my grandma had thought she lost herself. She did lose it for years. She even filed an insurance claim. Then one day, she was cleaning her cupboard and found it up on a high shelf. She'd meant to hide it from houseguests, but wound up hiding it from herself. And here it was, found again—an opportunity for redemption that I hadn't even known existed.

My mom continued sharing details, like how they were

planning to melt the gold and fashion it into a new ring.

A switch flipped, and I was suddenly starring in a Greek tragedy. Wailing about my misfortune. "Why didn't she give that ring to me? Hanna doesn't even know Grandma!"

My mom was stunned by my reaction. It wasn't a ridiculous question, but it was unexpected. She blindly searched for the answer. "She didn't think you wanted it... She didn't think you were going to get married..."

"Why not?!" I demanded.

I'd been with Wade for five years. We lived together. I was in a serious relationship. Plus, we'd been talking about getting engaged for a few months. I didn't realize I needed to tell the whole family yet. My mom already knew how wrecked I was about losing that ring—why hadn't she stepped in?

"They don't even want the ring, they're planning to melt it down!" I exclaimed.

I hated to throw a tantrum, especially since this would influence Hanna's first impression of me. But I couldn't help myself. I morphed into Gollum, fixated on the ring, my possessive mind spinning. I had to have that ring at all costs. I'd already lost my grandma's ring once; I wasn't about to let this one slip through my fingers.

My mom and my grandma spoke with my brother, and soon it was settled. He would bring the ring back on his next trip home. I'd been a big bossy baby, and it had worked. I felt both guilty and relieved. Guilty because now my introduction to my sister-in-law would always be—indirectly, but still rather forcefully—requesting her engagement ring to be returned to its rightful heir. A bad first impression, but the relief was worth it. No regrets.

My brother and Hanna got married in Okoboji in July 2022. Afterward, Wade and I road-tripped back to California. Our plan was to get engaged along the way. We made a stop in Sturgis and visited Mount Rushmore. Then we spent the night in Vail. Wade was planning to pop the question the next evening in Zion, but we got frantic messages from our dog boarder about Georgia's paw and had to expedite our trip.

Hurrying back, we drove straight from Vail to Vegas, instead of stopping in Moab. I was the DJ, and as we drove into Vegas, I blasted R. Kelly's "Marry the Pussy." We could not stop laughing.

I thought there was something poetic about getting engaged in Vegas. "Every relationship is a gamble," I quipped, half-joking, but also smiling at my confidence in our odds.

After a long day of driving, Wade got us a room at the Wynn.

Since Vegas wasn't the plan, we didn't have a dinner reservation. Everything was booked at all of the nice spots. We were both getting hangry, especially me.

We went back down to the fancy restaurant where we'd started to check one more time, and got lucky. During dinner, there was a waterfall light show with an animated emoji video set to the Sonny and Cher classic "I Got You Babe." Wade took the ring with us to dinner. I thought he was going to propose at the restaurant, maybe during Sonny and Cher, but I think he had a little stage fright.

We went back up to the room and lay on the bed. Finally, he pulled out the ring and asked, "Will you marry me?"

I laughed at how utterly anticlimactic it was.

I'm a writer. If I were proposing, I would have written a whole speech. But there was no speech.

There was just Wade asking, "Will you marry me?"

And me, letting out a laugh, stunned at the simplicity, but already knowing the only answer for me was yes. I teased him about his speech, but the important thing was not the speech. I love words, but they're impossible to hold onto. The important thing was the seven years that had brought us to this question.

Before we got engaged, Grandma Marge had met Wade several times and approved of him. Like most grandmas, she could appreciate a nice, reliable man. Her biggest recommendation was to marry someone you can talk to. Thanks to Dr. Donna, we can.

I love Wade so much, but sliding Grandma Marge's ring on my finger has made me realize that I will always be married to myself first. I will be married to everything that came before. I will be married to making mistakes and learning from them and doing it better the next time. I will be a wild wife, full of contradictions and untamed by conventions. I will exist in this union as a whole person, wholly myself in a version that I actually like. Those are my vows. That seems like a pretty good place to start.

Leaving Las Vegas, I looked down at my grandma's ring.

It's not quite as pretty as the first one. Chunky gold instead of delicate silver. And yet it's my most prized possession.

What's lost an absent reminder to treasure what has been found.

EPILOGUE: CURTAIN CALL

"This is your chance to fact-check me," I told my mom on the phone.

This was early fall, a few weeks before my fortieth birthday, and a few days before I would leave LA for a trip back to Minnesota to visit my family. My manuscript was almost complete, so I was asking my mom if she wanted to read it before I sent it to my agent.

She was hesitant but game. "Can I take it at my own speed?"

"Oh, yeah. I'll just get it printed and leave it with you."

I was surprised at my eagerness for her to read it.

My writing group cautioned me. But I was sure it was a good idea.

I got busy with last-minute preparations and didn't print it out before my trip. Maybe I was hesitant too, dragging my feet. I realized everything she would read—the details of my experiences with drugs, sex work, sexual assault… the list of revelations was pretty long.

It's not that she doesn't know me. She does, she knows I'm a wild woman, and she's read a few essays from this book, but I think she prefers ambiguities over specifics. In my late teens and early twenties, we adopted a sort of "don't ask, don't tell" policy, and for the most part, that worked pretty well.

The morning I left for my trip, I woke up to an email that began, "Hi Courtney, I like this Minnesota pot story a lot and would like to publish it as part of the Episode column, probably late October…"

"Yessss!" I yowled from bed, making Wade giggle from the kitchen. "Baby! I got my first story accepted by *The New York Times*." He was impressed, I was thrilled.

Running a quick errand in the car, I called my mom to tell her the news. After our hellos, I made my announcement, "I'm going to have my first byline in *The New York Times*."

"Yay!" she cheered. Then asked, "What's it about?"

"The first time I smoked weed."

"Oh," she replied weakly.

"Who cares what it's about? It's *The New York Times*!" I exclaimed, rolling my eyes.

The next day, back in Jackson, my mom and I sat across from each other at her kitchen table. The smell of the apple crisp warming in the oven wafted through the room, refreshed since belonging to Grandma Betty, but having retained its classic comfort and charm.

She smiled, but her eyes were tired. "That night you called me about your book, I couldn't sleep," she admitted.

"You don't have to read it," I said.

"It might be too hard for me," she said. "I want you to know that I'm still proud of you, even if I can't read it…"

I already knew our irreconcilable truth: If this were a memoir my mom wanted to read, I would have lived a completely different life. I knew my mom loved me, and I loved her, and maybe that was enough. Maybe I didn't need her approval, too.

"That's fine," I replied, quickly. But then again, maybe I *did* need her approval because I couldn't help myself. "I hope it's everywhere," slipped out of my mouth. "So successful that it's unavoidable—not for you, but for me." I let myself relish in this cocky flourish as my mind projected best-case scenarios—bestseller lists, a celebrity book club, adapted for the screen. After the fantasy highlight reel was over, I looked at my mom again. She had tears in her eyes.

"It's hard to believe that none of our kids turned out like us," she said, her voice wavering.

"What do you mean?" I asked.

"Everyone else we know has grandkids," she said glumly.

For a moment, I could see my mom's dreams as clearly as my own, and my heart flipped in my chest. This procreation responsibility doesn't rest solely on me—I have three younger brothers—but instantly, I felt guilty.

I never wanted kids; I wanted to make art. Yet despite my enduring quest to make it, I know that the most important things in life aren't about career success or external validation. My mom and I have made very different choices with our lives, but her desire to foster the next generation is equally valid. I've been ambivalent long enough to understand that the Divine Feminine and the Mother Goddess are often misunderstood and undervalued, no less by me.

"Don't get too excited," I warned my mom. "But we're thinking about freezing some embryos."

Later that night, in Grandma Betty's old room, I googled a thousand articles and research studies about egg retrievals and geriatric pregnancy and birth defects and could I take my thyroid medicines, etc., etc. The body horror of pregnancy and childbirth still freaked me out. However, there was a fledgling curiosity I felt compelled to explore.

The next day, my parents had already named their embryo-granddaughter "Hileria." They joked that they would be a hundred when she is one. I laughed. Maybe they wouldn't have to wait quite that long.

In my daydream, I yearned for a baby girl. I realized I felt uniquely qualified to help nurture a daughter in this world that wasn't built for her, even if she turned out as different as I am from my mom.

On the way to the airport, I mailed the baby books my mom kept for me to examine back in LA. A potential name for my daughter came to me on the plane.

I'd always believed myself to be unconventional, and in some ways I was. Still, I couldn't escape this most human instinct. I returned to Los Angeles with a half-eaten bag of prenatal gummies.

I don't know which ghost ship will carry me. Right now, they are engaged in naval warfare.

On one ship, I am happily childfree—so core to my identity

and the pursuit of my art, I wonder how I could ever let it sink.
If this motherhood question is answered with a no, I know I will
make a life full of meaning, love, and excellent art.

On the other ship, I reinvent motherhood in a way
that feels manageable to me and yet still stretches me beyond
recognition. Would the tension of this immense role and my
unlikely suitability lead me to revel or revolt? Is it at odds with my
ambition or additive? Maybe motherhood wouldn't stop me from
writing. Maybe it would give me more to write about.

I celebrate my fortieth birthday as I finish the manuscript for this
book.

The long arc of my girlhood finally comes to a close. My
metamorphosis is complete. I'm no longer a girl gone wild, I'm a
full-grown wild woman.

In my bed, with my laptop propped up on my knees, I
make some last-minute tweaks before sending it to my writing
group. My phone lights up with a sweet birthday message from
Doris, Wade's eighty-three-year-old aunt who I adore, a wild
woman herself. Her text ends with: "Now life begins."

As I finish writing this sordid, potentially scandalous treatise, I can't
help but hope my hypothetical daughter doesn't do ninety percent
of the shit I've done. I can't blame my mom for her opt-out—if this
daughter of mine refused my best guidance and insisted on not only
living a wild life, but writing it all down, I wouldn't be able to read
it either.

But I can't think of my hypothetical daughter anyway—it's
too precious and abstract a notion. Instead, I think of a younger me
or a young woman whom I love, or even a complete stranger who
makes me wistful.

To her, I say: This story is not a how-to guide written under
ideal circumstances. It is not a blueprint. It's a survivor's account.
It's a reclamation. Some of my bad decisions weren't empowered,
and they certainly weren't in my best interest—but some of them
didn't feel like genuine choices to begin with. Not everything in our

society is as cultivated, refined, and domesticated as it should be or pretends to be. Gender, class, and other people's expectations can be a cudgel. The patriarchy is a stricture for everyone involved. But we do not have to cooperate with cultural restraints that seek to keep us small. Untie the knots every chance you get. Write your own rules. Being wild for wild's sake isn't a virtue, but being liberated is.

My shapeshifting artistic ambitions have been the North Star of my life thus far, but perhaps the biggest dream I discovered along the way is to be free of any artifice that keeps us stuck, small, ashamed, and unable to inhabit our one wild and precious life. To be free, period.

What I have learned from my long arc of becoming a woman, and doubly so in the retrospect of writing this book, is that if you carve out time and space for inquisition and introspection and to peer into the mirror of your soul, you'll find yourself soonest. Don't rush. Everything meant for you will be waiting when you finally arrive.

It turns out making it is mostly a state of mind.

These days, I fancy myself less of a tornado and more of a spirited breeze—still in motion, without as much destruction— but I don't regret any of the wreckage. This wild life has been so beautiful. And now, it really begins.

ACKNOWLEDGMENTS

Though mine is the only name on the cover, writing a book takes a village. The gratitude I have for the people who helped me realize this dream—and what a dream!—is too deep for even a squishy memoirist to express.

First, I'm so grateful for this art form. Some authors get mad when writing is referred to as therapy, but my god, it gives even Dr. Donna a run for her money. To face the cold, hard accounting of your actions and impacts is the final boss of self-liberation. (But if you're looking for a human, no one is better than Dr. Donna.)

Thank you to Cheryl Strayed for showing me the trail and girding me with the patience to take the many steps needed to pursue it. I've never made your acquaintance, yet you made this book possible and have been my staff throughout its making.

Thank you to Chloé Caldwell for inspiring me and then sherpa-ing me through two whole years of working on this manuscript. You taught me how to start and how to finish. Thank you to the 2020 Catacult and 2023 Writing Workshops groups who gave camaraderie and thoughtful feedback as I was developing this book.

Thank you to Hannah Beresford and Sarah Lyn Rogers for your discerning editor's eye. You helped me mine the diamonds from the rough (and would have encouraged a better metaphor).

Thank you to Chris Belcher and Edgar Gomez, my Antioch University MFA mentors, whose insightful feedback helped elevate sections of this book.

Thank you to my last-looks readers: Stacey Garratt, Danielle Doyen, Amanda McNeil, Nan Bauer, and Laura LeMoon. I'm forever grateful.

Thank you to Ariel Gore, Hannah Howard, Mike Scalise, Brian Gresko, Amanda Montei, Krys Malcolm Belc, Diana Spechler, Alexander Chee, and all the other writing teachers who conducted workshops and gave feedback that helped me build this book bird by bird. Thank you to Susan Shapiro for your publishing prowess.

Thank you to my students, past and present, for giving me fresh eyes with which I return to my work anew.

Thank you to Chloé Caldwell, Antonia Crane, Bassey Ikpi, and Halley Sutton for your generous blurbs.

I'm mortified to be on the cover, but thank you to Brooke Olimpieri, aka Filthy Mouth Creative, for taking such a minxy photo of me that any alternative was unthinkable.

I recommend the work of the following writers who've had experiences across the spectrum of sex work and write about it eloquently: Antonia Crane, author of *Spent*; Chris Belcher, author of *Pretty Baby*; Christianna Clark, aka "Selena The Stripper" (their brilliant @prettyboygirl Instagram is suspended as of this writing, but you can find them on Patreon at patreon.com/therealprettyboygirl); Hannah Sward, author of *Strip*; and Margo Steines, author of *Brutalities*. Kaytlin Bailey offers impactful advocacy, history, and storytelling through Old Pros. The performance art of Kayla Tange, aka "Coco Ono," is mind-bending and evocative. All of you inspire me. We owe a debt of gratitude to the sex worker social movements that have secured labor, free speech, feminist, and queer rights, advanced HIV/AIDS activism, fought against police overreach, and demanded privacy protections that benefit everyone. Thank you.

Excerpts of this book have appeared in *The New York Times*, *The Sun*, *Slate*, *Los Angeles Times*, *HelloGiggles*, and TheGloss.com. Thank you to the editors of those early essays that eventually made their way into this memoir, especially Jim Windolf, Rachel Elliott and Staci Kleinmaier, Shannon Palus, Rene Lynch, and Rachel Sanoff.

Thank you to Kris Bigalk, Lili Gourley, Natasha Kane, Joel W. Coggins, and the Trio House Press team. Kris, it was love at first rejection. I'm eternally grateful that you gave my first book baby a good home.

Thank you to Michael Castañeda for your enduring creative partnership and for how, as with everything else, you made this audiobook clean, crisp, and alive.

Thank you to my family, friends, and former lovers for filling my life with such rich characters. I love you.

Thank you to my parents for not reading this book. I'm

sorry for all the awkward conversations it will force upon you. I'll tell you I love you in person.

Thank you to my husband for being incredibly chill about this weird work I do. You've been my biggest supporter from the first bulletin board on. Luckily an artist wife is the ultimate status symbol. ;)

Thank you to Georgia for molding me into a better human when I needed it most, and for being a sweet and stable witness while I was writing this book. Your paws are on every page.

Thank you to baby Courtney for daring to dream big and always having the chutzpah to chase. Look at that, you were right all along.

If you read this book and thought, *Why did you mention your eating disorder and not get into graphic detail?*, first of all, get help, and second of all, my next memoir is gonna be a fucking treat for you. Stay tuned.

ABOUT THE AUTHOR

COURTNEY KOCAK is a writer, podcaster, and comedian who splits her time between Austin and Los Angeles. She has written for Amazon's Emmy-winning animated series *Danger & Eggs*, Netflix's *Know It All*, and outlets including *The New York Times*, *The Washington Post*, *Los Angeles Times*, *Slate*, *The Sun*, *HuffPost*, and a viral essay for *Cosmopolitan*. She hosts the podcast *Private Parts Unknown*, which has over two million downloads to date. Her husband is hot and nice, and they have a cute dog named Joy-Joy (RIP Georgia). For more, visit www.courtneykocak.com.

Instagram: @courtneykocak

About the Book

Girl Gone Wild was designed at Trio House Press through the collaboration of:

Kris Bigalk, Lead Editor
Lili Gourley, Supporting Editor
Natasha Kane, Interior Designer
Joel W. Coggins, Cover Designer

The text is set in Adobe Caslon Pro.

About the Press

Trio House Press is an independent nonprofit press based in Minneapolis, Minnesota. We publish poetry and prose that moves, inspires, and encourages connection, empathy, and understanding, with a special emphasis on underrepresented voices and topics. To find out more about Trio House Press, please visit our website at http://www.triohousepress.org.